Religious
Interaction Ritual

Religious Interaction Ritual

The Microsociology of the Spirit

Scott Draper

LEXINGTON BOOKS
Lanham • Boulder • New York • London

Published by Lexington Books
An imprint of The Rowman & Littlefield Publishing Group, Inc.
4501 Forbes Boulevard, Suite 200, Lanham, Maryland 20706
www.rowman.com

6 Tinworth Street, London SE11 5AL

British Library Cataloguing in Publication Information Available

Library of Congress Cataloging-in-Publication Data Available

ISBN 978-1-4985-7629-1 (cloth : alk. paper)
ISBN 978-1-4985-7631-4 (pbk : alk. paper)
ISBN 978-1-4985-7630-7 (electronic)

∞™ The paper used in this publication meets the minimum requirements of American National Standard for Information Sciences—Permanence of Paper for Printed Library Materials, ANSI/NISO Z39.48-1992.

Printed in the United States of America

Contents

List of Tables and Figures

List of Tables and Figures

Acknowledgments

This book is ultimately a collective product or, if you will, the emotionally charged symbolic outcome of several years' worth of interaction ritual chains. I want to thank several people who supplied me with abundant emotional energy and cultural capital throughout my process. Numerous colleagues and friends read various drafts and sections of this book, and their ideas informed, challenged, and fed into mine.

First, I want to thank Paul Froese. The idea for this book began during conversations with Paul, and he provided essential feedback and support throughout my process. He is a truly brilliant sociologist and teacher, and a great friend.

In some ways, Jeff Takacs and I have been collaborating on this book for decades. Jeff provided crucial feedback and support from start to finish, and his editorial advice and creative intellect were essential. Randall Collins read an early draft and provided thorough feedback. As a young scholar at the time, this degree of attention really did mean the world to me, and has energized me ever since. Joseph Baker was another key contributor, hatching many of these ideas with me on my porch, and advising me throughout.

Other friends and scholars who gave the project valuable time and attention include Stephen Boyes, Megan Dixon, Penny Edgell, Martha Gault-Sherman, Mike McCallion, Patrick McNamara, F. Carson Mencken, Laura Olsen, Ashley Palmer, Jerry Park, Jon Singletary, Buster Smith, Julie Smith, Anne Spencer, Sam Stroope, Stephen Warner, and Andrew Whitehead. Thanks also to my excellent editors at Lexington Press, Sarah Craig and Courtney Lachapelle Morales.

Talented colleagues and students at the College of Idaho have collaborated with me for years through their conversation and encouragement, especially Sean Blackwell and Greg McElwain. My deep thanks to Ashley Smith for the cover's art design. Kirby Roberts, Zoe Roberts, Heather Vance, Alice Vinson, and Lucinda Wong provided crucial research assistance and technical expertise.

Although I cannot mention them by name, I also want to thank the generous congregations who not only welcomed me to practice alongside and write about them, but also volunteered to arrange and participate in focus groups. The organizations' leaders and focus group volunteers were all exceedingly gracious, and it was an honor and sincere pleasure to talk with all of them.

I also want to thank my family for all of their support over many years. Scott Smith, thank you for pulling off the road to visit The Garden. Thanks especially to Larisa Sergeevna Ryabokon, the love of my life, and my sons Vatslav and Stanislav Draper. Their love, patience, insight, and support is the foundation for every page of this book, and every moment of my life.

Introduction

Scan the contemporary religious landscape, and you will find people from all traditions fervently pursuing spiritual encounters. Look in one crowded church, and you find that everybody is jumping up and down and shouting, tears flowing freely. Across town, a well-dressed congregation stares at printed text and chants archaic words in unison. Over at the meditation center, twenty people sit cross-legged in a sweaty room and no one makes a sound. At the mosque, a dozen men, side-by-side, are digging their foreheads into a carpet while another man stands beside them and sings.

All of these people are engaged in "religion," and yet the contrasts in what they actually *do* during their rituals are striking. Do these differences matter? Religious *beliefs, after all, not rituals*, are what usually dominate contemporary conversations about religion. What matters is where one puts one's faith, one's pledge of allegiance to a particular god or creed. To be religious, it would seem, is to *think* certain things, or perhaps even to *call oneself* a certain thing. But then, what to make of all the rituals, which appear across all cultures and eras? What are all these people trying to do?

This book makes the case that, despite all the differences on the surface, rituals across religious traditions all strive for the same basic achievement: a feeling of the supernatural, or what I am calling "the spirit." The spirit is collective effervescence in rituals that focus on religion. As such, based on Émile Durkheim's argument, it is the source of not only religious beliefs, but also morality, identity, purpose, and even our ability to reason. I share evidence from fieldwork to show that the sources of the spirit are neither elusive nor mysterious. Rather, it will arise reliably when people in each other's company move and talk in certain ways.

[handwritten margin note: Focusing on practice]

1

Consider two moments recorded in my field notes:

Four grandmothers are clapping and singing about Heaven up at the front of the sanctuary. They want the rest of us to clap and sing too. Most of us don't seem to be feeling it yet. The oldest and smallest of the women gets playful. She leans forward, puts her hands on her hips, purses her lips; she is scolding us. Next, in rhythm with the digital organ, she starts jerking her body left and right, to-and-fro. The other grandmas watch her innovative dance moves and laugh. Someone says "Here she goes." A few seconds later, she's marching toward us, still in rhythm with the organist. Now she's walking in the aisle between the first few pews, hunching forward and clapping, looking in people's eyes, flashing contagious smiles. I have a quick vision of what this elderly woman might have looked like in her 20s. I'm feeling the music now. I look around. Most of the congregation is beaming. Many are laughing. Some are shouting her on. "Go girl!" "Mmm-hmm." Everybody's clapping. I'm too far back to make eye contact with her. Why didn't I sit closer to the front?

At another church, on another Sunday:

Pastor Craig asks us to stand up, turn to our neighbors, and greet them with the love of Christ. I never know what else I'm supposed to say at these moments, but I'll make a go of it. The married couple next to me is privately conferring with each other about something, so I turn to the pew behind me. I exchange good mornings with a family of four. The parents are cordial; their kids look at me suspiciously. The parents turn and greet someone else, and their kids sit back down. I just sort of stand there for a few seconds. There's another middle-aged guy next to the family, gazing toward the stage. "Good morning," I say. I seem to have broken his reverie. "Good morning," he says, with a half-smile and a nod. I extend my hand. We shake. He digs his hands back into his pockets. He's leaning back, looking at me quizzically. Maybe I'll tell him I'm a visitor, and ask how long he's been attending. "I'm Scott." He's Jack. That's as far as we get, since Pastor Craig is already telling us to turn to Hymn 143. I nod at Jack. He nods at me. While searching for Hymn 143, I have a chance to glance at my watch.

In the first account, a woman's sprightly dance moves transformed a Christian service. Something about her movements and sounds, and the way the congregation responded, clearly altered how the ritual *felt*. There was no mystery about the woman's intentions. As is very common in the black Protestant tradition of which she is a part, members of her church speak openly about their intentions to "feel the Spirit," and how they have to work together to make this happen. At home on Sunday mornings, they get "prayed up," trying to "get the Spirit going." They talk about Sunday School as though it is a "warm-up." When they talk about their services, they talk about *strategy*, almost like they are going into battle, or a competition of some sort. But who or what must they overcome, since they gather with *each other*? Based on their comments, it is the occasion itself that is the challenge. They have to work together to transform it from mundane to sacred. Success requires ingenuity and effort, and they admit that they do not always succeed. But they keep at it for hours if they have to, they usually *do* succeed, and they keep coming back for more.

The second account, from a different Christian church, was like many other moments during this research. It was hardly tragic, but like much of the rest of their service it looked and felt obligatory and halfhearted. Most of the congregation stood and greeted someone, but there was no chance to build up any interpersonal momentum. If a congregation thinks there is value in holding a greeting time, then why keep it so brief? This is not a merely rhetorical question, but rather is the sort of technical question I ask many times in the pages ahead. Worship leaders and congregants offer a variety of rationales for the practice itself. "Passing the peace" has been a formal feature of many Christian liturgies since ancient times, adapted by many contemporary congregations into a less formal "greeting," so one explanation is that they find inherent value in keeping up a long tradition. Additionally, this congregation prizes "fellowship," and looks to create opportunities, even brief ones, to build loving bonds with each other. The congregants also expressed, pragmatically, that they prefer not to sit still and listen for an entire hour. Standing and moving around a little "gets the blood flowing," and feels less like sitting through a lecture. I discovered after the service, though, the *main* reason for the brevity of this particular congregation's greeting practice: they pride themselves on prompt services that never extend beyond 60 minutes. Service length is an issue I consider closely in the pages ahead. No one wants a ritual to continue indefinitely, but comparison with other services suggests that this church's devotion to ending promptly is a simple ritual choice among many that impedes rather than advances their goal of a transformative spiritual encounter.

OBJECTIVE

The spirit is a powerful and unseen force that enters the scene when a religious ritual is clicking. By contrast, the spirit stays away when a ritual feels off, when those gathered are bored, distracted, or just going through the motions. With careful attention to the right details, we can confidently predict when this invisible power will arrive and vitalize.

I participated in a diverse range of religious rituals in order to decipher generalizable methods for capturing the spirit. The evidence I found suggests that the same small set of underlying social dynamics reliably determines whether a ritual succeeds or fails, regardless of which religious groups we want to consider and regardless of how different they might appear from each other on the surface. A ritual's effectiveness, and thus the spirit's arrival, routinely depends on issues that seem rather mundane by comparison—things like whether the church bulletin contains typos, where the door to the sanctuary is located, or how loud the organ is—but which nonetheless alter the social dynamics. Encounters with the spirit are collective achievements, dependent on concrete choices the congregation makes, even very subtle ones, regarding how to go about their ritual practices.

I joined in with Conservative Jews, Bible Belt Muslims, white Baptists, black Baptists, Latino Catholics, and Buddhist meditators. This sample design was motivated, in part, by a desire to account for organizations that fall outside the religious mainstream in America. Too often in the sociology of religion in the U.S., traditions such as Islam, Buddhism, Judaism, black Protestantism, and Latino Catholicism are effectively ignored due to relatively small numbers or lack of organizational records. Researchers frequently call for more work on non-Christian religious experiences and practices (e.g., Bruce 1999; Cadge et al. 2011; Edgell 2012; Poulson and Campbell 2010), and the nature of the research questions suggested that this study would be an excellent opportunity to consider some of these traditions in closer detail.

Focus groups from each organization spoke with me at length about their services and their past experiences together. I examine the microsociological details of these encounters over the course of five chapters. Each chapter focuses on a single ritual dynamic, and compares how it is handled by two separate religious groups.

Before providing more details on these methods, though, I should introduce the sociological theory that guided their logic.

A THEORY OF THE SPIRIT

This book's notion of spirit is based on ideas from Émile Durkheim. Durkheim used the phrase "collective effervescence" to indicate an intense emotional experience that emerges among people engaged together in a successful ritual. He argued that although the experience is *due* to the actions of a gathered crowd, they *attribute* it to sacred powers. In his study of ancient Australian and Native American religious rituals, Durkheim observed:

> Once the individuals are gathered together, a sort of electricity is generated from their closeness and quickly launches them to an extraordinary height of exaltation. Every emotion expressed resonates without interference in conscious-

nesses that are wide open to external impressions, each one echoing the others. The initial impulse is thereby amplified each time it is echoed, like an avalanche that grows as it goes along (1912, 217–18).

This self-perpetuating *force* is almost always considered by people who feel it to be mysterious and supernatural in origin. Durkheim, though, insisted that what they actually sense is collective emotion, catalyzed by particular patterns of social activity.

Durkheim argued that collective effervescence has enormous human consequences. Most fundamentally, as I will discuss in Chapter 1, he contended that effervescence opens up the possibility of shared "categories of the understanding," a basic mental framework that allows humans to reason together in mutually intelligible ways. His book *The Elementary Forms of Religious Life* is a bold attempt to settle a major epistemological debate, advancing a profound but frequently overlooked argument for the fundamental role of social practices (Durkheim 1912; Rawls 2004). Beyond this but related to it, he argued that effervescence produces "social solidarity," a long-term feeling that allows people to know with confidence who they are, what they are certain of, and what they want to do in the future.[1] Social solidarity preserves the feeling of force generated by collective effervescence. The individual recalls the ritual's power when she reencounters its sacred symbols, and the intense group experience thus continues to influence her perceptions, feelings, thoughts, and behaviors. The concept of social solidarity thereby opens a theoretical pathway for understanding how the group's collective spirit lingers and influences the individual even when she is alone.[2]

Durkheim's theory applies broadly in social life, to virtually any type of ritual. Religious rituals, though, when effective, are uniquely potent. Armed with authority over what is most sacred, they are particularly well-suited for generating feelings of certainty about identity, morality, and truth. The idea is that sacred beliefs and values are a *consequence* of religious rituals, not the other way around. In both Durkheim's era and our own, this argument for the priority of practice cuts against the grain of commonsense thinking about religion.

In recent years, Durkheim's theory has been updated and retooled by the sociologist Randall Collins. Collins' interaction ritual (IR) theory predicts when and how effervescence and solidarity will appear and what their consequences will be.[3] Although there is a growing interest in integrating insights from the sociology of religion and the sociology of emotions (Riis and Woodhead 2010), research on religious IRs is still in a very early stage.[4]

Collins' theory synthesizes accumulated knowledge from several of the discipline's most profound thinkers. Durkheim's work on religion and knowledge, George Herbert Mead's work on symbolic exchange and identity, and

Erving Goffman's work on the implicit rules of social interaction all provide microlevel starting points. Building up to higher levels of analysis, organizations are understood as groups of people who repeat certain kinds of rituals with each other, and whose ability to conduct emotionally intense rituals directs their degree of success in accomplishing collective goals (Collins 1975). Max Weber's work on organizational conflict, stratification, and power is integrated into the theory at this higher level of analysis. Along with these classic works, important contemporary work from exchange theorists, sociologists of emotions, phenomenologists, and symbolic interactionists is also integrated. The result is a cohesive body of concepts that serves the scientific purpose of offering generalizable explanations for a large range of particular social phenomena.

Society from an Airplane

Collins' conflict theory addresses several very "macro-" areas of social life, from the spread of bureaucratic cultures, to the management of violence by the state, to the success of ideologies across time and space. His stated intention is that all of these areas of research will be driven by "a sociology that builds up complex interrelations from the empirical realities of everyday interaction" (1975, 56). In other words, his approach is foundationally microsociological. Too often, he argues, sociologists work with abstract reifications like "structure" or "society" that effectively distance them from concrete observation. Like Georg Simmel and Erving Goffman, Collins prioritizes social interaction as the object of sociological investigation. He offers the following image:

> Imagine the view of human society from the vantage point of an airplane. What we can observe are buildings, roads, vehicles, and—if our senses were keen enough—people moving back and forth and talking to each other. Quite literally, this is all there is; all of our explanations and all of our subjects to be explained must be grounded in such observations (1975, 56).

The idea is that social scientists too frequently hypostatize. For instance, while much work in stratification identifies patterns of inequality in aggregated data, these patterns reveal little unless the researcher can also grasp how interacting humans create or sustain such patterns. The researcher may suggest that "social networks" sustain advantages for some groups over others, but even this concept forestalls deeper understanding until he can grasp why and how networks form and persist, and what interactional processes forge their bonds.

Interaction ritual theory is the part of Collins' larger conflict theory in which he proposes a handful of micro-level "dynamics," or "ingredients," that drive successful social rituals.[5,6] To the extent that the dynamics are effectively managed, participants are predicted to experience four main outcomes: *individual-level "emotional energy" (EE), social solidarity, symbols of social relationships (sacred objects),* and *standards of morality.* Anticipation of these outcomes, especially EE and solidarity, is what drives humans into each other's company. Because individuals differ in their interactional histories (their *interaction ritual chains*), there is much variety in which sorts of sacred objects and effervescent rituals will entice different individuals.

Emotional energy is the individual-level residue of collective effervescence. It is the buzz a person experiences immediately after a "stimulating" conversation or a "mind-blowing" live show. A person full of EE feels confidence, pride, and enthusiasm, evident in paralinguistic cues like eye contact and tall posture. By contrast, a person with depleted EE—after a bad date, for example—feels dissonance, shame, and lethargy, evident in cues like averted gazes and slouching (2004, 133–40). Collins argues that humans are "EE-seekers . . . [who] feel their way toward those situations in which, through the local combination of ingredients for making an IR happen, the EE payoff is highest" (2004, 157).[7] Interaction ritual theory takes as a starting point the image of individuals who are irresistibly drawn to social situations that, in one way or another, make them feel good.

Interactions that maximize individuals' sense of feeling good are interactions that successfully manage the following dynamics from Durkheim's and Goffman's ritual theories: *bodily copresence, mutually focused attention, a shared mood,* and *barriers to outsiders.* When these dynamics are proficiently managed, collective effervescence emerges and drives the above-mentioned outcomes of EE, solidarity, sacred objects, and moral standards. All of these variables reinforce each other in reciprocally influential feedback loops (Collins 2004, 48, 146). A model of IR theory is illustrated in Figure I.1.

For researchers, one of the advantages of this theory is its testability. The variables of interest can be measured and assessed in a relatively straightforward manner. This is not to say that the model has no gray areas. The dynamics and relationships are posited as recursive and overlapping, with, for instance, sacred objects facilitating social solidarity which, in turn, inspires more gatherings around sacred objects in the future. It is probably analytically hopeless to try to trace an indubitably unidirectional path from the "independent variables" to the "dependent variables." Nonetheless, the model provides clear ideal types that serve as a basis for research and discovery. Further, the propositional format of the model encourages systematic testing and revision,

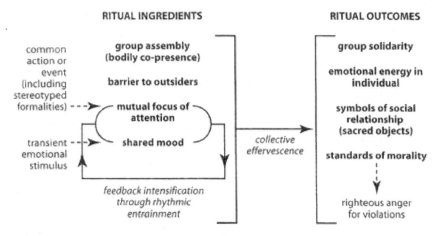

Figure I.1. Interaction Ritual Model
Reproduced with permission of the publisher from p. 48 of Interaction Ritual Chains, by Randall Collins.
©2004 by Princeton University Press.

promoting a sociology grounded in real, observable human interaction. Sociology is a vast field of inquiry that will benefit from continued rigorous analysis of big-picture, macrolevel questions. By the logic of IR theory, though, big-picture findings are virtually useless if we don't understand what they have to do with "people moving back and forth and talking to each other."

ON THE GROUND AND IN THE PEWS

I participated in rituals with six religious organizations located in different cities throughout Texas, where I resided at the time.[8] On the selected days of observation, I attended the services like any other visitor and participated, as well as I could, in the ritual activities. I joined in with members[9] as together we sang, moved, talked, looked, and listened. During certain moments of prayer or meditation, this research was conducted literally on the ground. After each service, I talked with focus groups[10] to inform my analysis regarding (1) how the ritual dynamics operated, (2) what emotions they experienced, and (3) what degree of solidarity they felt.

Sample of Rituals

This purposive sample is composed of rituals from religious traditions that I expected, based on existing research, to embody diverse IR dynamics. That said, it is crucial to note at the outset that this book is about the effectiveness of *rituals*, not *religious traditions*. In terms of method, a single ritual analyzed at the microlevel cannot adequately summarize defining features of a macrolevel concept like religious tradition.[11] Instead, the goal here is microsociological analysis of the rituals themselves.

Black and white Baptist denominations suggest different ends of the spectrum in terms of the typical levels of outward expression associated with their worship styles (Ammerman 1987, 1995, 1997; Bond 2002; Chaves 2004; Lincoln and Mamiya 1990; Nelson 2005). Although there are exceptions, black Baptist congregations commonly engage in highly expressive styles of worship.[12] White Southern Baptist congregations vary within the denomination, but the typical congregation tends to be more restrained during worship. These two traditions presented a good basis for comparing different strategies for generating social solidarity and intersubjectivity (Chapters 2 and 4).

I also compare rituals from two traditions that routinely have been marginalized in the U.S.: Judaism and Islam. The Jewish and Muslim organizations presented an opportunity to compare different strategies for managing barriers with outsiders (Chapter 5). These two organizations were also a good contrast in terms of historical tradition, the size of their memberships (large and small, respectively), the strength of their resource base (rich and poor, respectively), and their gender norms during worship (women openly participated in the Jewish service, but were segregated during the Muslim service). I suggest ways in which their contrasting attributes and worship styles shape their ability to capture the spirit (Chapter 1).

Rounding out the sample, I consider two organizations, one Vajrayana Buddhist and the other Latino-Catholic, that raise intriguing questions about the properties of physical copresence (Chapter 3). The Buddhists warrant consideration because their organization's central practice of mindfulness meditation would seem to suggest that physical copresence is not a necessary ritual ingredient; but what happens when they get together for *group* meditation sessions? The Catholic Mass allowed me to observe what I knew would be an extremely crowded IR. I had driven by the church on multiple Sunday mornings, and couldn't help but notice the throngs of parishioners competing for parking spaces and standing in line to get in the church doors. The raw numbers alone made the church a good candidate for research on copresence, and the sample was enriched with the inclusion of this understudied yet prominent religious tradition.

Indicators

Searching for signs of the spirit is a quest taken not just by social scientists; adherents often do it themselves. Timothy Nelson reports, for example, a "twofold problem" for the black Protestant Eastside Chapel: "how to success-fully invoke God's Spirit, and how to recognize the Spirit when he comes" (2005, 144). Adherents often insist that its presence is simply "felt," but they themselves are not always sure that the feeling is real and so look for observ-able signs to confirm their impressions (Inbody 2015).

By definition the spirit is immaterial, making its observation a formidable task. Still, the concept is too fundamental in social theory and human experi-ence more generally to abandon the effort. I wanted to proceed with caution, and for this reason I took a systematic and triangulated approach.

During the visits, I looked for specific indicators of effervescence and solidarity. For reasons explained later in this chapter, I knew that I needed to find out about two *types* of social solidarity: "membership solidarity" and "symbolic solidarity." I assessed membership solidarity by asking group members about the extent to which people in their organization experience a sense of belonging. To assess symbolic solidarity, I asked about the extent to which they share a common goal or vision.[13] I also asked members to tell me about any activities they partake in with the organization, apart from worship services. These prompts and follow-up questions initiated further conversa-tion in which the participants volunteered additional details relevant to both types of solidarity in their organizations.

Apart from the focus group questions, I also observed members as they in-teracted with each other and/or with me prior to, during, and after the rituals. This approach was more useful with regard to symbolic solidarity, and less so with respect to membership solidarity. Friendly interactions are simply too standard in such settings, and I knew it would be prohibitively difficult to try to distinguish which friendly exchanges signaled genuine feelings of membership solidarity and which were more obligatory or forced. I did, however, observe numerous signs of symbolic solidarity. The clearest signs of symbolic solidarity were: *repetitions* of words, phrases, or physical move-ments that were *characteristic* of the organization, by *different* members of the organization on *multiple* occasions.[14]

With respect to collective effervescence, focus group members were asked to describe their moods prior to, during, and after the service. Respondents almost never spoke negatively about their experiences in their organization's rituals.[15] But they usually provided clear reports regarding the degree of emotional inten-sity they had felt. These indicators ranged from words with more sedate conno-tations like "calm," "peaceful," and "relaxed" to words with more invigorating connotations like "uplifted," "energized," and "Spirit-filled."[16]

As much as the literal content of their responses, I also took account of the way members delivered their responses. Some responded quickly and defini-tively and received immediate affirmation from the group; these responses were always "positive" assessments of the rituals and were considered evidence in favor of effervescence. Other groups equivocated or asked me to repeat the question; these responses were always connected to less enthusiastic assessments of the ritual and were considered evidence of a relative lack of effervescence. In addition to questions about their moods, I asked if any aspects of the ritual had stood out to the focus groups on the day we all attended. This question provided an additional opportunity for participants to volunteer their emotional responses to the ritual.

Focus group members' responses regarding effervescence were highly informative, and received the greatest priority in my summaries of the services' levels of emotional intensity. Still, they needed to be supplemented with observations of the ritual itself. The clearest indicators during the rituals had to do with the *absence* of effervescence. Although there may be ambiguity in recognizing whether apparent effervescence is real or fake, there is little ambiguity in recognizing when effervescence is absent. Colloquially, Americans tend to refer to these moments as "*awkward.*" In moments of low emotional intensity, a high percentage of participants yawned, coughed, cleared their throats, sat or stood with passive body language, looked away from the action and around the room, refrained from singing and other collective liturgies, flipped through bulletins, or exited the room. These periods of low emotional intensity provided a stark contrast with other periods in the same ritual in which the emotional intensity was high.[17] Signs like yawns, slouching, and exits were replaced (or preceded) by signs that suggested greater emotional engagement by a high percentage of participants. These signs included crying, laughing, erect posture, looking intently in the direction of the action, singing or chanting with volume and synchronicity, and talking enthusiastically with other participants about the ritual.

Along with focus group responses and indicators during the ritual, I also report a number of physical behaviors that ultimately could be interpreted as either catalysts or expressions of collective emotional intensity. Consider clapping. Does clapping cause excitement?[18] Alternately, does clapping express an excitement that the clappers already possess? Or, does clapping merely *look like* excitement when in fact it is tangential to how the clappers actually feel?[19] Noting the complexities involved in definitively answering such questions, I found in practice that the combination of focus groups' responses and the totality of my observations of their rituals provided, in each case, a strong impression of the level of overall emotional intensity that their ritual achieved. While it is certainly possible that activities such as clapping, dancing, hugging, shouting, and kissing may instigate emotional intensity, they are treated as supplementary indicators of effervescence when the preponderance of indicators at a given ritual already supports that interpretation.

Each ritual exhibited a combination of behaviors that supported a clear overall assessment of effervescence. In each case, the combined indicators also supported my own subjective emotional response to the ritual, which I took seriously as relevant data. I acknowledge that my own biases, both recognized and unrecognized, may have impacted my emotional responses, priming my enthusiasm for some rituals over others. Additionally, I do not pretend to have noticed every detail of any of the rituals; it is possible (especially in larger congregations) that "pockets" of effervescence developed in some parts of the sanctuary but not others, and that the limitations of my own senses and attention prevented me from comprehending the total impact of each ritual. Emotional energy is not necessarily equally distributed and, to varying degrees in different observations, I may have been in a better or worse position than other participants to experience effervescence.

Despite these limitations on the validity of my subjective emotional response, evaluation of my response is important to the research questions because collective effervescence is supposed to be a collective emotional experience. My approach adheres to Riis and Woodhead's methodological recommendations in *A Sociology of Religious Emotion* (2010). In particular, the process of "critical emotional empathy" involves taking seriously the researcher's emotional responses to the rituals, comparing these with subjects' self-reported responses, and critically assessing both responses through triangulation of empirical methods. In research on emotions, the copresent researcher's own emotions are a necessary and interrogable part of the data.

In sum, analysis of each ritual's outcomes involved consideration of the following types of data, ranked from most- to least-decisive: (1) the content of focus group responses, (2) the manner of focus group responses, (3) observations of members' interactions before, during, and after the ritual, (4) observations of relatively unambiguous ritual indicators, (5) observations of more ambiguous ritual indicators, and (6) my own subjective emotional response to the ritual. In each case, the combined evidence left a distinct impression of the ritual's effervescence and the organization's solidarity.

THE PANORAMIC PICTURE: FINDINGS FROM THE USCLS

As a supplement to this book's qualitative analysis, I analyzed responses from *The United States Congregational Life Survey* (USCLS), a sample of over 70,000 worshipers from a wide variety of religious traditions. The goal was a mixed-methods approach that would ground this study's conclusions in both macrolevel patterns and microlevel specifics. Although analytic priority in IR theory needs to be reserved for the microlevel, the statistical patterns from the USCLS provided several new insights into congregations' efforts to capture the spirit. I will intermittently alert interested readers to relevant statistical analyses that can be found in Appendix A.

I conducted the survey analysis prior to the field work.[20] The process of operationalizing IR dynamics and outcomes based on survey data opened up new ways to think about the theory, and inspired several of the concepts and questions considered in the main chapters. Because of this, a brief summary here of the most striking and relevant USCLS findings will prepare readers for what follows.

The USCLS provides data from a large sample of U.S. religious congregations which includes evangelicals, mainline Protestants, black Protestants, Catholics, Jews, Mormons, and Buddhists. Randomly selected congregations throughout the U.S. were enlisted to distribute the survey to everyone who attended a worship service with their congregation on the weekend of April 29, 2001. The surveyors' approach allowed me, in analysis, to establish per-congregation averages on key variables, and then compare congregations with each other. Respondents provided information about what their congregation is like, what they do during their services, and, crucially, how their services impact their emotions. The questions on emotions allowed a rare statistical test of Durkheim's classic hypothesis that collective effervescence stimulates social solidarity. The survey also contains good measures of ritual dynamics, so I also test how physical copresence, intersubjectivity, and barriers to outsiders impact effervescence and solidarity.

The most important question is whether, as Durkheim contended, effervescence really does generate solidarity. Despite the long-standing theoretical importance of Durkheim's conclusion, no prior research has attempted to discern quantitative evidence of the relationship. The evidence from the USCLS, though, confirms it. This is a crucial discovery, as it lends much credence to Durkheim's hypothesis that the invigoration felt during successful rituals is the source of humans' most cherished convictions about the nature of reality, identity, and morality.

The USCLS analysis led to several other key discoveries, as well:

- Crowded assemblies entice to the spirit, unless the members of the crowd are too rich or highly educated (relevant dynamic: *bodily copresence*).
- The longer the ritual, the more likely the spirit will show up (*focus of attention*).
- When a high proportion of members attend frequently (creating *interaction ritual chains*), the spirit is inclined to join them.
- The spirit favors organizations who designate certain behaviors as stigmatic (*barriers to outsiders*).

In all of the above, the general rule is that more is better: more people, more time, more attendance, and more prohibitions. In one important and revealing area, though, less is more:

- Organizations who claim to value diversity *less* have the best chance of capturing the spirit (*barriers to outsiders*).

The USCLS analysis led me to rethink two concepts in particular, bodily copresence and social solidarity, which need to be discussed before proceeding.

Bodily Copresence/Bodily Density

When considering how to evaluate IR theory with survey data, my initial understanding was that bodily copresence is a simple either/or ("dichotomous") variable. You either have copresence or you don't, and without it a ritual cannot take place. This struck me as a simple precondition for analysis and thus an empirical dead-end.

The work of Erving Goffman, though, provided a crucial insight. Over the course of several books (1963, 1967, 1971) he meticulously archives different ways in which the arrangement of bodies influence the emotional dynamics of a social occasion. In particular, his essay "Where the Action Is" (1967) points to the power of the *crowd*. For example, imagine walking down a city street on a Friday night. You pass by a number of quiet bars and clubs that fail to attract your attention. Outside one club, though, a long line has formed with potential patrons waiting to get through the door. A roar of voices can be heard inside, and a glance inside the windows reveals individuals pressed shoulder-to-shoulder. Certainly, this type of social situation will entice some more than others.[21] One thing is clear, though: it is a gathering that exudes social excitement.[22] All rituals contain at least some social risk, but the most crowded rituals have a unique power to convey "action."[23] Further, a crowded situation increases the likelihood of physical contact, along with other incidental or intentional intimacies which require trust, and for this reason as well has the potential to stimulate effervescence. As bodies move closer to each other, copresence increases. Bodily copresence, then, should be treated as a continuous rather than dichotomous variable.

Based on this reasoning, I developed a new variable called "bodily density," or "crowdedness," from the USCLS data.[24] The concept refers to the proximity of human bodies in a given physical space, or the crowdedness of the ritual. It would not be sufficient just to compare congregations' raw attendance numbers. Rather, the sizes of their ritual spaces must also be taken into account. For example, consider how much action is conveyed by 50 people in a stadium vs. 50 people in a living room. I approximated the average bodily density in USCLS congregations' rituals with a formula that divides each congregation's average attendance by their seating capacity.

To my surprise, bodily density initially did not appear strongly connected to congregations' levels of emotional intensity during rituals. That is, not until I found a way to simultaneously account for the congregations' socioeconomic statuses (i.e., their average levels of wealth and education). When *class* was taken into account, a striking pattern emerged:

- Poorer congregations experience an *increase* in effervescence when the ritual is crowded.
- Wealthier congregations experience a *decrease* in effervescence when the ritual is crowded.

It turned out that Goffman had arrived at the same conclusion about 50 years ago, in his case based on microsociological observation: "Here . . . is one of the important differences between social classes in our society: . . . the higher the class the more extensive and elaborate are the taboos against contact" (Goffman 1967, 67). Mutual deference in the form of personal space is preferred in IRs of wealthier congregations, in particular.

It is important to keep in mind that, like most findings in the social sciences, this is a probabilistic rather than determinative relationship. Certainly, high-status individuals can be found in contemporary life who do not mind crowds, or even who thrive on them (a number of politicians and celebrities come to mind, for example). Rather than being some kind of essential quality of all people who possess wealth, the relationship can instead be traced historically to the cultural construction of manners (Elias 1978, 1982).[25] The emotional consequences of bodily density and class, as well as their combined consequences, are considered throughout the ensuing chapters.

Two Types of Social Solidarity

Social solidarity involves feelings of membership, and it also involves shared purposes. These two ideas represent different *types* of solidarity. The notion that there are different types of social solidarity guides much of the work of Erving Goffman, especially in books like *Behavior in Public Places* (1963) and *Relations in Public* (1971). Goffman was obsessed with cataloging the seemingly endless varieties of social ties, varying in permanence and intensity, and the numerous signs that express the status of those ties.[26]

The first type of solidarity I examine is the type I consider the most basic. I call it "membership solidarity." It is the feeling that one is welcome and properly belongs in a particular group or organization. The second type of solidarity is a more prolonged and intense kind of solidarity, "symbolic solidarity." This type involves an allegiance to the symbols and goals of one's group or organization.

In the USCLS analysis, collective effervescence boosted *both* types of solidarity. It had a more powerful effect, though, on symbolic solidarity. Membership solidarity was felt by at least 51% of the respondents in every congregation in the sample, suggesting that this type of solidarity may even be a baseline requirement for all religious organizations, regardless of how emotionally intense their services are. We can hypothesize, based on this, that voluntary organizations in which less than half of members feel membership solidarity will eventually just stop meeting. Symbolic solidarity has greater range and variation across congregations, and is more responsive to the effects of effervescent rituals. Throughout the book, I distinguish these types of social solidarity for qualitative analysis, as well, comparing them in terms of their sources and consequences.

OVERVIEW

Although the organizations I visited for this book symbolize the spirit in different ways, their efforts to capture it are fundamentally similar. Their degree of success depends on how they handle IR dynamics. These dynamics will be examined in sequence in the ensuing chapters. I use a comparative approach to analyze the rituals. Each qualitative chapter focuses on two rituals that differ in ways that help illuminate properties of the chapter's conceptual focus.

Chapter 1 scrutinizes the pivotal concept of effervescence. The two organizations considered in the chapter demonstrate that effervescence is not a random or static event, but must be strategically pursued. Congregation Shalom exemplified a cumulative effervescence, building toward an emotional climax with the resources of mini-IRs, free physical movement, and a patient orientation toward time. The Islamic Center, on the other hand, was disadvantaged for effervescence from the outset because of limited resources and cultural context. The marginality of their tradition in the U.S. compromises many Muslim organizations' efforts to (1) promptly gather on their holy day, (2) with an adequate number of participants, (3) with material resources that can catalyze effervescence.

Chapter 2 investigates social solidarity. Promised Land Baptist is an all-black church that exemplifies symbolic solidarity. Like effervescence, symbolic solidarity must be strategically pursued. Due to hard conditions in their local context, this pursuit is necessarily ongoing for members of Promised

Land. During the service I observed, the church recognized and acted on a communal need to reenergize their sacred symbols in the wake of a deadly shooting of two young men from their community. Promised Land held a highly effervescent ritual that functioned as a badly needed stimulus to symbolic solidarity. First Baptist Church is a mostly white church that clearly exemplifies membership solidarity. Compared with Promised Land, First Baptist's worship service, and members' comments about the same, revealed much less urgency and intensity in pursuing a collective goal. I argue that key differences in the two congregations' sacred symbols shaped the contrasting levels of urgency and intensity evident in their rituals.

In Chapter 3, I examine properties of physical copresence. The Meditation Center raised a fundamental question regarding the importance of copresence: since mindfulness meditation is recognized by many Buddhists as a practice that facilitates individual-level enlightenment, what is the benefit, if any, of meditating in a room full of other people? St. John's Catholic Church also held a ritual that prompted compelling questions about the properties of copresence. I knew in advance that St. John's was an active, well-populated parish that brought together a large proportion of the local community's Latino population, and I expected the crowdedness of the church to facilitate high levels of collective effervescence. To the contrary, my observations and members' reports suggested that St. John's had perhaps the least spirited IR in the sample. Why did St. John's present a challenge to the crowd hypothesis? Further, why did the somber mood inside the sanctuary conflict so much with the effervescent IRs I observed outside the church's doors prior to the service?

Chapter 4 explores intersubjectivity. This term refers to the sensation among interactants that their feelings and thoughts have more or less merged during a ritual, and encompasses the closely related dynamics of shared mood and shared focus of attention. Shared mood and shared focus of attention both depend on two subdynamics: *mutual monitoring* and *rhythmic entrainment*. I return to a comparison of Promised Land and First Baptist in this chapter. Despite their doctrinal similarities, the churches managed their IRs in distinct ways. First Baptist Church held an IR that was short, comfortable, and by members' accounts, "relaxing." Promised Land Baptist Church, by contrast, held an IR that was long, intense, and "energizing." The churches' contrasting methods of ritual management led to greater focus, shared mood, and overall effervescence for Promised Land, and lower levels of each for First Baptist.

Chapter 5 examines the final dynamic, barriers to outsiders, by again comparing rituals at the Islamic Center and Congregation Shalom. At the Islamic Center, barriers are both imposed by the surrounding culture and also generated from within. Because of cultural context, the Islamic Center experiences moral pressure to assure outsiders that they are neither extrem-ists nor terrorists. From within, the organization establishes barriers through the proficiency/cultural capital required to participate in the ritual. Like the Islamic Center, Congregation Shalom benefitted emotionally from engaging in ritual activities that require years of regular practice in order to know when to do what and how to do it. To a greater extent than the Islamic Center, however, Congregation Shalom's perceptions of barriers fueled their effer-vescence and solidarity.

The final chapter synthesizes findings and conclusions from the prior chap-ters, and suggests ways in which these findings inform other compelling is-

Table I.1.   Organizations and Points of Comparison

Organization	Tradition	Points of Comparison
Congregation Shalom	Conservative Jewish	• Rich material resources • Peak bodily density = 0.9 • 3-hour ritual • High barriers of ritual proficiency • Women participate alongside men • Recitation of enemy atrocities
The Islamic Center	Muslim	• Poor material resources • Peak bodily density = 0.05 • 42-minute ritual • High barriers of ritual proficiency • Women are segregated during services • Seeks interfaith harmony
Promised Land Baptist Church	Black Protestant	• Poor material resources • Peak bodily density = 0.25 • 3-hour ritual • Emotionally expressive • Collectivistic solidarity symbols
First Baptist Church	Evangelical Protestant	• Rich material resources • Peak bodily density = 0.33 • 1-hour ritual • Emotionally reserved • Individualistic solidarity symbols
The Meditation Center	Tibetan Buddhist	• Rich material resources • Peak bodily density = 0.75 • 45-minute ritual • Individualistic solidarity symbols
St. John's Catholic Church	Latino Catholic	• Poor material resources • Peak bodily density = 0.9 • 1-hour ritual • High ritual stratification

sues in the sociology of religion. I consider the dimensions of religiosity, Max Weber's views on the naturalistic origins of religion, images of God, rational choice theory and related theories of religious identity, William James' views on religious experiences, and the spirit's role in social conflict.

Two appendices are also provided. Appendix A discloses and explains key findings from my analysis of USCLS data. Appendix B lists the questions asked during focus groups, along with basic demographic details of the focus group members.

CONCLUSION

In religious life, what are the social sources and consequences of the spirit? While pursuing these questions, I'll also tackle related questions like:

- How do material aspects of rituals impact the spirit? For example, does it matter how many people are gathered, how much money they have, or even which musical instruments they choose to play?
- Does a ritual's location affect the spirit? Does the design of the worship space make a difference? Does a group's ability to conjure it depend on where they happen to live?
- Is the spirit influenced by timing? Does it matter how long a ritual lasts, or which events happen during which moments? Related, can the spirit be hurried?
- How does the spirit conjoin discrete minds?
- When the spirit drifts away, how can it be recaptured?
- Is the spirit enticed by certain kinds of symbols more than others? How does it respond to individualism? How does it respond when some participants, all the men for example, are given privileged statuses during worship?
- How and why does a spirit of solidarity metamorphose into a spirit of conflict?
- How and why does a spirit of conflict metamorphose into a spirit of solidarity?

Interaction ritual theory offers clear ways to use evidence to answer these questions. If its predictions are accurate, then identity, morality, and ideology are collective accomplishments that depend on congregations' choices about how to arrange their ritual practices. Chapter 1 takes the next step by looking at how contrasting ritual strategies by a Jewish synagogue and a Muslim masjid impacted each congregation's ability to reach collective effervescence.

NOTES

1. The dark side of solidarity is conflict, as people learn who they are *not*, what lies they want to expose, and what kind of future they want to prevent. This concomitant theme will be examined throughout this book.

2. Chapter 2 and the Conclusion will consider how individuals' *private* religious experiences are tied to collective rituals.

3. Pieces of IR theory can be found throughout Collins' body of work, but two of his books give the most sustained attention to interaction rituals. *Conflict Sociology* (1975) expresses IR theory with a set of testable propositions within a broader conflict theory. *Interaction Ritual Chains* (2004) also provides testable propositions, adding several new twists.

4. Some of the studies that have led the way include Baker (2010), Barone (2007), Collins (2010), Heider and Warner (2010), Inbody (2015), Summers Effler (2010), Wellman et al. (2014), and Wollschleger (2012).

5. The word "ritual" is tricky because it is defined in a multitude of different ways within and between academic disciplines (e.g., Bell 1992, 1997; Freud 1989; Levi-Strauss 1958; Rappaport 1999). Goffman (who coined the phrase "interaction ritual") and Collins mean the term to apply very broadly in social life. Collins defines ritual as "a mechanism of mutually focused emotions and attention producing a momentarily shared reality, which thereby generates solidarity and symbols of group membership" (2004, 7). That IR theory considers rituals to be nearly omnipresent in social life does not render the concept useless for analysis. The key is that rituals can be analyzed as a set of variables, with ritual intensity (effervescence) and social solidarity as outcomes that range from low to high. See Collins (2004, 9–32) for distinctions between the conceptualization of "ritual" in IR theory and in other 20th-century scholarly movements.

6. Interaction ritual theory's emphasis on Durkheimian theory can be misunderstood. Durkheim and many 20th-century Durkheim scholars assumed functionalism, the idea that rituals (along with every other social phenomenon) serve a larger "society" by helping it function properly (cf. Rawls 2003, 314, 332). IR theory rejects functionalism, social Darwinism, and code-seeking programs, drawing instead on Durkheim's "subcognitive ritualism." Subcognitive ritualism conveys the idea that group symbols, moralities, and identities are *products* of emotionally powerful rituals.

7. This image of "EE-seekers" has a parallel in the assumptions of exchange theories. IR theory's individual actor is, like Coleman's (1990) rational chooser, predisposed to maximize his own self-interest. The difference is that IR theory's self-interested individual strives after *emotional* profits that may or may not be (but often are) related to material profits. I consider this theoretical synthesis in Chapter 5 and the Conclusion.

8. The names and locations of the six organizations, as well as the names of all individuals associated with the organizations, have been changed or withheld.

9. I use the term "members" loosely throughout this book, meaning "people who attend the organization's rituals with some regularity." I do not make a distinction between official members and nonmember participants who regularly attend.

10. My initial contacts, all leaders in their organizations, generously assisted me by finding willing volunteers for the focus groups. Obviously, then, the focus groups were not randomly selected. They likely are biased in the direction of more active and enthusiastic members whom the leaders felt could be relied upon to attend a focus group after the service.

11. Any of these organizations could be outliers within their tradition. For example, only a minority of American Buddhists (and an even smaller proportion in "New Buddhism" movements) regularly attend formal services (Coleman 2001; Wiist et al. 2012), so it would be reckless to conclude that the rituals examined in this book represent "The American Buddhist Experience" or other generalizations of this sort. Similarly, analysis of a single ritual does not allow speculation about an organization's *other* rituals which I did not observe. For this reason, I rely entirely on focus group members' reports, sometimes supplemented with existing scholarship, when considering anything that falls outside the bounds of the observed ritual, itself. Members informed me, for example, about their organizations' histories, current programs, and community relations, and they also helped me understand ways in which the service I observed was or was not typical of their other services.

12. Note that I do not equate "highly expressive styles of worship" with "collective effervescence." Rather, expressive and restrained styles of worship represent different strategies for pursuing intersubjectivity, different forms of emotional management which can potentially help or hinder shared emotions and thoughts. The sample considered here does suggest that, at least when considered in combination with other ritual dynamics, emotional expression does generally seem like a commendable strategy for achieving intersubjectivity, but overall I proceed from the assumption that collective effervescence can result from quiet assemblies as well as loud ones, among introverts as well as extroverts. As light empirical support for this theoretical assumption, analysis of the *United States Congregational Life Survey* shows no significant differences in levels of effervescence for congregations who frequently shout "Amen!" compared with those who do not.

13. Both of these solidarity questions were borrowed directly from the *United States Congregational Life Survey*, the source for Appendix A, discussed in more detail below.

14. Another good method for "measuring" symbolic solidarity is to track the display of physical emblems. An example can be found in Collins (2012), where he counted the number of American flags displayed in certain locations over a period of months following the 9/11 attacks on the U.S. In this case, he was thus able to trace the rocket-like trajectory over time of post-atrocity national solidarity.

15. Only at St. John's Catholic Church did a focus group member directly criticize his organization's ritual. I report this criticism in Chapter 3. Other focus group members, however, especially in the Buddhist and Muslim organizations, did report their own personal struggles remaining focused and engaged during their rituals. These reports were framed as self-criticism, not as something amiss with their organization's rituals.

16. Inbody (2015) highlights additional self-reported bodily sensations that researchers should look for, all having to do with the worshiper's skin. These include

"goosebumps," "tingling," "chills," "warmth," and "heat." Inbody's innovative study of IR methods was published after I had already collected the data, but I now whole-heartedly agree that asking respondents to describe their somatic sensations during rituals is a smart direction for future IR research.

17. As I will show, the Islamic Center, Congregation Shalom, and Promised Land Baptist all moved from lower intensity to higher intensity over the course of their gatherings. In the other direction, First Baptist, the Meditation Center, and St. John's all moved from higher intensity to lower intensity over the course of their gatherings.

18. To the extent that it does, this would be an example of what Reddy (1997) refers to as an "emotive." Emotives do not simply express an inner state, nor are they purely performative. Rather, "Emotives are themselves instruments for directly changing, building, hiding, intensifying emotions" (331). Emotional utterances or acts of this type can have an affective impact not only on the actor herself, but also on those around her.

19. I have attended seminars and classes where the leader tried to rev up the group by getting us to clap, do "the wave," and other supposedly fun activities. When mor-ally imposed on an unwilling audience, such activities can be emotionally draining.

20. Some of the USCLS findings shown in Appendix A were originally published in Draper (2014).

21. Those who would prefer to avoid it might include, for example, bookworms, rebels, the elderly, germaphobes, and, as we'll see, many members of the upper class.

22. Promoters of live events such as concerts, plays, and stand-up comedy shows understand quite well this basic principle. Theater troupes, for example, will often "paper the house," giving away free tickets for early performances. This helps publi-cize the show through word-of-mouth and, more important, ensures that the perform-ers don't have to play to an EE-depleting empty house.

23. As I discuss in Chapter 4, this feeling is likely to intensify as participants share a common focus of attention. At the low end, consider a crowded elevator or subway car. At the high end, consider a wedding or public execution.

24. See Morgan (1996, 132–33, 137) for a discussion of bodily density within family practices.

25. As Norbert Elias details in his two-volume history of civilization, the prefer-ence for personal space among cultural elites has historical origins in early modern court societies, where careful regulation of one's own body (i.e., "manners") signified legitimate membership in the class of nobles. Prior to that era, "[t]he old nobleman-as-warrior had no need of good manners, had such a concept even been clearly defined. Since his nobility inhered in his blood, whatever he did was by definition admirable" (Ehrenreich 2006, 115). Medieval knights could prove their high status, if necessary, through acts of individual valor in battles or duels. As military priorities shifted in the early modern era, though, kings increasingly amassed standing armies and required their closest competitors—the knights—to stop gallivanting around the countryside and instead live within the king's court, where the kings could keep a watchful eye upon them. No longer proving their valor on the battlefield, nobles gradually arrived at a new method of status-display. It was in this setting, according to Elias, that man-ners as we know them today first emerged. Good manners in this context had nothing

to do with hygiene, but everything to do with presenting a demeanor worthy of deference. As Ehrenreich puts it, "The notion of 'personal space' and the horror of other people's bodily processes that set limits on human physical interaction in our own time arose, originally, out of social anxiety and distrust" (2006, 116).

26. Also see Collins (2004, 25).

Chapter One

Collective Effervescence

When introduced in sociology courses and textbooks, collective efferves-cence[1] is often depicted as an exciting crowd experience which sometimes happens during exotic tribal festivals or, closer to many students' life ex-periences, fun live events like concerts and basketball games. Often missed in these discussions is the phenomenon's foundational importance in *all* of social life. If Durkheim was right, it is much more than a way of describing moments of exhilaration in large crowds. Rather, regular doses of collective effervescence make human culture possible. Without it, we would never be able to form basic convictions about who we are, what we're supposed to be doing with ourselves, or what the world is really like. Without effervescence, argues Durkheim, we wouldn't even be able to understand each other.

This chapter examines how two religious congregations, one Jewish and one Muslim, manage their ritual practices to pursue and achieve this critical group experience. First, though, Durkheim's ideas about effervescence need to be contextualized within a fascinating theory of knowledge that is at the center of *The Elementary Forms of Religious Life*.

HOW DO WE COME TO KNOW WHAT WE THINK WE KNOW?

Anne Rawls' (2004) *Epistemology and Practice* shows that Durkheim's main purpose in *The Elementary Forms* has been consistently overlooked: a socio-logical solution to the epistemological impasse between Humean skepticism and Kantian apriorism. Put simply, this is a debate over how humans can ever come to know anything at all.[2]

Based on Rawls' analysis, the problem Durkheim was attempting to solve is how individuals secure "the categories of the understanding," a small and

limited set of notions—time, space, classification, force, causality, and totality—without which human thought as we know it could not operate (Rawls
2004, 1–2; Durkheim 1912, 8–9).[3] The categories, Durkheim explains, "are
like solid frames that confine thought," and "seem to us as almost inseparable
from the normal functioning of the intellect" (9). Although the contents of
thoughts vary across individuals and cultures, these basic forms of thought
appear to be universal. The notion of basic categories of understanding is
found throughout the history of philosophy, from Aristotle to Kant and beyond. But where do these categories originate in human experience? David
Hume considered whether a person could derive the categories through empirical observation of natural phenomena, and concluded that individuals'
ever-shifting sense perceptions are entirely insufficient for securing this kind
of understanding. "Reason," then, is nothing more than a habit. Immanuel
Kant, though, thought that we are able to overcome the limits of our perceptions because the categories of the understanding originate in the mind itself,
"a priori" in human consciousness.[4]

In *The Elementary Forms*, Durkheim offers a solution to the dilemma
posed by the conflicting epistemologies of Hume and Kant. He found neither
position satisfactory. Both positions are fatally flawed, he argued, because
both focus on the individual *in isolation*. If the individual is assumed as
the "artisan" who constructs the categories based on her sense impressions,
Hume's skepticism ends up as the only conclusion (12). Durkheim writes,

> [J]ust as [the categories of the understanding] are not attached to any particular
> object, they are independent of any individual subject. They are the common
> ground where all minds meet. What is more, minds meet there of necessity:
> Reason, which is none other than the fundamental categories taken together, is
> vested with an authority that we cannot escape at will. . . . But the characteristics
> of empirical data are diametrically opposite. A sensation or an image is always
> linked to a definite object or collection of definite objects, and it expresses the
> momentary state of a particular consciousness. It is fundamentally individual
> and subjective. (13)

Rawls sums up the problem with the individual-as-artisan-of-the-categories
thesis as follows:

> When knowledge is thought to begin with individual experience, certain prob-
> lems arise: the things that persons experience change from day to day and from
> moment to moment. Nothing is ever exactly the same twice and the stream of
> experience (if persons have not already acquired general categories of thought)
> is constantly changing and undifferentiated (in a state of flux) (1996, 432).

Although Durkheim agreed with the empiricists that the categories must originate in experience, he emphasized their own conclusion that there would then be no way to determine how different individuals at different times derive universal, empirically valid categories of understanding. On the other hand, although he agreed with the apriorists that the categories must be universally valid, he argued that they were intellectually lazy to assume that the categories must therefore be innate in individuals' minds.

Durkheim's solution was that the categories of the understanding do not originate in individual experience, but only in the *collective practices of ritual*. Only ritual can produce moral feelings that convince participants of the categories' force and necessity. An individual's sensory perceptions of the natural world, Hume's focus, are always particular, bound within subjectivity, and can always be doubted. Moral feelings, by contrast, are not subject to such doubts because the group's common experience produces and confirms them.[5] Sensory perceptions fluctuate from person to person and occasion to occasion, whereas moral feelings necessarily are shared, internalized in individuals' consciousnesses, and confirmed over time through ritual repetition. Durkheim's thorough analysis of ancient religious rituals, the bulk of the content in *The Elementary Forms*, is an effort to show how humans generate through religious rituals the moral feelings that structure the fundamental categories of their understanding and their basic interpretations of reality (Durkheim 1912, 13–18; Rawls 2004, 63–68).

Collective effervescence links ritual practice to humans' identities, moral laws, and ideologies. This is because it has the unique capacity to impress on ritual participants the sensation of an external force. In this line of thinking, our basic conceptions of who we are, what we should do, and what is true are impressed upon us by emotional forces produced when we interact in certain ways in the presence of sacred objects with other members of our group. It follows that those organizations which are most successful at generating collective effervescence, thus most successful at conveying moral force, will most successfully approach consensus regarding their identities, laws, and beliefs.

COMPARING EFFERVESCENCE

Interaction ritual theory extends Durkheim's theory by rendering it as a series of testable relationships. Which organizations have the strongest evidence of social solidarity? In IR theory, these should be the organizations that manifest the strongest evidence of collective effervescence. Which organizations have the strongest evidence of collective effervescence? In IR theory, these should be the organizations that manifest the strongest evidence of skillful ritual management. Collective effervescence is neither automatic nor static. Rather, participants strategically work to achieve it, and once achieved its magnitude varies. Interaction rituals range from unfocused and emotionally draining to intense and invigorating. This variation is evident between organizations, between rituals within single organizations, and even within particular rituals. Although intensity varies between rituals of a single organization, some organizations are better attuned to the tools that tend to produce their desired results. *Ritually proficient organizations more* consistently draw on tools that lead to high levels of effervescence. Proficient organizations have more invigorating IR chains.

Rituals at two organizations, Congregation Shalom and the Islamic Center, are compared in this chapter. In both organizations, the rituals were initially unfocused. Congregation Shalom pursued and ultimately achieved an extended period of vibrant effervescence that was evident in their enthusiastic sounds and movements during and after the service. They did this by bolstering copresence and intersubjectivity with the resources of mini-IRs, freedom of physical movement, and time. The Islamic Center initially lacked effervescence, evident in members' passive body language, lack of visible engagement with the words of their imam, and especially their comments afterwards. However, they ultimately achieved a few moments of effervescence by making technical adjustments that enhanced physical copresence and intersubjectivity.

These organizations provide a useful contrast in terms of initial advantages due to resources and cultural context. Congregation Shalom appears to be the wealthiest organization in the sample, and the Islamic Center appears to be the poorest.[6] Congregation Shalom's tradition dictates that they gather all day on what happens to be a weekly U.S. holiday from work, and the Islamic Center's tradition dictates that they squeeze a gathering into the middle of the afternoon on a U.S. workday. The evidence in this chapter suggests that resources and cultural context played an important part in conditioning the rituals' emotional outputs. As I will argue in Chapter 4, however, resource base is not a reliable predictor of effervescence; in fact, it can even drain emotions when the resources are mismanaged. Although the Islamic Center's ritual did not convey as long and strong a sensation of emotional force as Congregation Shalom's, the Islamic Center nonetheless made use of other resources from their tradition to ensure that a brief period of effervescence was achieved. Both organizations' rituals demonstrate that effervescence is elusive, but both eventually found it by reconfiguring their ritual dynamics. To see how they did this, I touch on all of the IR dynamics (copresence, intersubjectivity, and, to a lesser extent, barriers) in this chapter before returning for closer scrutiny in subsequent chapters.

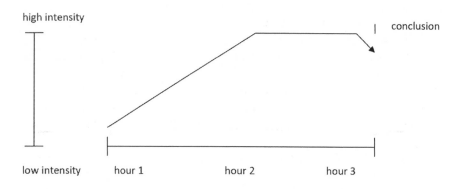

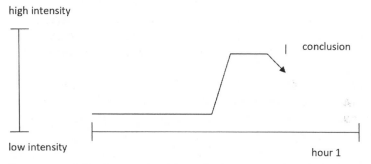

Figure 1.1. Collective Emotional Intensity in Congregation Shalom's and the Islamic Center's Rituals

CONGREGATION SHALOM:
GATHERING EMOTIONAL FORCE

Congregation Shalom is a well-attended and well-resourced urban synagogue that also runs a school, a family center, and numerous weekly and monthly educational and community-building programs serving all age groups. On two different campuses, the organization holds daily prayer services, large holy day celebrations, and multiple Shabbat services for over 1,000 partici-pating families. They identify with Conservative Judaism, and their services offer a blend of old (e.g., traditional melodies from Europe) and new (e.g., prayers set to well-known pop music) worship styles. They also identify as an "Egalitarian" Conservative congregation, which conveys their commitment to more equal participation for women in worship and prayer.[7] I observed a Shabbat morning service merged with a Bar Mitzvah, a ritual in which a Jewish community collectively affirms a 13-year old boy's transformation into adulthood and religious leadership. When I attended, a boy named Michael was being honored.

Jews prioritize Shabbat as a sacred time of the week. Shabbat begins on Friday evening near sundown and continues until after dark on Saturday night. This sacred day has been called "the very foundation" of the Jewish faith, and Jews expect joy and restfulness to flow from it (Grunfeld 2003). Conservative and Orthodox Jewish organizations maintain that no work is to be done during this time, and that energies should be spent on activities such as prayer, Torah study, and interaction with the community (Grunfeld 2003; Ribiat 1999). The primary sacred object during Shabbat morning services is the Torah. In conjunction with rabbinic laws and Jewish traditions (together these sources are known by Jews as *Halakha*), the Torah symbolizes Yahweh's special relationship with Jacob's descendants throughout history (Mariner 1996).

When I entered Congregation Shalom's spacious main sanctuary just before 9:00 am, I encountered only about 20 participants. Three rabbis began the service, leading reading and singing in Hebrew of selections from the Torah. My impressions during the first 20 minutes were of a low-impact IR. Not only was it sparsely populated, but participants did not appear enthralled by the worship activities. As the 3-hour service progressed, however, late arrivals gradually filled the sanctuary. During the second hour, most of the sanctuary had filled and the focus had become noticeably more intense. During the third hour, the sanctuary was standing-room-only and the congregation was ecstatic. Members enthusiastically danced, sang, cried, hugged, and laughed, conveying the impression that they had achieved high levels of effervescence. After the service, focus group members confirmed this impression when they all agreed that they felt "uplifted."

During the Bar Mitzvah ceremonies, Michael's closest friends and family members took turns telling the congregation about their love and pride for Michael and his dedication to Judaism. Many of the stories, especially from Michael's devoted father, were emotionally poignant. At one point, I noticed a woman in the row in front of me leaning to another woman in her row to provide a tissue. Both women had tears in their eyes. A third woman, sitting in my row, leaned toward the first woman and asked if she could have a tissue as well. When a fourth woman sitting next to the third woman asked if she could also have a tissue, all four broke out laughing, as did others sitting nearby.

All were aware of their shared emotional state and enjoyed the moment of mutual recognition. This was one of many moments during the middle and latter parts of Congregation Shalom's service in which I observed strong and shared emotions, as the organization generated emotional force through their use of mini-IRs, uninhibited physical movement, and time. These strategies mainly coincide with the dynamics of copresence and intersubjectivity.

Mini-IRs

The concept of *mini-IRs* recognizes that, alongside individuals who attend and observe on their own, crowds are typically composed of discrete subgroups of people engaging in small IRs within the larger IR. The individuals within a given subgroup often travel to the event together, remain physically close throughout most of the event, and engage in their own interactions. Prior research demonstrates that crowds vary in the number and average intimacy of their subgroups, and the aggregate can thus be understood as more or less "anonymous" (Aveni 1977; McPhail 1991). A less anonymous crowd would be one in which a large proportion engage in emotionally invigorating mini-IRs with close friends.

At Congregation Shalom, I was struck by the organization's proclivity to engage in frequent and enthusiastic mini-IRs. This was evident from the earliest moments of the service when family members and friends sat together and talked within small clusters throughout the sanctuary. This continued throughout the service. As new participants entered the sanctuary, members of in-progress mini-IRs would often wave or call across the room and ask the newcomers to join them. The conversations were often at full-volume, causing me to wonder whether some at Congregation Shalom considered them a distraction from the focus of the larger ritual. In other settings, for instance, members of crowds sometimes reprimand individuals who distract the group with candy wrappers, cell phones, loud conversation, and the like. Early in my observation, I considered the mini-IRs a possible indicator of unfocused attention.

However, no one was noticeably shamed at Congregation Shalom for talking aloud within their smaller groups. At times I even observed the group of rabbis taking part, holding their own mini-IRs or, in one rabbi's case, audibly greeting late-arriving friends from his station at the front of the sanctuary. Nor did it appear as though the mini-IRs caused Congregation Shalom to neglect their sacred object. They continued to hear, recite, sing, and interpret the Torah. However, their *style* of attention was distinct from more reserved crowds I have observed. Congregation Shalom appeared to have an organizational culture in which mini-IRs were encouraged and complementary to the main action.

As Congregation Shalom's ritual gradually increased in emotional intensity, I began to understand that the mini-IRs were a resource that *increased*
the organization's overall focus of attention. The data indicate that Congregation Shalom (1) engaged in active mini-IRs throughout their service, (2)
maintained focus on the Torah, and (3) achieved a highly effervescent ritual.
The coincidence of these factors does not logically require that (1) promoted
(2) and (3), but there are good reasons to think this is the case. The style of
attention at Congregation Shalom was to allow for mini-IRs with their own
local properties, but that maintained a basic focus on the events of the formal
ritual. For instance, two women in my row spoke together throughout much
of the second hour of the service. At one point during the Bar Mitzvah, the
woman closest to me interrupted her friend to tell her "I love this part!" The
woman's friend responded, "Oh, I know!" They watched intently as Michael
recounted memories of the ways his friends and teachers at school had helped
him learn to be faithful. The women's reactions during Michael's comments
were nearly identical, verbally affirming or laughing at the same moments.
This exemplified the basic orientation exhibited in most of the mini-IRs I was
able to hear. Members appeared to be generally attentive and reverent toward
the Torah and the larger ritual, but free to simultaneously engage with their
friends and families.

In other settings, mini-IRs could possibly derail the larger IR. Two conditioning factors have to be considered, however. First, participants in mini-IRs
must intend to promote, not impede, a shared focus and mood with the rest
of the crowd.[8] To laugh with a friend during a funeral, for instance, would
be to dismiss the symbols and emotions of the rest of the funeral-goers. By
contrast, when two children at story time talk excitedly with each other about
what will happen next, it tends to promote the other children's enthusiasm.
In the case of Congregation Shalom, the mini-IRs did not render the main
events inaudible, nor did they compete with the main event in emotional tone.
Rather, they coincided with and complemented the main event.

Second, mini-IRs are likely to be most effective when the organization
emphasizes the *collective* rather than the *individual*. Unlike members of the
Baptist and Buddhist organizations that I will consider in Chapters 2 and 3,
Congregation Shalom's members did not indicate that their purpose in attending the event was an individual-level religious experience. If this had been
a prominent goal at Congregation Shalom, members likely would have been
more prone to sit quietly, focusing on their internal dialogues or the voice of
God, morally objecting to other members' sounds.

Because of Congregation Shalom's emphasis on the group experience,
mini-IRs were not distractions, but rather confirmed their shared symbols
and had the effect of invigorating attention and emotional connection to the

events of the larger ritual. Members were oriented toward each other *and* their sacred object, as though the Torah was the source of the good feelings produced in their mini-IRs.

Freedom of Physical Movement

Just as Congregation Shalom's members felt free to engage in mini-IRs, they felt free to move about the sanctuary as they wished. By contrast, the unspoken norm in the other organizations in the sample was to remain in or near one's seat throughout the service. Especially during the first half of Congregation Shalom's service, members' movements often coincided with the arrival of newcomers. As newcomers arrived, other members moved to greet them. New mini-IRs sprouted in different locations around the sanctuary. These movements were neither constant nor chaotic—the majority of the congregation remained in or near the seats they had initially chosen—but free movement was clearly normal and acceptable to members, and a significant proportion travelled the room during the ritual.

Mini-IRs and freedom to move around both conveyed the impression that Congregation Shalom was surprisingly informal about certain aspects of their ritual. This was surprising because of the formality of other aspects of the ritual. The dress code was formal, for instance, as most men wore jackets, ties, and yarmulkes, while most women wore dresses and covered their hair. Other aspects of the service evinced ritual formality, as well, such as the use of Hebrew and the precise handling of the Torah. These formal features of the ritual, however, did not function as constraints on members' ability to interact whenever and with whomever they wished. There were no significant barriers evident between insiders.

Congregation Shalom felt free to move around the sanctuary, and they also felt free to move their bodies around when remaining in a fixed location. Throughout the ritual, members sporadically drew on traditional customs involving rapid twisting or bowing.[9] I first observed this during the first hour on occasions when the congregation would stand to pray, sing, or read aloud. Several members twisted their torsos forward-and-back or to-and-fro, a custom known in Yiddish as *shuckling*. Some, such as a woman in my row, twisted very casually and lightly as though the intent were to "keep the blood flowing," as in tai chi. A similar effect might have been achieved if members were to lightly bounce, jog in place, or stretch, but shuckling gave them a way to maintain attention in a manner that reinforced their Jewish identity. Members of the focus group confirmed my interpretation of these movements. Ellen, a widow who was in her 50s, explained, "Moving a little bit during prayers feels good to me. I get tired if I just sit there or stand there, so I move a little and I feel like this helps."

As the ritual progressed, I noticed a growing proportion of the congregation twisting or bowing. This arguably could have been related to a growing proportion of the congregation who were losing (and trying to recapture) interest. However, my impression was that intersubjectivity increased as members were encouraged by each other's visible engagement with the ritual. In short, the movements were a resource from the tradition that helped focus attention and mood through rhythmic entrainment and mutual monitoring, as well as stimulating circulation of the blood.

Congregation Shalom turned out to hold the most "charismatic" ritual in my sample. In many ways, they even resembled Pentecostal and charismatic Christian organizations whose members dance, speak in tongues, get slain in the spirit, and so on (Poloma 1982; Cox 1995). Congregation Shalom incorporated a different set of movements and sounds than charismatic Christians, but they were similarly expressive, especially during the more cathartic moments of their ritual. I noticed, however, a difference in the emotional quality of Congregation Shalom's movements compared with the quality of movements I have observed in charismatic Christian organizations. To Congregation Shalom's members, emotional engagement was understood not as a precondition for physical movement, but as a potential yet nonessential by-product. The movements were performed *in order to invigorate* an experience rather than *because of* an experience. Ellen and other members confirmed that their orientation to the movements was very pragmatic and not necessarily motivated by inner sentiments or mystical experience.

A late moment in the service not only brought together all of the elements mentioned thus far, but also introduced a new one: collective physical reorientation to the sacred object. Activating another resource from Jewish tradition, the rabbis carried the Torah scrolls from the front of the sanctuary, into the crowd, and finally to a glass ark against the front wall. The process took several minutes, and members gathered close to the scrolls, sometimes touching them with prayer books as the rabbis carried them through the aisles. This process was a visual demonstration that the Torah belongs to the community, brings them together, and (especially since physical contact with the scrolls was mediated by prayer books) is sacred. During this time, enthusiastic mini-IRs persisted all around the sanctuary. Members moved around, sang, twisted, and bowed as each saw fit. This produced a heightened situation of energy, movement, and intersubjectivity that I consider the most effervescent period within their ritual, and possibly within this whole sample of rituals.

Time

As mentioned, the mini-IRs and physical movements made Congregation Shalom's ritual feel surprisingly informal despite their formal dress code, use of Hebrew, and careful handling of the Torah. Congregation Shalom's informal orientation, which appeared commensurate with their effervescence, was largely due to their orientation toward time.

As a Jewish organization, Congregation Shalom views their morning prayers as merely one period during a full day of worship and prayer. Shabbat takes place from Friday night to Saturday night, and all activities within that time frame are supposed to have a sacred orientation (Grunfeld 2003).[10] Awareness that they are within a sacred span of time conditions their IRs throughout Shabbat. For Congregation Shalom members, in contrast to many non-Sabbatarian organizations, sacred IRs neither began when they entered the sanctuary nor concluded when they exited.

This impression was supported by comments from the focus group. Bryan, a married man in his 30s, explained that Congregation Shalom does not pressure members to attend the prayer service. He added, "When I don't come [to the morning service], I'm observing Shabbat with my family. If we're not at the synagogue, that's fine. Wherever we are, we're doing the same thing." Sam, a widower in his 50s, added, "This is what we do during Shabbat. Most of us have been doing it for most of our lives. Wherever we are, we pray with our community."

Sacralizing all of Shabbat helps reduce a certain stress that might otherwise be felt in IRs when the organization's sacred time is more limited. A counterexample might be useful here. At the non-Sabbatarian white Baptist church that I examine in Chapters 2 and 4, a one-hour service distinguished sacred time from profane time. During worship, members pursued individual mystical experiences with God. After worship, members tended to go out to lunch, watch football, or otherwise relax at home. This means that First Baptist's sacred time had to be *efficient*. Mini-IRs, for instance, would mostly need to be postponed. Physical movement needed to be limited because members had only a brief period in which they needed to exert silent effort to ensure a moment with God. By contrast, Congregation Shalom members knew that, wherever they happened to be during Shabbat, they would need to refrain from work and either pray, read the Torah, or spend time with friends. All of these experiences are part of their sacred time, reducing the burden that otherwise would fall entirely on the morning prayer service.

Put differently, Congregation Shalom was able to ease into effervescence because they could take it slow and relish each other's company. The service became emotionally intense, but I doubt that this would have been achieved if Congregation Shalom had a more anxious orientation toward sacred time. Further, because Shabbat stretches across a 24-hour period, collective prayers are largely a chosen activity of participants, rather than morally enforced. Observance of Shabbat *is* morally enforced, but attendance at particular rituals is not. In other words, it is likely that most Congregation Shalom members

Does the IR have to have a physical presence?

attend Shabbat morning prayers because they *enjoy* doing so, much as they
enjoy moving across the room to greet friends, engaging in mini-IRs, or
twisting back and forth. They are deeply committed to the idea that Shabbat
is a different sort of day, and so they are inclined to stretch out and relish the
moments within it.

THE ISLAMIC CENTER:
REPOSITIONING FOR EFFERVESCENCE

The Islamic Center is a one-story house surrounded by a failing white fence.
A hand-painted sign hanging on the fence reads simply, "Masjid." On the
ground outside the front door is a mat for removing one's shoes. Inside the
house, a narrow lobby separates the front door from the Islamic Center's spacious prayer room, and connects to washrooms designed for *wudhu,* the ritual
cleansing of one's body in preparation for prayer.[11]

I visited the Islamic Center during Jum'ah, the prayer service held on
Muslims' holy day of Friday. The Muslim prayer ritual, *salat,* is multifaceted.
Muslim apologist Maududi explains, "This systematic method of worship
includes recitation of the Quran, repetition of selected words for praising
Almighty God, standing, kneeling, sitting, prostrating, and other postures and
movements" (1977, 97).[12] The primary sacred object is the Quran, which is
read or sung throughout and serves as a rhythmic device to prompt specific
movements. The Quran is also central in the *khutba,* a sermon delivered before salat during Jum'ah.

Like Congregation Shalom, the Islamic Center's ritual demonstrates how
strategic human choices are necessary to summon the spirit. Their brief ritual
felt unfocused, even emotionally draining, during the first 30 minutes. Near
the 30-minute mark, however, they activated a Muslim ritual resource that
decisively altered the dynamics of physical copresence and intersubjectivity. By repositioning their bodies and engaging in a group prayer sequence,
members achieved a 12-minute period of moderate effervescence that allowed them to depart with a new store of good feelings and confidence in
their organization.

Members' comments after the service supported my impression that much
of the service had lacked collective energy. I asked the Islamic Center's focus
group about their moods during and after the service. Tyler, a middle-aged
IT worker, and one of the few white members of the masjid, spoke first: "My
'mood'? What do you mean?"

Before I could respond, a black construction worker in his 50s named
Antoine interjected, "I feel good. Because I know I am doing what Allah has

commanded. The Quran teaches that <u>when Allah gives a blessing to one, he</u> <u>blesses all of us who are present."</u>,

[handwritten margin note: Physically present?]

As Antoine spoke, Tyler continued to think about my question. He looked deep in thought and a bit bothered, not misunderstanding my question, but skeptical of its relevance. Antoine was something of a leader and mentor in the organization, and it was clear that the other men liked and respected him. When Antoine was done responding, Tyler added, "Yeah. I do it because it's my duty. It doesn't really matter if I feel happy or sad or whatever. But I agree with Antoine; I feel good because I am doing what the Prophet said I should do." The group echoed Tyler's remarks repeatedly during our conversation: salat and Jum'ah are duties. This is consistent with the theme of *submission to Allah*, the meaning of "Islam." The focus group members considered feelings to be nonessential artifacts of their service. Much more consistent in their comments were the themes of dutiful submission and the practical guidance offered in the khutba.

Ahmed, a middle-aged small-business owner, said,

> I come to Jum'ah because this is the duty of Muslims. We pray five times a day, and come to hear the khutba and pray with other Muslims. I can't always come because of my job, but whenever I find a way to leave work I come. Coming to Jum'ah reminds me that I am a Muslim and to follow Allah. I pray on my own every day, but the khutba helps give me guidance on how the Quran applies to my life.

Similarly, a college student named Fawaz explained, "Khutba is good here because it helps me understand what the Quran is saying in some places. I know how to read Arabic since my family all learned it, but I don't understand all of it. Khutba helps me learn parts I don't know."

These comments lend support to my observation that effervescence was mostly missing from the Islamic Center's ritual. However, Durkheim's work and IR theory propose that collective effervescence is essential for establishing and confirming organizations' notions of truth, morality, and identity. <u>If members don't gain EE from their services, why do they continue to meet?</u> Three interrelated responses to this question fit both the data and the theory. The first and most obvious response is that the Islamic Center is not a vibrant organization. As I discuss in greater detail below, their numbers are low, their resources are scarce, and I would not be shocked to hear in a few years that they had disbanded. Their shortage of effervescence is consistent with their shortage of organizational vitality.

A second response is that members of the Islamic Center typically *do* gain EE from the Islamic Center's rituals, but not chiefly by reaching a state of ebullience together. Rather, they gain EE by sacralizing the shared symbol of "duty." Comparable to many soldiers, athletes, and clergy, the Islamic Center's members' prior IR chains have turned symbols of discipline and submission into sources of EE. Symbols such as "duty," "responsibility," and "work ethic" imply a certain doggedness to persist despite difficulty or even boredom. While "duty" may not always look appealing to the outsider, it can be emotionally powerful to the insider. Indeed, to Durkheim, duty and emotional energy feed off of each other: "We feel a *sui generis* pleasure in performing our duty simply because it is our duty. The notion of good enters into those of duty and obligation just as they in turn enter into the notion of good" (1974, 45). Perhaps due to Western individualism and a resistance to feeling "trapped" by obligations to others, this connection between duty and pleasure can be easy to overlook. Still, even the sacred symbol of duty requires effervescent rituals from time to time in order to keep the symbol emotionally resonant.[13]

The third response is that the Islamic Center *did* achieve effervescence, even if they didn't consistently articulate this in the focus group. By my observation, the final portion of their service intensified members' focus, copresence, and intersubjectivity. This made their worship experience feel different from the mundane; confirmed their identity, morality, and beliefs; and inspired them to return for more on subsequent Fridays. Their khutba may not always invigorate, but members feel good about fulfilling their duty; beyond that, the raka'ah sequence during salat (discussed below) lets them leave with the feeling that a sacred encounter has occurred.

I will proceed by considering, first, why the first two-thirds of the Islamic Center's Jum'ah lacked collective energy. I argue that this was largely due to a series of factors related to the marginalized status of Islam in the U.S. The Islamic Center was disadvantaged for effervescence because of (1) an inability to gather promptly, (2) with an adequate number of participants, (3) with material resources conducive to effervescence. Next, I show how the Islamic Center was finally able to achieve a moderate level of effervescence despite these difficulties by drawing on the Muslim resource of raka'ah.

An Inconvenient Holy Day

American Muslims' religious practice is disadvantaged by their cultural context.[14] Although they are legally free to practice as they wish, their faith is not accommodated by the culture as it is in majority Muslim nations. In Turkey, for instance, public *adhans* can be heard throughout the day calling the faithful to prayer. By contrast, many Americans are unfamiliar with or antagonistic toward the tenets and practices of Islam (Cainkar 2002; Council on American-Islamic Relations 2009; Rubenstein 2004; Singh 2002), and this can pose a number of practical problems for those who wish to leave work or other commitments and attend Jum'ah on a Friday afternoon.

Masjid (or "mosque") attendance is quite low among American Muslims, with less than 15% attending Jum'ah (Mujahid 2001). American Muslims tend to practice salat in private, alone or with families, more often than in larger corporate settings (Wuthnow 2005).[15] The minority of American Muslims who are able to visit a masjid on Friday are usually forced to keep their visit brief so they can get back to work. Although prior research has focused on Muslims in the workplace (Read 2004), or gender and family views among American Muslims (Predelli 2004; Read and Bartksowski 2000), little has been written regarding constraints on American Muslims' religious rituals. Their low attendance rates can be taken as indicators of a tradition that is struggling to flourish in its current context. To better understand the sources of these struggles, close attention to ritual dynamics should prove useful.

The most obvious obstacle to effervescence at the Islamic Center was the inconvenience of gathering for worship during a non-Muslim work week. Congregation Shalom, as discussed above, is able to set aside a full day for worship. This impacts the quality of members' focus during the morning prayer ritual. After a night of prayer and reflection, the Saturday morning service is a three-hour period during which members can ease their way into effervescence. When Congregation Shalom's morning prayers are over, members can continue to spend time in prayer, reflection, and community. The Islamic Center's members, by contrast, rush from jobs and errands to the masjid, where they speed through a ritual and then rush back to their jobs and errands. The disparity between cultural norms and organizational aims conditions the quality of the Islamic Center's attention during Jum'ah.

One exchange between focus group members at the Islamic Center indicates the sort of psychological shift this rapid worship experience can require. I had asked about members' experience of Jum'ah, and Fawaz explained, "Life is so busy and fast-paced, but you come to Jum'ah, and everyone is together in the room, and I pray to Allah, and it sort of puts me in a different state of mind." Antoine replied, "And then we rush back to our jobs and everything gets hectic again." Antoine's reply prompted empathetic laughter from the group, and suggests an important contrast in the quality of holy day rituals for American Muslims compared with Jews and Christians. Because Saturday and Sunday are embedded in the culture as times of moral freedom from professional obligations (with some exceptions), most Jews and Christians can worship and reflect on their community for a full day if they so desire. Muslims' holy day is not similarly culturally advantaged. Due to timing, their corporate experience is necessarily a diversion from their daily chains of interaction. Although this may be a welcome diversion to devout

Muslims, it forces them to exert extra time and effort adjusting to the group experience. For example, they have little opportunity to engage in activities like Christians' "Sunday School," which can serve as an emotional warm-up to the main event of corporate worship.[16]

Another way in which the timing of their holy day conditions the quality of the Islamic Center's attention is that it forces a staccato rhythm and flow on their ritual. When I arrived, 10 men (including myself and the imam) were present. Newcomers arrived throughout the ritual, up to and including the closing prayer. The 12 latecomers arrived at the following times during the 42-minute service (1:30–2:12), with the number of latecomers for each entrance indicated in parentheses: 1:35 (1), 1:40 (2), 1:41 (3), 1:45 (1), 1:46 (1), 1:50 (1), 1:55 (1), 2:00 (1), and 2:02 (1).

Each new arrival was a diversion from the khutba, an interruption of focused attention and rhythmic entrainment. Each time the door opened, several heads turned and watched, drawing attention away from the khutba. The imam, Omar, often tracked the latecomers, as well, from his position behind the podium.[17] Each entrance caused the organization to momentarily stop and restart the ritual.

Of course, Congregation Shalom's members also arrived intermittently during their Shabbat service, but in that case I considered the gradual accumulation of members to spur rather than impede effervescence. I think three other ritual factors conditioned the impact of late arrivals on effervescence at Congregation Shalom and the Islamic Center. The first is the design of their physical spaces. At Congregation Shalom, the entrance was at the back of the sanctuary. If a participant at Congregation Shalom were to feel distracted by late arrivals, it would have been easier to ignore them. At the Islamic Center, by contrast, the doorway was located at the side of the room, within the periphery or full view of all of the participants.[18] This difference is related to the respective stores of ritual resources in the two organizations. Organizations with the means to do so, such as Congregation Shalom, can minimize the distraction by building inconspicuous entrances and/or designated sections for latecomers. At the Islamic Center, scarce financial resources meant that remodeling their modest house was, out of necessity, low on their list of organizational priorities. Further, it wouldn't suffice to simply reposition the congregation with their backs to the room's entrance. As an additional ritual constraint imposed in this case by religious tradition, Muslims must face in the direction of Mecca during salat.

The second factor is the difference in their rituals' levels of bodily density. The Islamic Center's khutba had the lowest bodily density of any ritual I observed during this research. In a room that could fit at least 300, ample "personal space" was available to all throughout the ritual. This rendered the late arrivals more noticeable and consequential than they would have been otherwise, much as scarcity of economic resources tends to increase their value. Congregation Shalom knew from experience that their sanctuary would eventually fill up, so late arrivals became less relevant to participants as indicators of the organization's vitality. At the Islamic Center, each new arrival was significant and drew attention from the ritual's intended focus.

The third factor conditioning the impact of late arrivals is the organizations' respective orientations to time. Congregation Shalom had developed an organizational culture in which all of Shabbat is devoted to sacred activity. A full 24-hour period removed some of the burden placed on their morning prayer service to generate collective energy. In effect, Congregation Shalom was able to ease into effervescence by engaging in practices they enjoyed in a way that supported the focus of the larger ritual. At the Islamic Center, by contrast, time constraints meant that every moment of the prayers and every word of the khutba mattered. As with scarcity in attendance, scarcity of time increased the significance of every minute. Late arrivals jeopardized the focus during the limited time frame in which the Islamic Center was able to worship.

Repositioning for Effervescence with Raka'ah

After 30 minutes of an emotionally uninvigorating khutba, Omar invited the congregation to come to the front of the room to practice salat together. The 20 men who were present moved from their spots around the room and formed a horizontal line from one wall to the other, facing the front.[19] The men allowed about two feet of space between each other. For 12 minutes, they prayed, knelt, stood, and bowed together. Their movements were extremely well-synchronized.

During the prayer sequence, in stark contrast to the khutba, the participants mustered considerably higher levels of copresence by forming a horizontal line across the room. This reduced their "personal space" and made necessary a degree of trust that had been unnecessary during the khutba.[20] Physical contact was built into this ritual moment. Immediately prior to the raka'ah sequence, Omar helped an elderly man into a chair at one end of the line of men. Immediately afterwards, men who had been standing near each other engaged in hand-shaking, shoulder-clasping, and warm embraces.

Although emotional entrainment and shared attention appeared low during the khutba, it clearly accelerated during the raka'ah sequence. The sequence allowed the group to experience their shared identity by enacting physical and symbolic unity. Durkheim argued that such behaviors facilitate the coming together of otherwise discrete individual consciousnesses:

> It is by shouting the same cry, saying the same words, and performing the same action in regard to the same object that [groups] arrive at and experience

agreement. . . . The individual minds can meet and commune only if they come outside themselves, but they do this only by means of movement. It is the homogeneity of these movements that makes the group aware of itself and that, in consequence, makes it be (1912, 232).

In the Islamic Center's ritual, the coming-together of individual consciousnesses was prompted by the movement of bodies in the room. Before the raka'ah sequence, each participant seemed fixed on an isolated island of personal space. To begin the sequence, they left these islands and formed a shared continent. Led by the skillful singing of the muezzin, they rhythmically kneeled, bowed, stood, and vocalized, peripherally monitoring each other's movements and concentrating together on the words of the Quran. The raka'ah sequence was relatively brief (12 minutes), but feelings of shared emotion permeated the room as soon as it was done. Thus, the raka'ah sequence appeared to secure strong feelings of effervescence that were absent during the khutba. Overall, the evidence indicates that collective effervescence was dramatically boosted by an intentional mid-ritual shift that increased bodily density and physical contact, and also rhythmic entrainment.

I asked Islamic Center members to describe their experiences during the raka'ah process. Tyler explained, "Sometimes my mind sort of wanders a little. Like my foot will get a cramp or something, but I keep coming back to the verses and what they're saying." Antoine replied, "That's good. That's very human. That's right. Sometimes you think about something about your body or whatever, but you keep coming back to the prayer." Other members of the group nodded and sounded affirmations.[21]

I wanted to know whether the Islamic Center members' experience of corporate salat differed from their daily experience of private salat. Alex, a college student who recently converted to Islam from Christianity, explained, "Salat with the group intensifies how it feels. It's good when I'm alone, but when you know you're there with all your brothers, it's somehow a more intense experience."

Antoine added,

> We're all from different nations and backgrounds. We're all very different. So it feels good to come together and worship Allah together despite our differences. I get a real feeling of unity from being all together, almost shoulder to shoulder, praying to Allah together.

Although Tyler and Antoine had acknowledged that their minds sometimes drift during the raka'ah sequence, Alex and Antoine also indicated that it is an intense and bonding part of the ritual.

CONCLUSION

Congregation Shalom and the Islamic Center both conjured the spirit through choices and shifts that altered the ritual dynamics. Their examples suggest that the choices and shifts can be relatively minor: get everyone to stand closer together, for example, or find a way to keep the meeting from feeling rushed. If Durkheim was correct, such decisions are of enormous consequence because the sensation of emotional force is the very source of humans' understandings of reality. Along with Durkheim, we may bracket the issue of whether entities called God or Luck work through human choices to stimulate the spirit. In terms of social science, there is good evidence that the right human decisions about how to conduct the ritual will produce the effervescence people crave.

I argued that Congregation Shalom's achievement of effervescence followed a gradual accumulation of bodies within the room. Equipped with potent traditional and material resources, members were in a good position to ease into effervescence.[22] Their management of mini-IRs, physical movement, and (especially) time maximized the benefits of copresence and intersubjectivity, so that the second and third hours were filled with tears, laughter, dancing, and celebration of the organization. The Islamic Center struggled throughout their khutba because of limited resources and cultural constraints. Unlike Congregation Shalom, who could take time to enjoy their IR, the Islamic Center faced daunting pressure to get in, encounter the sacred, and get out. Nonetheless, the dense and rhythmic raka'ah unified the men as "brothers" who are affectionate toward each other and committed to their common duty.

Mini-IRs, physical movement, time, traditional resources, and material resources all condition a ritual's copresence, intersubjectivity, and barriers. I will return to each of these dynamics in greater depth in subsequent chapters. I will also return to Congregation Shalom and the Islamic Center for a close examination of barriers to outsiders in Chapter 5. Before moving on to these ritual dynamics, we need to consider further the process by which ritual practice leads to identity, morality, and ideology. On its own, collective effervescence would not be able to convey the experience of emotional force beyond the ritual itself. Collective effervescence transforms into solidarity as it is preserved in organizational symbols and the secure feelings of membership. If effervescence is to matter in the long term, it has to be preserved in social solidarity.

NOTES

1. Some authors, such as Joas (2000) and Ehrenreich (2006), instead translate Durkheim's concept as "collective *ecstasy*," mostly because "ecstasy" is more

common in contemporary discourse. I sometimes refer to it as "ecstasy" here, as well. Although I see the alternate terms as equally valid and basically synonymous, I favor "effervescence" for two reasons: (1) "Effervescence" evokes imagery that is theoretically relevant: effervescence in rituals, like effervescence in soft drinks and chemistry experiments, indicates a transformation, a new product which emerges from the constitutive elements of a successful ritual. Moreover, it is a transformation that moves upward. Once generated through the cooperation of discrete consciousnesses, this product rises above and beyond each of them, and exerts a new kind of force back upon them. (2) "Collective effervescence" is the terminology used by Collins.

2. Presumably, animals "know" things, too, instinctual knowledge that prompts them, for instance, to run from larger predators. But as far as we know, they are unconcerned with rationality and logic. Humans have an instinctual sort of knowledge, as well, but the question is how humans developed the ability to *reason* together in mutually intelligible ways and thereby create human morality and society.

3. Anne Rawls shows that Durkheim's philosophical argument is hardly an afterthought on his part, but actually guides the logic by which the chapters in *The Elementary Forms* are organized. He examines the categories in succession and, one after another, shows their derivation from ritual practices. Sociologists have mostly been missing the full significance of Durkheim's argument to the epistemological viability of our discipline (2004, 316). As Rawls writes regarding classical theory more broadly (in the context of discussing *The Elementary Forms*): "While it is often argued that contemporary social theory has gone beyond the classics, . . . the classics may still, in fact, be ahead of us" (27).

4. Hume (1748, 1777) pursued the origin of the categories of the understanding by considering whether humans are able to derive them from nature based on sense perceptions. Hume's empirical approach ended in skepticism, though, when he concluded that there is no necessary connection between the unchanging categories and our ever-shifting perceptions of natural phenomena. For instance, the category of causality cannot be established through an individual's perceptions. The individual might perceive that y has always followed x in the past, but how can she definitely determine that y occurred *because of x*, and that the pattern will necessarily persist in the future? Such a conclusion would require an additional assertion related to the category of time: the future is necessarily like the past. But, again, how could this additional assertion be justified based on sense perceptions? We might say that the future will *probably* be like the past, but there is no way to be certain that it will. In fact, the future often turns out to be quite different from the past. Based on arguments of this kind, Hume concluded that there is no way for the categories to develop out of individuals' sense perceptions (Durkheim 1912, 12–14, 145–149; Rawls 2004, 8–11).

Kant (1781) "solved" Hume's dilemma by positing that the categories of the understanding exist a priori in the mind of the individual. This solved Hume's empirical dilemma by assuming it away. Durkheim harshly criticized this position, calling it "lazy" and "the death of analysis" (1912, 148). To Durkheim, apriorists had cheated by shifting the problem from the origin of the categories to "the justification of innatism" (Rawls 2004, 61). Unable to empirically explain their derivation, the apriorists conclude that the categories must be innate. Durkheim argued that Kant's solution also posed an additional problem: if humans possess a priori categories of understanding, all of our perceptions of reality necessarily will be mediated by those categories. Thus, we have no way of being certain that our interpreted perceptions actually do correspond with reality "out there." Kant's solution thus introduced an unbridgeable gulf between the world as an object of experience and the world as it really is. There is no way of knowing that my observations of "the world" are accurate representations since all of my observations are filtered through my preexisting mental categories. Empirical observation becomes largely irrelevant to accurate correspondence.

5. "[I]t is the cult that stimulates the feelings of joy, inner peace, serenity, and enthusiasm that, for the faithful, stand as experimental proof of their beliefs" (Durkheim 1912, 420).

6. I use the terms "wealthy" and "poor" here with respect to *organizational* resources. I do not know members' average income, although Congregation Shalom appears to be much wealthier in this way, as well, based on indicators like car models, clothes, mannerisms, and stated occupations. In terms of organizational indicators, Congregation Shalom reports high levels of financial giving, meets in an immaculate building on a large campus, and has a large paid staff. The Islamic Center has a small and fluctuating membership, meets in a meager and neglected house, and has one paid staff member who pleaded members for volunteer hours when I attended.

7. Since the 1970s, Conservative Judaism has been gradually relaxing restrictions on women's participation in worship and prayer. The most recent decisions of the Rabbinical Assembly (the movement's chief governing body) have established that women can serve as rabbis, participate in minyans, and participate equally in liturgy and worship (see Fine 2002 for a thorough review of these decisions). More traditionally oriented congregations are still permitted to maintain strict divisions between genders without fear of being stigmatized as "sinful" by other, more inclusive, Conservative congregations. Congregation Shalom embraces the more progressive approach, and has even hired a female rabbi.

8. In *Behavior in Public Places*, Goffman discusses this issue more generally while elucidating unspoken rules for "occasioned mutual involvements." Interactants within a larger ritual must be careful not to let their subrituals "drift from the spirit of the occasion" (1963, 173–76). Goffman emphasizes regulation of mood, to which we can add regulation of attention.

9. These movements are most associated with Hasidism, but Congregation Shalom incorporates them as part of their eclectic approach to sacred rituals.

10. The Shabbat behavioral proscriptions can be rather extensive depending on the community. Congregation Shalom enforced several such regulations that are discussed in Chapter 5 with respect to barriers to outsiders.

11. I consider wudhu in the context of IR barriers in Chapter 5.

12. Winchester (2008, 1763) describes salat as follows:

"Performed five times a day, salat is a complex act of worship involving specific movements of the body such as standing, bowing, prostrating and kneeling coupled with recitations of Quranic verse at particular moments in time. Performed by . . . experienced worshippers, the complex movements appear fluid and artful—'meditation in motion,' as one convert aptly described it. . . . At the end of the last cycle of prostration (called a rakat), the worshippers utter a unified 'Ameen' and stand up from their positions on the floor to embrace one another and give reciprocal greetings of 'Asallam Alaykum' and 'W'alaykum Salaam.'"

As Winchester explains, salat is performed five times per day by devout Muslims. During Jum'ah, salat is practiced collectively, so that the movements are done in unison while the Quran is sung or chanted.

13. For comparison with a quite different sort of ritual, consider the boxers in Wacquant (2004, 66-69). Success in the boxing ring requires much personal sacrifice and a "monastic devotion" to one's training (see also Oates 1987, 28–29). This leads some boxers to experience a "joyful masochism" as "training becomes its own reward." The boxers, though, rely on regular IRs in the gym with their coaches and fellow boxers in order to reenergize symbols of self-discipline and thus persevere in their grueling exercises.

14. Estimates of the number of Muslims in the U.S. population vary. Their numbers are growing at a fast rate, but they have always comprised only a small proportion of the population. A 2017 study from the Pew Research Center estimates the total population of U.S. Muslims at about 3.45 million. This is about 1% of the U.S. population.

15. For comparison, see Killian (2007). In France, the privatization of Muslim rituals is driven in part by a 2004 law banning public displays of religiosity such as headscarves worn in public schools. As American Muslims do not face such legal restrictions, the fact that they mostly worship in private highlights the power of informal social controls in shaping styles of practice.

16. I consider warm-up rituals in Chapter 2 with respect to Promised Land Baptist Church.

17. Another interruption came in the form of a ringing cell phone during the khutba. I saw only one head turn toward the passive moral offender. Ironically, the call coincided precisely with a moment when Omar was discussing the dangers of technology.

18. And, related to ritual stratification, the entry was positioned directly adjacent to the women's screened-off section. I consider gender-based ritual stratification at the Islamic Center in Chapter 5.

19. An additional member joined the line shortly after the sequence began. I did not participate, as I had little personal experience with salat and didn't want to impose a distracting influence on their practice. I discuss this methodological decision further in the context of ritual barriers (Chapter 5).

20. Bodily density, as evident here, is more than an issue of the ratio of attendance to room capacity, as measured in Appendix A. Density can vary further according to the alignment of bodies within the room. A density shift of this type, however, is really only possible if the room has a low enough initial level of density to allow significant realignment.

21. Tyler's comment is comparable to the experience of the Meditation Center members in Chapter 3 whose meditation was at times a struggle to move beyond

body awareness to meditative self-solidarity. Like Meditation Center meditators, Tyler and Antoine dealt with the physical distraction by rhythmic devices—here, the raka'ah movements. Unlike the meditators, Tyler and Antoine intentionally activated conscious thought by "coming back to the verses and what they're saying."

22. I am referring specifically to the *organizational* ritual resources that I have been describing. Individual-level cultural capital is also an important issue. Well-designed rituals can still fall apart if participants are not properly trained. I will consider the issue of cultural (or "religious") capital in Chapter 5.

Chapter Two

Social Solidarity

Collective effervescence is ephemeral, and will slip away as soon as the ritual dynamics shift. Eventually, someone or everyone will need to go have lunch, take a nap, or pick up the kids at school, and in the process they will start fresh IRs in different locations with other people, generating new feelings of a different sort. Because it is ephemeral, collective effervescence cannot establish identity, morality, or truth beyond the fleeting IR that arouses it. These more permanent experiences are properties of social solidarity. Solidarity may also be ephemeral in the long run, but it nonetheless provides humans with their most palpable impressions of the eternal.

Solidarity is the spirit stored in symbols. As Durkheim put it, "Without symbols . . . social feelings could have only an unstable existence" (1912, 232). Shared sacred objects and symbols are necessary for (1) bringing people together and also (2) reminding them of each other after they depart. The objects symbolize the group, and foster identification by calling to mind the special experience that once occurred or usually occurs in the group's presence.[1] Shared ways of talking, thinking, talking about thinking, and thinking about talking also symbolize the group. Deviance, for instance, is a way of talking and thinking about censured behaviors; by agreeing about what is inappropriate, *member a* and *member b* remind each other that each of them, fortunately, understands and stays within the bounds of what is acceptable to their group. The two members find solidarity by expressing their common identity and agreed-upon morality.

Durkheim's arguments about sacred symbols of solidarity add a second "layer" to his theory of knowledge. Chapter 1 of this book described the first layer, his epistemology. His epistemological argument is that the experience of effervescence makes it possible for humans to universally share a small set of categories of understanding, a framework for thought that makes it

49

possible for us to comprehend and reason with each other. The first layer is foundational, a way of explaining how humans become able to reason. The second layer, though, is about the contents of thoughts, a "sociology of knowledge" rather than an epistemology.

This second layer is where we find "collective representations," the ideas and images that have meaning within one's culture, the cache of particular sacred symbols that accrue over time in a particular society. The categories of the understanding and the collective representations both are made possible through the emotional forces of ritual, but in different ways. The categories emerge because of the *experience*, as the force of society impresses itself upon the individual consciousness and thereby transforms it. The categories do not "represent" anything; rather, they are a prerequisite for representations, the very logic with which different representations are configured in relation to each other (Rawls 1997b). The collective representations, by contrast, are the sacred symbols themselves, including *beliefs*. Although the emotional conviction behind beliefs emanates from practices, beliefs do have important consequences of their own once in circulation. Relevant to the current chapter, for example, they influence individuals' preferences for certain practices over others.

To experience social solidarity is to feel oneself as part of a larger collective, sharing reverence for its sacred symbols and submitting to its programs. In the USCLS analysis, I examined two types of social solidarity: (1) a collective sense of belonging, and (2) a collective sense of shared goals and "vision." The first, *membership solidarity*,[2] is evident among at least 51% of members in every religious organization in the USCLS sample. This suggests the possibility that most participants need to feel like they belong if the voluntary organization is to persist at all. *Symbolic solidarity*, however, has greater range and variation across organizations.[3] It is this type of solidarity that boosts the collective power of social movements, from worker strikes to student protests to large-scale political organizations (Dixon et al. 2004; Goodwin et al. 2007; Hirsch 1990; McAdam 1986; Snow et al. 1986; Summers Effler 2010). Shared symbols and commitments drive collectives to persist in their cause, even when their prospects look dim.

The USCLS analysis points to a strong relationship between effervescence and both types of solidarity. Of the two types, though, symbolic solidarity is even more responsive to the influence of effervescence.[4] Here and in Chapter 4, I compare rituals from two Christian churches: the all-black Promised Land Baptist and the mostly white First Baptist. These two organizations are similar in denomination and doctrine, but sharply divergent in the practice of ritual. In short, Promised Land exemplified effervescence whereas First Baptist often appeared distracted and bored. Promised Land's spirit was evident in their clapping, enthusiastic singing, shouting, alert postures, and visible and audible engagement with the content of the sermon. By contrast, First Baptist's lack of spirit was evident in congregants' rustling of bulletins, unenthusiastic singing, inattention to the activities on stage, yawns, and exits from the sanctuary. Members' comments after the service supported these impressions, as I report below.

Promised Land displayed more obvious signs of symbolic solidarity, whereas First Baptist displayed more obvious signs of membership solidarity. Still, close consideration of First Baptist's ritual suggests that they do not lack symbolic solidarity (nor does Promised Land lack membership solidarity, as Table A.1 in Appendix A would lead us to expect). Rather, the symbolic solidarity that unifies First Baptist is of a very different sort than Promised Land's, and has different organizational consequences. Figure 2.1 illustrates the relationships I observed at First Baptist and Promised Land between their solidarity symbols and the levels of collective effervescence generated in their organizations' IRs.

Promised Land evinced a collective commitment to overcoming violence in their area, and their service was an active effort to rejuvenate solidarity symbols in the wake of an extremely dispiriting incident. Their circumstances instilled a clear sense of threat, and this helped them rally around a shared symbolic cause. First Baptist's members, by contrast, evinced the common goal of individual enlightenment through a personal encounter with God. They did not develop a rallying cry or a strong sense of collective mission. As I will discuss in this chapter's conclusion, the distinction between the two groups' symbolic solidarities supplements Emerson and Smith's (2000) conclusions regarding black and white evangelicals in the U.S. The evidence here suggests ways that these traditions' contrasting orientations, collectivist vs. individualist, are cultivated in the practice of religious IRs.

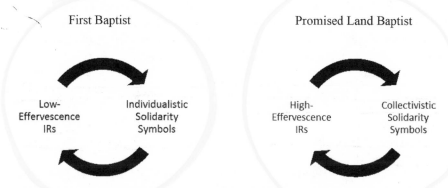

Figure 2.1. Comparison of Effervescence and Solidarity Symbols

Before comparing solidarities (this chapter) and evaluating ritual strategies for intersubjectivity (Chapter 4), I will share evidence from the focus groups supporting the interpretation that the two rituals resulted in contrasting levels of effervescence.

PROMISED LAND: UPLIFT, ENERGY, AND JOY

Promised Land's achievement of high levels of effervescence was evident in members' comments. Asked about their moods following the service, an older lady named Sylvia responded quickly and definitively: "I feel uplifted." Everyone agreed, and Wendell, a married man in his 40s, added that he felt "energized." Another woman, Addie, offered that she always felt "overjoyed" after services, and a woman named Alice said that she usually leaves Promised Land's services with "peace" in her heart. The participants all agreed with Sylvia's additional claim that the church's worship services are "Spirit-filled."

As suggested by their comments, the high-energy service I observed was not unusual at Promised Land. The organization cultivates effervescence by letting prior high-energy rituals spur momentum into subsequent rituals in an IR chain reaction. Promised Land assured a sense of "uplift" through their preparation, or buildup to the ritual. Wendell explained: "Church starts before you get to church. You have to be prayed up. When Sunday comes, we're prepped, we're ready to go. We've already got the Spirit going. And when the pastor gets into it, it's like adding wood to the fire." Addie offered, "Every Sunday when you're getting ready to come, you have that expectation. And we get it. I mean, we always have Spirit-filled worship services, and we go away with a sense of happiness and joy. And it starts with our Sunday School."

Wendell's and Addie's statements draw attention to two important points. First, their prior experience with Promised Land's rituals led them to expect that future rituals would produce joy and spiritual uplift. Both had ample experience to support this expectation since they had been attending for 20 (Wendell) and 35 years (Addie).[5] This lends evidence to the idea that high familiarity with a group's rituals enhances the ability to proficiently generate effervescence and solidarity. Reciprocally, emotionally charged rituals inspire participants to return repeatedly for rejuvenation. Second, IR analysis needs to account for smaller rituals that build up to the main event, or *pre-ritual rituals*. In the case of Promised Land and countless other American churches, Sunday School serves a ritual function that can be compared to warm-ups before a big game, or pre-party drinks before a gala. The focus

Does this create a barrier to outsiders?

group at Promised Land informed me that less than half of the congregation attends Sunday School regularly. Those who do attend, however, are positioned to be the "Spirit-filled" energy conductors during morning worship.

FIRST BAPTIST CHURCH:
INFORMATION, THOUGHTS, AND APPLICATIONS

When I asked First Baptist members to describe their moods after the service, a young married woman named Cherith responded that she felt "restful." Rest had been the topic of that morning's sermon, and the group laughed with Cherith after her response. Ron, a married man in his 50s, added, "Looking *forward* to rest." I nodded and asked for any other descriptions of their moods.

There was a pause of several seconds. Cherith spoke again:

> One of the great things about Pastor Craig is the fact that he puts a lot of common life in his preaching. I feel like we all get kind of drawn into his [approach of], "Has anybody ever felt this way before?" and then [we think], "Oh, I need to rest." You have that "ah-hah!" moment where you go, "Oh. That makes sense." We all know today was about rest, and we all go away thinking, "Maybe I should think about that."

Cherith's response highlighted First Baptist's emphasis on practical application of biblical lessons. I was still unsure, however, about how she felt. Cherith and Ron were simply restating the subject of the sermon. They had given valid responses to the query—even if "restful" doesn't qualify as a mood, perhaps "peaceful" or "calm" would be equivalents—but, as Ron's comment ("looking *forward* to rest") suggested, the restfulness spoken of by Pastor Craig had to do with incorporating moments of rest into one's daily life. He had not stated that congregants would walk out of that day's service literally feeling rested. I asked the question again: "How else would you describe how you felt after the service?" Ron responded again: "There's information, too. That's what we got from it." Debbie, a married woman in her 50s, added, "It just creates thought process. You go away with something to think about, to either influence the way you live or to take away and do something about." Debbie's statement suggested that First Baptist's sermons stimulate the symbolic resources of shared ideals and practical guidance for daily life. Again, though, the response circumvented the question of how they felt.

At this point in the discussion, Diane, a married mother of three, said:

> This time I will leave feeling a lot better because I know my children were listening today. And I really have to fight on a personal level trying to get them

to rest, to get adjusted to life without school and *structure* [during a vacation
from school]. And so I believe [the pastor] talked about, you know, "You do
that," but I will go away feeling relieved that I'm not the only one sitting there
talking about that. It's coming from a Word from God. And I can use that with
my children and myself.

Diane felt good after the service because she had reason to believe that the
content would have a beneficial impact on her kids. The Word of God confirmed something she had been trying to convey to her children, in effect
legitimating her authority regarding a particular household dynamic. I asked
Diane whether her children had talked with her about the sermon yet. She
responded, "No, but I question them during the service: 'Did you hear that?'
But it's still a challenge for me to keep them still, to keep them focused."
Diane expressed good feelings as a result of the sermon, and they had to do
with the symbolic content that was being imparted from God to her kids, with
Diane as the intermediary.

The comments of First Baptist's focus group revealed an interpretive
framework for religious practice that does not dwell on assessment of
one's emotions. In this sense, First Baptist resembles the Islamic Center, as
discussed in Chapter 1. Emotional invigoration did not appear to be their
motivation for going to church. Instead, as is evident below, the members of
First Baptist's focus group were seeking a mystical encounter in which God
would communicate personalized information about their individual choices
and behaviors.

I will return to the organizations' respective outputs of effervescence in
Chapter 4. Here, I will proceed by focusing on their contrasting types of solidarity and their consequences. I begin analysis of each ritual by focusing on
the portion of the service most obviously pertinent to symbolic solidarity: the
sermons and their immediate aftermaths.

PROMISED LAND BAPTIST CHURCH:
REVITALIZING ORGANIZATIONAL SYMBOLS

Pastor Dave is a heavy man with gray hair in his early 50s. He wore a light
blue suit and snakeskin boots. He has been pastor of Promised Land for over
a decade, and seems completely comfortable in the role. He is a virtuoso
of the energetic call-and-response preaching style that is common in many
black American churches. He began his sermon by telling the congregation
of about 100 that he had been at a funeral on Saturday. He said that the young
people at the funeral had "looked lost, like they had lost their identity." He
then explained that the sermon today would be addressed to the young people

of Promised Land. In fact, "Old people, if you want, you can tune me out." I glanced around the congregation at this point to see how the young people were responding. This presented a puzzle: there weren't any. At least, not many. There were, at most, 15 people who looked under 30. Of these, perhaps 5 were young men in their late teens or early 20s. If young people were largely absent, I wondered, and old people are free to tune the pastor out, who is the sermon for? Why preach to an imaginary audience?

From additional comments by Pastor Dave and congregants who spoke with me after the service, as well as from local news reports, I was able to gather additional information about the prior day's funeral. It was for one of two young men who had been shot to death on the Monday before. The victims were aged 17 and 20. They had been sitting in a parked car along with two other men in their early 20s. Another group of men wearing hoodies walked up to the car and opened fire with pistols and a shotgun, leaving 20 bullet holes in the side of the car. The two in the front seat were wounded but escaped. The two in the back were killed. The shooting had happened only a few blocks from Promised Land, and the victims were well-known by the church community.

Pastor Dave continued to address "the youth." He wanted them to recognize in the wake of the murders that no one ever knows when death will come. Those who aren't prepared for death will go to Hell. Not only do young people face immediate mortal dangers, he argued, they are living in "the last days." Apart from violent crime, natural disasters such as earthquakes and hurricanes could come at any time. The schools are being torn apart. Families fail to provide support, to the point where "children are suing their parents" and "parents are disowning their children." Where are young people to turn for direction?

Pastor Dave brought out a prop at this point: a white bandana. He held it up for the congregation to see. He pointed at it and yelled, "Young people, *this* is not where it's at! This is not where your family is!" He put the bandana away. He then held up his fingers and tried to contort them into a gang sign. He obviously had no idea how to make the sign and spent time playing up that fact, to the comic delight of his audience. He gave up and took a more serious tone: "young people, *this* is not where it's at!"

The energy in the room intensified as Pastor Dave identified other false sources of meaning and direction. Too many youths, he argued, try to find it in things like bling and tennis shoes. Too many youths think they can find it in parties, dance clubs, drugs, alcohol, and tattoos. Pastor Dave warned the youths in the church that he sees how they cover up their tattoos when they come to church. At this point, he erupted: "You want a tattoo? Get the cross of Jesus tattooed upon your heart!"

Pastor Dave challenged the youth to identify with the church and the cross rather than the world and its empty pleasures. At this point, he began to address the adults in the congregation. "They watch us when we're in church," he said. "When I was a child, I pretended to be like the grownups in our church. We'd have fun and pretend to be them." He proceeded to imitate eccentric older ladies who attended the church he grew up in, again to comic effect. "The young people watch us. They want to be like us."

He returned his attention to the youth. "Keep on markin' us, young folks. You gotta learn how to act in church." The message of the rest of the sermon was clear: the church provides family, meaning, and direction that can't be provided elsewhere. Have faith in Jesus and his church, and avoid the dangers and temptations of the world. The energy in the room grew palpably as the pastor preached and the congregation answered back. Late in the sermon, the pastor started singing. The organ joined in at high volume. Clapping began at different spots around the room. Some stood, some smiled, some nodded their heads, and some raised their hands high.

After about 10 minutes of this, Pastor Dave said, "I need someone who is Spirit-filled to sing 'Amazing Grace.'" An older assistant pastor took up the challenge. Then, for the final five minutes, we all swayed together and sang the same song, grasping hands within the pews and across the aisles.

Promised Land's Imaginary Audience

Why was Promised Land's sermon preached to a largely imaginary audience? Pastor Dave had stated at the top of his sermon that the old people could tune him out because this sermon was for the young people. Although he was clearly kidding about the older participants tuning him out, there was no irony in his statement that the sermon was for the young.

Surely Pastor Dave and the other members genuinely wanted to edify the few members of the church in their teens and 20s, and these young people must have felt the weight of their pastor's attention. However, the sermon would likely have been comparably effective if these younger members were absent altogether. This is because the effect of the ritual was to enliven symbolic solidarity, and this was done by rejuvenating confidence in the group's most valued symbols after these had been battered by the group's enemies in the prior week. The ritual can be understood as a hiatus and regrouping in the midst of a heated and ongoing conflict. The shooting of the young men had been deeply discouraging. As one member, Wendell, remarked softly during the focus group, the shooting made him "sad." He added, as if to himself, "You look back and wonder what's going on in the world." Had Pastor Dave ignored the shooting, or the ongoing problem of gang violence in their city, the sermon might have seemed oddly irrelevant to the congregants, and more importantly it would have left them in a weak position when they again encountered or heard about their opponents in the following week.

The symbols of the opposing sides of the conflict could not have been more apparent. The enemies' symbols were displayed by Pastor Dave for all to see in the form of a bandana and gang signs, and referred to by words when he spoke of "drugs," "clubs," "tattoos," and so on. Pastor Dave also made clear which symbols Promised Land was to call upon to combat their enemies' symbols: the cross of Christ that the young members needed to tattoo upon their hearts. Clearly, this activity supported the IR hypothesis that barriers with outsiders enhance commitment to an organization's symbols.

Barriers with "Outsiders" and Symbolic Solidarity

In Collins' general conflict theory, violence and the potential for violence always lurk beneath the surfaces of organizations' symbolic conflicts (1975, 351–413). For Promised Land and other urban churches all around the U.S., violence emerges as a necessary and explicit feature of the symbolic content. It is immediately evident "in the streets" every time a gunshot is fired or sirens are heard. The threat of violence catalyzes organizations' symbolic solidarity.[6] Evidence in favor of this point was readily available at Promised Land.

This observation, though, raises a pressing question: Is there a problem with arguing that Promised Land's service symbolized conflict with "outsiders"? Many of the young men who belong to the gangs in question live in the local community and are good friends and relatives of the Promised Land church family.[7] In effect, the gangs war against the community they are a part of. In the IR I observed, then, the "outsiders" were simultaneously "insiders" who belong to the local community. This creates a delicate situation in terms of how the congregation discusses the gangs. To accuse young men by name, for instance, would overlook the fact these young men are also the primary (though not the only) victims.

How, then, can the conflict be symbolized without diminishing solidarity with their local community? One way for the congregation to maintain a degree of solidarity with the young men in these circumstances is to ritually emphasize the organizational features of the gangs rather than the personal failings of individual gang members. The ceremony made clear, in other words, that the enemy *organization* and the broader secular culture that informs its symbols are the problems. Note that this position is pretty consistent with empirical research on gangs. Gangs swallow up young men through their social networks (Anderson 1999; Pattillo-McCoy 1999). Gangs are powerful and offer valuable incentives which are extremely difficult for underprivileged

Barriers to Outsiders

youths to procure on their own. In addition to material resources like income
and weapons, these incentives include intense feelings of membership and action, and symbols of agency and power. Such rewards become available after
a series of rituals aimed at recruitment and initiation (Sánchez Jankowski
1991, 47–58). Although the choice to join a gang is considered by Promised
Land to be an individual-level moral failure, the culprits that they identify in
ritual are the disembodied entity known as the gang and the corrupt secular
culture that provides its symbols.

Promised Land ritualized their opposition to the enemy organization by
deriding its symbols rather than the particular youths who use the gang's
symbols to assert their own power and agency. As discussed above, Pastor
Dave held up the bandana and mocked the gang signs, explicitly identifying
these symbols as inferior to the congregation's sign of the cross. We can abstract from this activity a specific function served by symbolization. In this
case, symbols serve as a device that allows interactants to respond to painful
conflicts from a more bearable distance. The symbols rouse emotions, but
they also create a buffer from other emotions related to the apprehension that
the "enemies" are often the same loved ones they want to protect.

Another way of using barriers to rouse solidarity is to direct attention to a
mythological Enemy. Pastor Dave asserted several times during the service
that the gangs were a work of Satan. At one point he exclaimed, "Young
people, your family is not on the streets. That voice you hear calling you
belongs to the Devil!" During the focus group, I asked what problems Promised Land faced as a congregation. Without any hesitation, an elderly woman
named Sylvia answered, "Like all the rest of the congregations throughout the
world: Satan. The Devil is busy." I asked her for examples. She responded,
"He could be right inside of a lot of our churches. Sometimes we slip. And
then it takes one slip and then the Devil gets into you and you go dividing
the church. Satan is busy." To Sylvia, the Devil sometimes gets *inside* her
church and "divides" them. It is noteworthy that Sylvia's instant reply when
asked about problems in her church was to cite breaches in solidarity. Given
the extent to which Promised Land members depend on each other and their
shared symbols to make it through each week, her reply seems quite sensible.[8]

FIRST BAPTIST CHURCH:
GETTING TOGETHER TO BE ALONE WITH GOD

Pastor Craig is in his mid-30s, and had been hired recently following First
Baptist's long search for a young pastor who might appeal to teenagers and
young adults. He wore a thin, inconspicuous headset microphone. He deliv-

ered the sermon with energy and confidence, often pacing the large stage and looking toward different sections of the congregation. Pastor Craig had just returned from a vacation, and his sermon focused on the value of rest, on "nurturing unhurried moments" in a fast-paced world. He mixed in several colloquialisms, stating for instance that "[The Apostle] Peter could be a little bit redneck," or, at another point, that a crabby character in a story he was telling was "a goober."

[margin, handwritten: Was the lack of Bible reading a draw?]

The pastor read aloud from the Bible three times. All readings were less than two verses. He consistently emphasized practical tips for applying the lessons in contemporary life. For instance, when discussing a verse in which Jesus takes his disciples to a deserted place to rest, he contrasted their experience with vacations in contemporary life which are overfilled with emails and texts. "Jesus wasn't tethered to a smart phone," and we likewise need to "unplug and tune in to God."

Although the pastor was a proficient public speaker, the congregation became noticeably shifty after about 15 minutes. Five minutes later, the restlessness had increased. Eyes glanced around the sanctuary, bulletins rustled, and some members exited the sanctuary. Pastor Craig spoke and moved more emphatically, but did not appear to recapture the congregation's attention until he announced that he'd conclude with a few practical tips for their rest time.

After the sermon, an altar call was held while we sang a hymn. The congregation watched as a woman and her young daughter approached the stage during the second verse. She spoke with the pastor, and then an assistant pastor took her aside. Another assistant pastor then invited a young family to the stage and announced the family's decision to become members. He told them to "consider this church your family," and the congregation welcomed them with a collective "Amen." Pastor Craig then led a final prayer and gave a benediction. The 10:30 service was over promptly at 11:30.[9]

[handwritten: My kind of church]

Extended Family

[margin, handwritten: Membership solidarity]

Membership solidarity was strongly apparent in members' comments after the service. The church's website had given an initial indication that this might be the case, as the home page reports, "We are a church in which you can really experience a sense of belonging." Members tended to confirm this, especially those who had been attending for many years. Glen, who had attended for nine years, explained, "We feel very close. The church is part of my family." The family motif came up numerous times. Glen's wife Diane explained that she looks forward to worship services because, "It's kind of like rejoining your family. [You] find out what's going on during the week, and you find that these people live like you do, basically."

Cherith agreed, stating, "You come into church and you see the people you love. Just like [Diane] said, it's like a reunion. You see the people around you. We have five generations in the church, so of course we see family. But not just that, we [also] see our church family, and they kind of tell us, 'We love you.' You know: 'Here's all our love.'"

As Cherith suggested, the familial feelings at First Baptist seem to be bolstered by their multigenerational demographics. In Sunday worship and other events, different age groups interact, as indicated by Diane: "We intermix and intermingle with each other. And I think that keeps us a whole as a church."

Outsiders Wanted   *Transforming into worldly*

Prior research demonstrates that collective identity in many conservative Protestant congregations is shaped by symbolic boundaries with outsiders such as atheists, secular humanists, and evolutionists (Draper and Park 2010; Edgell et al. 2006; Smith et al. 1998). Smith et al. (1998) show that evangelicals' sense of being embattled by a corrupt surrounding culture shapes their identity and helps them thrive as a movement. Other recent work, however, has suggested that many within the tradition may be moving in a more world-affirming direction (Draper and Park 2010; Lindsay 2006; Shibley 1998; Webber 2002). As Shibley's (1998) arguments suggest, such changes within the tradition would be consistent with theory on a "sect → church" cycle wherein "otherworldly sects" initially gain vitality from high levels of cultural tension, but then gradually lose vitality over time as they gain cultural legitimacy, succumb to social pressures, and transform into "worldly churches" (Johnson 1963; Stark and Finke 2000).[10]

Consistent with the position that many evangelicals have become more "world-affirming" in recent years, First Baptist did not appear to have serious boundaries with anyone in the surrounding culture. The sermon displayed no "fire and brimstone," and the primary behavioral mandate was that Christians should take time to enjoy life's goodness. Pastor Craig alluded to a "fast-paced world" and warned against tethering oneself to technology, but the tone of the comments was lightly self-critical.[11] The pastor did make one potentially divisive comment when he used the term "redneck," but it was clear from his delivery that he was using the term colloquially to broaden the sermon's appeal (recall that this takes place in Texas). Members of the focus group did not mention conflict with homosexuals, secular humanists, atheists, or any other social group. Promised Land's strong sense of boundaries, by contrast, catalyzed their symbolic solidarity. First Baptist would likely have strengthened their symbolic solidarity had they been conscious of an external threat.

Does this prevent Symbolic Solidarity?

Symbolic Solidarity in Individual-Level Religious Experience

Studies of evangelical Protestants highlight the central role of the Bible within their communities, particularly among Baptists (Ammerman 1987, 1995; Luhrmann 2012). For the most part, the interest is not with the material object itself but the contents of the text as interpreted by those present, especially the preacher. Although there are differences among Baptists regarding how "literally" the Bible needs to be interpreted, there is little disagreement about its symbolic importance (Ammerman 1995). Consistent with this, attention to "God's Word" was the primary source of symbolic solidarity at First Baptist.

Members frequently expressed that they benefited from the service because they were able to hear the Word of God in various ways. The Word of God was thought to operate indirectly through the stories and applications of the pastor and the quiet reflection of congregants. As Ron and Debbie commented (above), the sermons provide "information" and "create thought process." These thought processes "influence the way you live." As Diane mentioned, the idea that her children need to find time to rest comes "from a Word from God."

Hearing the "Word of God for their lives" appears to be the main goal of First Baptist's private and corporate worship. Members consistently invoked personalized applicability as the ultimate benefit of both. Debbie was struck by the personalized nature of God's communication during Sunday worship:

> I think it's so impressive when I come on Sunday. There's always a point in the sermon where something is said that is something I've thought about during the week. I'm a note-taker and I'll write it down and put a little star. . . . The sermons are always so timely. It seems it always happens: there's something that brings it right back to me and makes me understand that I need to listen and apply this, that it's not for *everyone else out there*, but my responsibility is to walk away with something that God has said to *me*.

Continuing, Debbie emphasized that hearing God's personalized instructions was her *duty*, an obligation that was first impressed upon her when she was young:

> If I *don't* walk away with a Word from God, *I'm* the problem. Someone challenged me when I was a youth to never go to church and walk away without God. God is there and God is *speaking*, and if I leave and haven't heard him, then *I'm* the problem. And it just made me think, "Oh my goodness, if I don't get something out of a prayer, a song, whatever. . . ." [trails off] It's sort of that moment for me, realizing, "This was for me."

Diane picked up on Debbie's comments, stating:

> It's kind of funny afterwards to talk about the message. Because the things that
> just *really* struck me are for me only. We'll hear the same message from the
> same person, but the person I'm talking to will say, "Oh, but what about such
> and such?" I mean, something *different* struck them. And so I think it's all about
> when your heart connects.

By Diane's statement, worshipers' hearts "connect" with God in unique
ways and at different moments. This suggests the realm of religious experience, defined by Glock and Stark as "all those feelings, perceptions, and
sensations which are experienced by the actor or defined by a religious group
or a society as involving some communication, however slight, with divine
essence, i.e. God, with ultimate reality, with transcendental authority" (1965,
42). When the believer feels her heart connect (Diane), or has an "ah-hah"
moment (Cherith), or realizes "this was for me" (Debbie), she perceives that
God is speaking directly to her. First Baptist's members seek these mystical
moments, express pleasure when they are achieved, and blame themselves
when the experience is absent.

CONCLUSION

[margin note: Rules about sacred objects]

Promised Land's ritual revitalized the organization's symbols in the midst
of an ongoing and violent conflict. After being emotionally battered by the
murders of young men from their community, Promised Land responded by
deriding the enemy's sacred symbols and celebrating their own. The pastor
accomplished this in a sermon preached to a mostly imaginary audience,
suggesting that "audience" is a flexible social construct that still can be effective even when the supposed listeners are absent. Here, the "audience"
was the "young people" who must choose allegiance to either their church
or the church's enemies. In symbolizing the enemies as either a disembodied
organizational entity, a corrupt secular culture, or the figure of Satan, the organization allowed members a more emotionally manageable distance from
which to address a conflict that involves their own loved ones as not only victims but culprits. Promised Land's service exemplified the powerful human
drive for solidarity, the torment when solidarity symbols are under attack, and
the power of ritual to restore them. Their symbolism applied directly to their
organization as such. In effect, Pastor Dave had told his congregation, "Our
sacred symbols and the community they represent came under brutal attack
this week. Come and join me in reviving our symbols so that our organization
can continue to give us all strength this week."

First Baptist's approach would be better summarized as, "God speaks to you as an individual. You may have had difficulty hearing his voice this week. It is your duty to come to church and concentrate on our shared sacred symbol of the Bible so that you will be more open to God's individualized instructions today and in the week to come." Symbolic solidarity at First Baptist is found in common identification with a solitary religious experience.

In this sense, First Baptist has much in common with the Buddhist Meditation Center examined in Chapter 3. Group meditation at the Meditation Center was valued not because members were energized by an intense collective IR, but because the group provided moral pressure in support of solitary meditation. For the most part, the rituals at First Baptist and the Meditation Center do not emphasize the group. Because the goal is an independent and inimitable religious experience, the experience of the person in the nearby pew or on the nearby meditation cushion becomes much less relevant to the encounter (although it feels encouraging to see that they are trying to do something similar). This speaks to the ways in which participants orient themselves to the ritual, and suggests that individualistic symbolism will yield relatively low levels of mutual monitoring, emotional entrainment, and collective effervescence. Additional details from the Meditation Center's and First Baptist's rituals, reported in the next two chapters, support this interpretation.

To the extent that mutual monitoring does take place during First Baptist's rituals, it might be of a similar nature to mutual monitoring at the Meditation Center. There, other people served mainly as distractions from solitary practice. Some Meditation Center members spoke of the need to incorporate distractions into their meditative awareness, but in general it was best if other meditators remained quiet and still. Likewise, the baseline expectation at First Baptist is that hearers of the Word will remain still and attentive.[12] Early in Pastor Craig's sermon, for instance, a young child near the stage began to cry. This went on long enough for several members to turn their heads in the child's direction. A woman several pews ahead of me expressed a loud "Shh!" and the child's mother hurried the child out of the sanctuary. This is not an unusual scene in public life, but it draws attention to the moral pressure at First Baptist to permit other members of the organization to pursue independent mystical moments.

A similar scene could conceivably occur at Promised Land, and I would not suggest that individualistic religious orientations are entirely absent there. However, the moral management of noise and individual expression at Promised Land is a stark contrast to the Meditation Center and First Baptist. Quiet and stillness are not required during Promised Land's worship because there is little incentive to ensure that others don't intrude on one's consciousness.

Promised Land's ritual openly depends on the experience of other people, and noise and movement alert the individual consciousness to that experience. When the organ plays improvised music, hearers are alerted to the emotional engagement of the organist. When congregants exclaim "mm-hm" or "preach it," hearers are alerted to the emotional engagement of other listeners. Spontaneous sounds are less welcome at First Baptist because members are listening closely to something internal.[13]

These observations supplement Emerson and Smith's (2000) conclusions about white evangelicals' often-unwitting contributions to America's racial divide. Emerson and Smith argue that white evangelicals' preoccupation with "accountable freewill individualism," "relationalism," and "antistructuralism" has the effect of obscuring from them the racialized nature of American culture. Their argument has been criticized for overlooking that these patterns merely echo a perspective on race that is readily evident among white Americans in social institutions other than religion (Bonilla-Silva 2003; Feagin and O'Brien 2003; Lamont 2000; Williams 2004). Emerson and Smith's data show, though, that evangelicals are indeed *more* likely than other white Americans to express individualism, relationalism, and antistructuralism. But it remains unclear why this is so. Comments from their interviewees typically do not help in this regard, since they rarely tie these views on race to their faith. Is there something unique about the evangelical tradition that perpetuates circuitous racism among white Americans?

In order to contrast different types of social solidarity between a black Baptist and white Baptist church, I found that the black Baptists' worship ritual focused attention on symbols of the collective, whereas the white Baptists' worship focused attention on symbols of the individual. Durkheim's logic is that emotionally charged symbols convey fundamental understandings of how the world operates. Emerson and Smith's work reveals that white evangelicals have a distinct tendency to hold attitudes that perpetuate racial inequality, especially insofar as an exclusive focus on the individual diminishes attention to the racialized nature of American life. This chapter's findings suggest ways in which these contrasting orientations of black and white Baptists are generated and cultivated in weekly ritual practices that focus heightened attention on, respectively, "we" and "I."

A focus on ritual dynamics in religious settings can thus contribute to a more complete understanding of the sources of racial discord in the U.S. In *The Dignity of Working Men: Morality and the Boundaries of Race, Class, and Immigration* (2000), Michèle Lamont shows that black and white working class American men *both* express deep respect for individualistic values like work ethic, discipline, and responsibility, but black men are much more likely than white men to also extol collectivistic values like solidarity and

altruism. Lamont's explanation is that both demographics realize the importance of self-reliance in order to survive near the bottom of a harsh capitalist
marketplace (e.g., lazy workers may quickly find themselves without a job
or home). The American sacred symbol of individualism is well-ingrained
in both groups. White American workers, though, have decreasingly participated in two types of organizations that have historically championed
symbols of collectivism: labor unions and progressive mainline Protestant
churches. Unions and mainline denominations both clearly have been declin-
ing in numbers and influence since the mid-twentieth century (Chaves 2017;
Finke and Stark 2005; Lantzer 2012; Panagopoulos and Francia 2008; Western and Rosenfeld 2012). By contrast, Lamont argues, although black workers, too, have declined in labor union participation, they continue to be highly
active in black Protestant churches, which continue to preach the benefits and
necessity of collective solidarity. The growth of evangelicalism over the same
time period has meant that more and more white Americans are participating
weekly in rituals that emphasize the experience and responsibilities of the
individual, often to the exclusion of attention to the experience and responsibilities of the group. Participants in churches like Promised Land, by contrast,
can gain EE from symbols of collectivism almost any Sunday morning.

The spirit appears in intense moments of religious worship, and returns
repeatedly when deftly reinvoked with sacred symbols. There is much more
to consider, though, about how intense emotions are generated in religious
worship. A precondition is for human bodies to more or less crowd together.
This dynamic, though, is more complex than it appears on the surface. Chapter 3 considers how a Buddhist and a Catholic organization manage bodily
copresence during their rituals. Hidden motivations that inspire the rituals,
and unintended consequences that flow from them, will help establish why
and how copresence is so important.

NOTES

1. Durkheim writes, "If society is to be able to become conscious of itself and keep
the sense it has of itself at the required intensity, it must assemble and concentrate.
This concentration brings about an uplifting of moral life that is expressed by a set
of ideal conceptions in which the new life thus awakened is depicted" (1912, 424).

2. For some readers, this book's concept of membership solidarity might bring
to mind the anthropological concept of "communitas." Edith Turner writes, for example, that communitas "is togetherness itself" (2012, 4). Communitas also shares
similarities with the concept of collective effervescence, and in some cases communitas and effervescence have even been treated as equivalents (Olaveson 2001;
cf. Berger 2016). Although there is clear conceptual overlap, though, the logic of IR

theory requires that membership solidarity and collective effervescence must both be distinguished from communitas.

Victor Turner (1969, 1974) describes communitas as an experience of unstructured community, where individual roles and statuses are absent and egalitarian fellow-feeling flourishes. Turner consistently emphasizes what communitas is *not*; it is *"anti-structure,"* an experience where feelings of social hierarchy and stratification are *absent*. Turner notices communitas, for example, in collective and liminal rites of passage, in the egalitarian feelings of traveling bands of pilgrims, and during communal happenings in the 1960s hippy counterculture.

Is communitas equivalent to effervescence? Although there are good reasons to expect a generally negative relationship between social stratification and collective effervescence, this negative relationship cannot just be assumed. In fact, situational stratification is routinely evident in a wide range of effervescent deference rituals in, for example, the military, education, families, and religion. Interaction ritual theory treats stratification as a conditioning factor that *impacts* a gathering's ability to reach effervescence. From this perspective, it would be an analytical error to assume that effervescence is always an egalitarian experience. Communitas, by contrast, is always by definition an egalitarian experience. Along with Berger (2016, 163–65) on this point, I'll suggest that effervescence and communitas are best conceived as distinct but "partly overlapping analytical concepts."

With respect to membership solidarity, Victor Turner (1969, 132) and Edith Turner (2012, 5) both argue explicitly that social solidarity must be distinguished from communitas. This is because Durkheim thought that solidarity depends on processes of social exclusion, on a contrast between in-groups and out-groups that is contrary to the entire notion of communitas. Consistent with this, exclusion (barriers to outsiders) is understood in IR theory as an independent variable that *impacts* social solidarity; as with communitas and effervescence, communitas and membership solidarity must not be conflated.

3. See Table A.1 in Appendix A.

4. See Figure A.1 in Appendix A.

5. The group I spoke with was extremely well-accustomed to the church's rituals. The members of the focus group had been attending the church for an *average* of 26 years. The "newcomer" to the group had been a member for four years. They informed me that most of the rest of the congregation similarly had been attending for a very long time.

Promised Land and Congregation Shalom held the most effervescent rituals in the qualitative sample, and their congregants also appeared to be the oldest, on average. In multivariate analysis of the USCLS sample, average age is unrelated to the ability to achieve effervescence, confirming my own ever-increasing bias. Older congregations, though, have a small positive relationship with membership solidarity and a small negative relationship with symbolic solidarity (Draper 2014).

6. Proposition 21.52: "The more that members of a group are threatened by violence, either from its own hierarchy or from outsiders, the more intense the commitment to the group and its symbols" (1975, 379).

7. This is common in neighborhoods with prominent gang activity. Consider Pattillo-McCoy's account of Groveland's "Black Mobsters" in *Black Picket Fences*

(1999). Although a notorious and powerful (i.e., proficient at violence) national gang, the Mobsters were known by Groveland residents as friends, sons, brothers, uncles, etc. They also provided needed services to the community such as combating graffiti, breaking up fights, helping shut down a liquor store, and even providing security for school events. Along similar lines, see Alice Goffman's riveting portrayal of Philadelphia's "Sixth Street Gang," whose members are also affectionate and loyal family members and friends of the community in *On the Run: Fugitive Life in an American City* (2014).

8. Some churches are quite conscious of the interdependent relationship between solidarity and the spirit. In Nelson's (2005) ethnography of a South Carolina African Methodist church, members regularly remind each other that attendees who are not saved or are insufficiently devout "result in a diminished sense of [God's] presence in the worship." The pastor explains during one sermon, "When we come to the Lord's house on Sunday morning and there's no Spirit of God, that means that somebody has come without the Lord on their mind" (139). Such demands for undeviating symbolic solidarity increase the moral pressure on the individual attendee to display his own commitment through expressive worship, which in turn tends to boost intersubjectivity and effervescence.

9. USCLS data reveal that service length has positive relationships with both effervescence and symbolic solidarity, but no relationship with membership solidarity (Draper 2014). This is consistent with what I observed at First Baptist's brief service, which showed substantial membership solidarity but little effervescence and relatively weak symbolic solidarity.

10. I revisit this theory and its relation to the current study in closer detail in the Conclusion.

11. Supporting this impression, the church has a pastoral blog and congregational Twitter account, both of which were regularly updated before and after my visit.

12. Hearing God's individualized message can be hard work, especially for the conscientious. Luhrmann's *When God Talks Back* (2012) examines the process in depth. Based on interviews with evangelicals, she describes how they work to "train the mind in such a way that they experience part of their mind as the presence of God" (xxi). This requires discipline in learning to "pay attention" in the right way:

"[E]vangelical Christians . . . not only have to accept the basic idea that they can experience God directly; they must develop the interpretive tools to do so in a way that they can authentically experience what feels like inner thought as God-generated. They have to pick out the thoughts that count as God's and learn to trust that they really are God's, not their own. . . . To an observer, what is striking is how hard people work to feel confident that the God who speaks to them in their mind is also the real external God." (41)

It takes discipline and concentration to get better at this process, introducing an exam-like quality to church.

13. The intended object of internal concentration differs from that at the Meditation Center, though. Whereas Meditation Center members were attending to reflexive inner dialogue, First Baptist members were listening for the voice of God.

Chapter Three

Bodily Copresence

Bodily copresence, the first of three IR "ingredients" to be considered, facilitates emotional intensity by allowing interactants to become more closely attuned to each other's thoughts and emotions. Erving Goffman argued that persons in each other's presence, even in the most mundane of moments, continuously "are tracking one another and acting so as to make themselves trackable" (1981, 103). Randall Collins points to biology to explain this, and the idea that "humans as animals have evolved with nervous systems that pay attention to each other: there is always the possibility of fighting, or spreading an alarm; or, on the positive side, positive sexual contact" (2004, 54). Based on these arguments, bodily copresence stimulates attunement and risk, which in turn have the potential to speed the spirit.

Still, the properties and consequences of copresence are complex and far from fully understood. For example, what is the minimum threshold for "copresence"? We might imagine a continuum of *proximity of bodies* ranging from close to far apart. At one end of the continuum, we find sexual intercourse and violence. The other end of the continuum would have to be the maximum distance at which individuals can either see or hear each other – imagine a farmer waving at her neighbor from across a large field. Along with proximity, we should also consider the *number of bodies* that are copresent. Do the ritual outcomes shift as we move from two people to three, from three to four, and so on? Finally, what are the consequences of different *arrangements of bodies* within the physical space? What happens when some bodies are literally higher than others, as on a staircase, or when the bodies shift from a vertical to a horizontal line? The consequences of all three variables clearly depend on other factors, as well (e.g., being up close with your lover vs. a fellow subway passenger), but we can nonetheless isolate independent effects of different types of copresence.

[handwritten margin note: How does it create risk?]

69

In analysis of USCLS data, I reconceptualized bodily copresence as "bodily density," a continuous rather than dichotomous variable. In other words, we can examine copresence as a matter of degree, or how *crowded* the gathering is. I found that the relationship between bodily density and effervescence is generally positive, as I expected, but also that the relationship actually depends on a third, intervening factor: the socioeconomic statuses of those who are gathered. For this reason, this chapter compares high-density rituals at one rich and one poor organization.

At the Meditation Center, the wealthier organization, my research question was simple: why meditate with a group? The enthusiastic discussion that ensued in the focus group highlighted the importance of moral pressure and symbolic empowerment, both of which require copresence with other Meditation Center members. During my observation of St. John's Catholic Church, I was struck by the contrasting collective moods inside and outside the doors of the sanctuary. Although both of St. John's rituals were very crowded, a mood of action and glee prevailed outside, and a mood of boredom and sobriety prevailed inside. This contrast points to the influence of physicalized ritual stratification, another key factor that conditions the effects of copresence.

Before delving in to those rituals, though, we should pause and consider *non*-copresent interaction rituals, an unescapable issue in "the virtual age." The existence of the internet (along with earlier innovations like telephones and TVs) creates a natural laboratory in which we can more precisely discern what bodily copresence adds to rituals.

NON-COPRESENT INTERACTION RITUALS

Telecommunication technologies have diversified the ways in which humans can communicate. But is it possible to hold an interaction ritual from a distance? Drawing on Goffman, Collins defines ritual as "a mechanism of mutually focused emotions and attention producing a momentarily shared reality, which thereby generates solidarity and symbols of group membership" (2004, 7). There is little reason to think that the telephone and other electronic communication formats can't provide participants with a momentarily shared reality which generates solidarity. These formats fit the definition. However, lack of bodily copresence severely limits the heights emotional intensity can reach.

Radio and telephone technologies made it possible for humans to carry out IRs that are exclusively oral. Mutual focus of attention can be achieved in exclusively oral IRs by maintaining a topic of conversation, and emotional entrainment can be achieved through vocal intonation, volume, rhythm, or the use of emotionally loaded terms like "love," "hate," or "pissed off." What is missing from these IRs, however, is the risk of physical consequences. For example, two lovers might have an emotionally poignant interaction over the phone, but there is no way for the interaction to culminate in kissing or sex. Exclusively spoken IRs are relatively safe. The lovers might tell each other things like, "I want to hold you," or even engage in phone sex, but their physical distance is a decisive limitation on their intimacy. They know that it is impossible during the ritual to achieve the highest levels of solidarity.

Just as the most intense forms of intimacy cannot be reached over the phone, neither can the most intense forms of conflict. Although two people might become angry with each other over the phone, there is no way for the anger to culminate in immediate violence. Because immediate physical risk is eliminated, because the most acute expressions of solidarity and conflict are not options, interactants in exclusively oral rituals cannot gain the sense that they are truly "where the action is" (Goffman 1967).

The internet has made additional types of distanced rituals possible. Messaging technologies facilitate exclusively verbal interactions. Mutual focus of attention can be achieved, as in a phone call, by sustaining a topic, rhythm of exchange, or perhaps a style of conversation. However, these technologies do not allow for interactants to send and receive unambiguous emotional cues,[1] making misunderstanding a constant threat to solidarity. Kruger et al. (2005) point to an inescapable "egocentrism" that governs email relationships: "[P]eople tend to believe they can communicate over email much more effectively than they can" (925). Without "paralinguistic cues such as gesture, emphasis, and intonation," emails and texts lend themselves to misinterpretation. Emotional entrainment and overall intersubjectivity are in this sense hindered by internet media, as is, again, a sense of immediate risk and action.

Internet technologies have also made it possible to transmit pictures and videos to accompany oral and verbal interaction. Services such as Skype and Google Talk, for instance, allow for videoconferencing, or oral interactions accompanied by live video feeds of the interactants. Although slow transmission speeds and technical glitches can impede rhythmic entrainment, these technologies help recover paralinguistic signals that are unavailable in emails and texts. Nonetheless, as with phone calls, videoconferencing cannot result in the most intense forms of solidarity and conflict. Interactants know that their ritual cannot climax in a kiss or a fistfight, and there is an inherent constraint on ritual intensity and action.

Collins (2004, 53–64) considers copresence in several specific types of rituals. In each case, it is clear that face-to-face contact would lead to greater emotional intensity than remote contact. In intense formal rituals like weddings and funerals, for example, copresence conveys "that one is paying one's respects" (54). Although these rituals can be "virtually" attended, actual attendance does much more to honor the sanctity of the occasion and convey solidarity. Physical copresence allows one not only to feel the full force of the occasion, but also to make one's own emotional involvement available *to* the occasion.

Collins also considers less formal scenarios, such as watching sports or election results on television. Emotional excitement is attainable for someone who views the event in solitude, but viewers typically want to share their excitement: "At peak moments of victory, or suspense followed by dramatic success, the excited viewer reaches out to hug, touch, or kiss someone" (56). This is probably the main reason why Americans hold Super Bowl and election night parties. Without feedback and intersubjectivity with friends, their excitement cannot be maximized or sustained.

Explicitly religious rituals, too, tend to be more emotionally intense, sacred, and unifying when they are in-person. What, though, does copresence add to Buddhist meditation? I turn now to a group of Buddhists who gather several times per week for this ancient religious practice. Their goal, over the long term, is to cultivate personal qualities such as peace, mindfulness, and wisdom, which are among the foremost sacred symbols of their tradition. Collins has drawn upon symbolic interactionist arguments to argue that meditation is a ritual of "self-solidarity," one that takes place "inside the self" rather than in "external social assembly" (Collins 2010, 23; Mead 1934; Wiley 1994). As a deeply introspective religious practice, meditation is an excellent test case for considering how copresence works.

THE MEDITATION CENTER: WHY MEDITATE WITH OTHER PEOPLE?

There are numerous different branches and variants of Buddhism, including the major world traditions of Theravada, Mahayana, and Vajrayana. The Meditation Center practices a westernized form of Tibetan Buddhism in the Vajrayana tradition.[2] As many observers have pointed out (e.g., Cadge 2005; Numrich 2000; Smith and Froese 2008), American Buddhism is largely separated into immigrant communities ("cultural Buddhists") and convert communities ("convert Buddhists"). The Meditation Center clearly belongs in the latter category, as several members discussed not only their own adult conversions[3] but also the group's distinction from a more "traditional" Buddhist temple in their city. Numrich (2000) identifies several characteristics common among convert Buddhists that were evident in my visit to the Meditation Center: members are predominantly white, financially stable, highly educated, and dissatisfied with their non-Buddhist religious upbringings. They are also extremely open-minded. Meditation Center members frequently mention that all are welcome and can benefit from participating in their community (*sangha*), even those with no interest in religion per se. The community believes that everyone can benefit from meditation, in particular, and this practice is the stated foundation of all that the group does.

There are a variety of types and rationales for Buddhist meditation.[4] The Meditation Center practice "shamatha," which is meant to facilitate personal development as the practitioner trains to "peacefully abide" with her own mind. Meditation Center members expect to become more mindful, wise, and calm through the regular practice of meditation. Shamatha involves sitting on the ground (or cushion) with legs crossed and hands resting on one's knees. The meditator attempts to maintain an upright yet relaxed posture while lightly focusing attention on her breathing. In that position, she then tries to gently turn away from distracting thoughts and outside concerns as they pop into mind (Chödrön 1991; Mipham 2005; Ray 2004).

This type of meditation is clearly not a time for social interaction. Meditators learn to avoid all verbal and nonverbal communication during the practice. But this raises a question: if mindfulness meditation is a personal process that is by and for the individual, why do the Meditation Center and many other Buddhist organizations regularly hold *group* meditations? The question is not whether Buddhists value community. Along with the Buddha and his teachings, *sangha* is one of the "Three Jewels" in which Buddhists take refuge. Sangha refers to monastic communities or, especially in the West, lay Buddhist communities. In either case, the social component is highly valued. But it is nonetheless clear that mindfulness meditation is fundamentally solitary. Group meditation is rare in Tibet, and practitioners even suggest that it must be practiced regularly when *away* from the group in order to be effective (Chödrön 1991; Coleman 2001; Mipham 2005).

The Chant and the Sit

In the main shrine room of the Meditation Center, 25 blue cushions in neat rows take up most of the available space on the wood floor. Each cushion (known as a "gomden") rests on a small blue mat, is a little under a foot tall, and is designed to help a person sit comfortably with legs crossed for a long period of time. A short raised stage with three small shrines stretches along the front wall of the room, and to the right of the stage is a lower platform with an extra cushion. Six large and colorful banners adorn the front and side walls.

On the day of my observation, nine women and seven other men took their cushions (three individuals entered late, for a total of eleven women and nine men). Seventeen of us were white, and there was one Latino, one Latina, and one Indian-American male. Andrea, the Latina, handed each person a folder containing written chants. Connie, a local artist in her 20s who works as the group's office manager, walked to the front and prepared the stage.[5] Next, she sat on a cushion next to the stage and explained to us that she would ring a bell three times: to begin the chanting, and to begin and end "the sit."

Connie instructed us to read aloud the first four chants in the folder, all of which were praise songs to god-like beings.[6] She rang the bell and we began. The group recited together in an unexpressive monotone. Some punctuated the first beat of each line with a high-pitched whine. We tended to begin at contrasting speeds and gradually fall into a common cadence, with the loudest voices setting the pace and the quiet voices following along. After the four chants, Connie rang the bell and we began to meditate.

Before describing this period of the ritual, I should explain why the tone of this analysis is about to shift, temporarily, to an emphasis on my own subjective sensations and internal dialogue during these moments in the ritual. I follow researchers such as Caughey (1984), Collins (2004), and Wiley (1994) in reporting remembered excerpts of internal dialogue as relevant data on cognitive and affective processes. In research on Buddhism, in particular, Preston (1988) uses the same approach in his analysis of Zen practice. As discussed above, meditation is consistently framed as a way to work on one's own internal thoughts and perceptions; focusing closely on what other meditators are doing is generally discouraged. Because this approach has implications for copresence and intersubjectivity, I want to convey the meditative experience from the perspective of someone who is in the process of working to engage the practice as directed by the tradition. Later in this chapter, I will also provide accounts from the focus group regarding their personal thoughts and sensations during the meditation session. Here, detailing some of my own novice struggles with meditation seems the most accurate way to convey the occasion.

I had received meditation instruction from one of the members (Louise) during a preliminary visit to the Center, and I attempted to follow her guidelines.[7] I directed a soft gaze toward the ground a few feet in front of me. I wiggled my head a little to maneuver it into a good resting place at the top of my spinal column. I relaxed my jaw and left my mouth slightly open. I listened to my breath. I tried not to think about anything in particular, and redirected focus to my breath when conscious of conscious thought.

There were few "external" distractions. I noticed the individuals who arrived late, but they quickly found cushions and began to meditate. Two individuals in my periphery shifted positions more often than the others, but for the most part everyone was very still. The most prominent object of my external awareness was the hum of the air conditioning unit, which shut off about halfway through the exercise. Shortly after, beads of sweat began to form on my face (it was over 100° outside). This made me anxious until I remembered Louise's advice to "welcome" distractions as opportunities to redirect attention to my breath. My mind "settled," although I was relieved when the AC resumed a few minutes later.

With respect to my internal awareness, I was able to avert disruptive thoughts for some but not all of the session. Louise had suggested a technique that proved useful: I counted my breaths from 0 to 21 and back down again. Some worries did cross my mind, though. For instance, I thought anxiously about practical issues related to my role as a researcher. Related to this, I also engaged in too much self-assessment, sometimes happily affirming to myself that I could meditate just fine (thereby hindering my ability to meditate just fine). The following recalls what some of my thoughts would have looked like if written down:

> 18... Remember to ask Perry to read some of his poems. Wait, Perry isn't here today. Ha. I was eager to ask so I didn't realize he's not even here... Could be sitting behind me, but I don't think so...... This is stupid. Get back on track. 17............ Was it 17? .... 16.... who knows .... not bad that I forgot what number I'm on. A sign that I'm not being dominated by conscious thought. Really in the right state, now, I think.... That's ridiculous......... 17............................ 16.. My God it's hot.....................15..........

When Connie rang the closing bell, I was surprised that, despite my struggles, the entire event had passed so quickly.

Solitary and Collective Rituals

Members at the Meditation Center mentioned several times that mindfulness meditation is by and for the individual. They believe that society would benefit from a growth in the prevalence of the practice, but the practice per se is devoted to individual-level experience.[8] When I asked members of the community why they meditate *as a group*, they often appeared surprised to hear the question. Perry, for example, a highly educated poet who has come to the center for 25 years and now coordinates all of the meditation instruction, replied: "That's a good question. I'll have to think about that."

The practice is so heavily focused on individual self-improvement that even the most experienced members can overlook that they regularly

participate in a collective religious ritual. When discussing the presence of
other meditators, members often stated that other people serve as distractions.
According to Steve, a single man in his 40s:

> When you meditate with the group, the issue to deal with, and that we're trained
> to think about and talk about, is possible interruptions. People walking in and
> out the door and sitting, or somebody being restless. . . . Just being with the
> group is . . . challenging.

Alan, an energetic single man in his 30s, explained that he sits near the
front during group meditation in order to avoid distractions: "That makes it
easier for me to meditate. But that's not necessarily the goal . . . to make it
easier. It's sort of like a cop-out." Alan's sentiments were consistent with
others in the group. A major goal of meditation is cultivating a new awareness of one's immediate surroundings, and distractions from meditation are
considered opportunities to train this capability. Bree, a single woman in her
30s, explained:

> When you begin, you start with a type of meditation that is very closed in your
> field of awareness and vision. And as you progress, you open up until it's almost
> a 360° awareness of what's surrounding you in the physical space. The sounds.
> Other bodies. Everything.

Whether or not other people are *welcome* distractions, they are considered
distractions nonetheless. Members' hesitations regarding collective meditation were also evident in their comments about the physical space. Steve
commented,

> Space is a problem here. Sometimes I want to go to the main shrine room, and
> there's some guest speaker or something that I didn't know about, and I'm
> like, "there's all these *people*" [with a look of mock disgust]. And I think, "We
> should *expand*! We should build a larger center."

For Steve, crowdedness was a problem that obviously needed to be corrected.
Other members concurred, and explained that the Center was planning an
expansion that will include a second main shrine room. Having meditated
with the group in the main shrine room, I understand their impulse. There
were only 20 participants in my session, but almost all of the cushions were
filled and "personal space" was limited to no more than a couple of feet in
any direction.

The group's expressions of discomfort are consistent with the USCLS
finding shown in Appendix A (Figure A.2) that socioeconomic status conditions how bodily density affects effervescence. Religious organizations with

high levels of education and income tended to report decreases in emotional intensity when bodily density was high. Goffman (1967) observed a similar phenomenon in ethnographic study, and attributed it to an expectation of deference that is distinctive of upper-class cultures. Consistent with this, Meditation Center members reported a number of negative emotions after the session. Gina, a single woman in her 20s, reported, "Today I had a lot of anxiety. I was still preoccupied afterwards, but maybe a little more settled." Terry, a woman in her 30s, explained, "Today I was just tired. My objective was just to get in. It was something I had committed myself to for some period of time. So I was just glad I did it." Similarly, Steve described his struggle with fatigue in detail:

> I was just battling the entire time. So I was just glad I got through it. I was realizing how my body was functioning, what's going on with my body, all that body awareness stuff. I'm really tired. My eyes were going [demonstrates a struggle with heavy eyelids] and I thought, "I need to keep them open. I'm trying to keep them open."

For these members, the practice did not lead to shared ebullience. Participants expressed feelings like anxiety or fatigue as much as they expressed feelings like joy or empowerment.

When it came to the chanting, however, participants consistently described it as fun and energizing. Terry, for example, said, "I look forward to doing the chants. The unity that comes from doing that. And the voices joining together. I think it's really cool. I get joy from it." Terry's comments suggest that chanting tends to be a highly effervescent IR at the Meditation Center. First, she "looks forward" to the chants, which means that her prior IRs energize her for future IRs of the same type.[9] Second, she suggests that "voices joining together," an action that requires rhythmic entrainment, generated "unity." Third, she gets "joy," a positive form of EE, from doing the chants.

Similarly, Matt's description of the chanting corresponds extremely well with descriptions of collective effervescence in Durkheim and IR theory:

> I lose myself in the chanting. When the whole group is doing it and you find yourself in sync with everybody else . . . nothing exists but the words. I become completely focused. I kind of lose myself in the activity of it, which is nice.

Again, Matt's choice of words suggests the energizing force of the chanting IR. He reports losing himself in the group activity, as though his individual awareness was temporarily colonized by the group awareness. He reports being "in sync with everybody else" (rhythmic entrainment), with "nothing exist[ing] but the words" (shared object of attention).

Alan claimed that one chanting ritual at the Meditation Center actually jolted his perceptions of physical reality: "The room sometimes changes size. . . . One time when I was leading a chant, there were a whole bunch of people there, like 60. I felt very close to people. It felt like the stage was about seven feet tall and the ceiling was gonna scrape my head." The IR Alan recalled would have felt exceptionally crowded in the main shrine room. With 60 bodies, many would have been pressed into physical contact. The sound of so many voices in unison would have generated significant reverberation, priming the group for a spiritual experience. Alan's account of altered awareness is consistent with Durkheim's description of effervescence: "The vital energies become hyper-excited, the passions more intense, the sensations more powerful; there are indeed some that are produced only at this moment. Man does not recognize himself; he feels somehow transformed and in consequence transforms his surroundings" (1912, 424).

My observations, and especially members' comments, lead me to think that group meditation at the Meditation Center is not a reliable source of collective effervescence, whereas chanting tends to facilitate relatively high collective effervescence. In the ritual I observed, the two practices had virtually identical levels of copresence/density. A brief review of the other IR dynamics, however, suggests why chanting was the more invigorating group experience: (1) chanting facilitates a more obvious mutual focus of attention, which according to one participant is "the words themselves"; (2) chanting requires higher degrees of rhythmic entrainment and mutual monitoring, thus increasing sensations of intersubjectivity; and (3) chanting activates higher barriers to outsiders because it requires participants to verbalize symbolism that is foreign to most American English speakers. It is consistent with the theory, then, that chanting is more invigorating than collective meditation.

 Still, chanting is peripheral in members' descriptions of their experiences at the Meditation Center. It is also peripheral within the structure of the IR—the chanting period is brief and is followed by a much longer period of meditation. It is clear that members enjoy the chanting as part of their overall experience of the organization, just as they enjoy various social events and volunteer opportunities that are sponsored by the community. In this respect, they are a vital organization. A sample of events during the month I visited includes the following, to name only a few: Zen archery, Buddhist art classes, meditation instruction to prison inmates, classes on Buddhism at four different levels of experience, movie night ("Kundun"), public discussion about Buddhism, and a gay men's group. The rigorous training sessions, in particular, featured prominently in members' responses to my questions about membership solidarity.[10] For example, Alan explained:

We get a real family feeling in these classes that we have on the weekends. They go from 7–9 on Friday, 8–5 on Saturday, and then the next morning too. And we graduate together and see each other every 2 months. So there's a real camaraderie on these weekends. Like we're all in the galley together, or army barracks or something.

The Meditation Center helps members get to know each other in supplementary activities designed to build solidarity. And they are effective at building "a real family feeling." The weekend trainings, especially, facilitate solidarity by stimulating a galley-type experience. For fellow graduates, memories of the trainings serve as emblems of their shared success in overcoming physical and emotional challenges. These activities enhance both types of solidarity, and yet they are considered tangential to the primary experience of ongoing meditative practice.

Moral Pressure and Empowerment

Although members spoke in detail about the drawbacks of collective meditation, especially crowded sessions, they made additional comments that suggested why they persist anyway. Members value the collective ritual because it strengthens their solitary practice. They expressed clearly and consistently that the individual's independent spiritual journey is primary. The group's symbolic allegiances, then, were consistent with research that points to the centrality of individualism in American culture, generally, and religion, in particular (Bellah et al. 1996; Goffman 1967; Madsen 2009).

Collective meditation at the Meditation Center supports the solitary practice of the individual in two ways. First, collective meditation makes the individual morally responsible to the group. Second, collective meditation reassures members that their practices and symbols are well worth their time and commitment.

After the focus group had discussed the challenges of collective meditation for several minutes, Alan began to speak of its rewards. He explained, "I think it's easier to meditate here than at home. The time is a set thing. . . . Everything is just really here for the purpose of meditating." The focus group nodded and orally confirmed this observation. Terry added, "That's right. I probably wouldn't have even meditated this morning if it weren't Sunday [the day on which she regularly attends the Meditation Center]. We've all made a commitment to do the practice. And sometimes you feel like it, and sometimes you don't."

Alan's and Terry's comments evoke the moral components of time and place. Durkheim addresses these at several points in *The Elementary Forms* (1912, 9–12, 311, 353–54, 441–42). Time and place socially construct humans' responsibilities to each other. Calendars, for instance, impose sacred and profane periods. Durkheim writes, "The division into days, weeks, months, years, etc., corresponds to the recurrence of rites, festivals, and public ceremonies at regular intervals. A calendar expresses the rhythm of collective activity while ensuring that regularity" (10). A similar example is the drive for punctuality. When we try to be punctual, we are not trying to serve a disembodied entity called "Time." Rather, we are attempting to please other people who expect us to be at place x at time y. Efforts to be on time for a lunch date, birthday party, business meeting, etc. are primarily efforts to avoid disappointing significant others. Rushing to the appointment, one might imagine the shame that will follow the late arrival. Latecomers often point to uncontrollable external factors that made them late, and this is meant to alleviate personal responsibility: "It was the damn *traffic* . . . [Please understand that I would never willingly ignore my obligations to you by showing up late]." Meditation Center members illustrated the morality of time by mentioning repeatedly that late arrivals are distractions during meditation. The organization agrees to meet at a set time and place, and they expect each other to remain physically still and quiet until the final bell rings. Members like Alan and Terry welcome the social pressure of having a set time and place for meditation because it prods them to persist in the practice.

Matt expressed a second way in which collective meditation supports the solitary practice:

> There's something about the shrine room, and being in there. After years of coming here I've never been able to put my finger on it exactly. But when you walk into that room and you sit there with that group of people who are also meditating and you're doing something *completely* solitary—you know, it's just you working on your own mind—but somehow being in a room full of other people doing it is empowering. I always find it easier to meditate here than at home.

For Matt, the presence of the group added a sense of "empowerment" to what he nonetheless considered a "*completely* solitary" activity. Practicing as a group emboldens the individual because it confirms that others are committed to the same pursuit. This is not to suggest that meditators are somehow cognitively unaware that other people in the world meditate. Rather, the cognitive awareness is insufficient on its own to embolden the meditator. A copresent intersubjective experience is required.

Loïc Wacquant (2004) shows a similar pattern in his ethnography of boxers in Chicago's South Side. Although boxers could do most of their training at home, they prefer to do their exercises in the gym where they can scrutinize

Would this work in other traditions?

and imitate the movements of other boxers (116–17). Along with this tacit method of knowledge transmission (see Polanyi 1967), the boxers gain emotional sustenance for the individual practice by experiencing the collective rhythms of the gym. Wacquant's gym organized boxers' exercises (hitting the bag, jumping rope, doing sit-ups, etc.) in three-minute segments. Similar in function to the bell in a boxing ring, Connie's bell at the Meditation Center served as an auditory device entraining individual meditators into the physical tempo of the group. Whether boxing in the South Side or meditating in Texas, the individual can gain skill and confidence by practicing in the same room with other people.

Note that this emboldening experience requires little, if any, spoken communication. Michal Pagis' (2010) ethnographic study identifies two types of nonverbal cues that signal intersubjectivity during collective meditation: movement and nonmovement. Pagis noticed that movement during group sessions was often contagious. Meditators would get caught up in little clusters of nonverbal movements and sounds. For example:

> In one incident a loud cough was heard. . . . As the man continued coughing, a woman in the third row moved her leg and changed her posture. Her movement was loud and activated two other movements—another woman moved her hand, and another straightened her back (319).

These clustered movements typically are short-lived, and the persistent stillness of other meditators serves as a reminder of what everyone is supposed to be doing. Nonmovement, then, signals that a meditator is proficient and probably very experienced. As such, a superior ability to remain still could potentially serve as an indicator of participants' high status in the organization. Meditators, especially novices, can gain confidence and knowledge from being physically copresent while other meditators model stillness.

David Preston drew a similar conclusion in his study of a California Zen community: "Practitioners sense each other's commitment," and this promotes "the emergence of a sense of reality shared by these others and support for one's efforts to experience such a reality" (1988, 130–31). In this sense, group meditation can be considered a solidarity ritual that increases confidence in group symbols. Ironically, the shared symbols usually refer to the potential of the individual. A good contrast is found in Promised Land's solidarity ritual from Chapter 2. There, sacred symbols of group unity were rejuvenated through a highly charged emotional experience of the group as a unit. At the Meditation Center, confidence in the sacred symbol of individual enlightenment is supported mainly by being copresent with other people who are doing (or not doing) and saying (or not saying) the same things in the same place at the same time.

ST. JOHN'S CATHOLIC CHURCH:
CROWDS AND EFFERVESCENCE INDOORS AND OUT

American Catholic services tend to display more ceremony and less overt enthusiasm than their Protestant counterparts (Chaves 2004). Latino Catholics,
however, are changing this perception as they alter the demographic characteristics and worship styles associated with the U.S. Catholic Church. According to a large national survey conducted by the Pew Forum on Religion
and Public Life (2007), close to 70% of Latino Americans identify as Roman
Catholic. About a third of all U.S. Catholics are Latinos, and this proportion
will likely continue to grow. According to the Pew study, the growing proportion of Latino Catholics is transforming the image of American Catholicism.[11]

I learned from their website and conversations with leaders that over 1200
families attend St. John's Catholic Church. St. John's thus falls under the
category of "huge" urban parishes, 25% of all American Catholic churches
which comprise the tradition's fastest-growing population in the U.S. (Davidson and Fournier 2006). From preliminary visits to St. John's, I learned
that it is an extremely well-attended organization that holds multiple services
each Sunday and throughout the week. Although I anticipated that this could
diminish the numbers at any single service, I found that the service I attended
was more crowded than any other ritual in the sample.

Initially, bodily copresence may seem the simplest IR dynamic. The
analysis in the first half of this chapter has begun to show why copresence is
actually quite complex. I argued in the Introduction that copresence is best
understood as a continuous variable called bodily density, and that its impact
on effervescence is conditioned by socioeconomic status. Consistent with
this, the Meditation Center's high-SES members expressed that they were
instinctively bothered by bodily density, but crowd together anyway because
doing so provides moral pressure and symbolic empowerment.

An additional complication surfaced at St. John's Catholic Church. I had
gained the impression prior to the visit that St. John's was a vibrant church
that was "home" to several hundreds of Latinos who lived in the area, and
I knew Sunday Mass was likely to be very crowded. I also was aware that
Latinos in their city earn less than half of the per capita income of whites,
and the lowest levels among all races and ethnicities in the area (U.S. Census
2010). Thus, the observation controlled for economic factors that appear to
weaken the stimulating effects of bodily density. Contrary to my expectations, however, the service appeared to instigate very little effervescence. I
again encountered the complex properties of copresence, and found that the
emotional excitement gained in crowds can be rapidly obliterated by ritual
stratification.

Density and Effervescence Outside the Doors

When I approached the church at 10:15 for St. John's 10:30 a.m. English-language service, I encountered what is best described as an outdoor party. The front doors to the sanctuary enclosed the 9:15 service, and a line of about 20 people were waiting to get in. This conveyed an immediate impression that St. John's was a Sunday morning hot spot. As in the cases of dance clubs or restaurants, long lines outside the front door communicate that something very fun or otherwise valuable is inside.[12] The door functions as a physical barrier to outsiders that suggests at least some degree of exclusivity: more people want to participate than the space will allow. The resource inside the doors is perceived to be quite valuable, and those who arrive too late may not get to enjoy it. Waiting in line at St. John's, I anticipated a powerful jolt of EE in their 10:30 service.

This impression accelerated during the next 30 minutes. By 10:27, the line stretched from the door to the street, roughly 30 feet from the entrance. By 10:35, approximately 80 people were in line behind me (about 100 total) and the line now stretched a long distance down the sidewalk. Additionally, a new line had formed to the side of the church, comprised of over 100 youths who had been released from Sunday School and catechism class.[13] Over 100 cars were parked in the church lot and in the streets surrounding the church.

Although lines suggest high-value products at the front, they do not always result in positive collective moods. At St. John's, however, the wait was a celebration. All ages were present. Some of the nearby mini-IRs were comprised of multigenerational families, and others were comprised of people from the same age group. I observed lively conversation, laughter, hugging, hand-holding, and kissing. In three different mini-IRs, adolescents were showing off dance moves.

Over the roar of the crowd, four different vendors hawked products near the entrance, including cowboy boots, kids' toys, sweets, and fruit drinks. On the sidewalk, another man sold Mexican ice cream treats from a cart. I also noted a barbecue smoker near the entrance which, according to a sign, could be won in an upcoming raffle. Down the sidewalk a bit, a group of teenagers from the church were holding a car wash, holding signs and waving at passing cars.

In short, I observed a large, informal, and exciting IR outside St. John's. Bodily density was high, attention was focused on the church community, membership was signified by shared symbols of ethnicity and religious commitment, and the mood was festive. Finally, at 10:45, the doors opened and participants from the 9:15 service poured out. All of us who had been waiting corralled ourselves into the church. Within moments, the mood shifted drastically.

Density and Drain Inside the Doors

St. John's sanctuary is long and narrow. There are more than 30 pews, divided by an aisle, with space for 15 to 20 people in each. All of the rows were filled, so that at least 500 were present when I attended. The design of the building is in the Gothic style often found in Roman Catholic churches. The ceiling is high and vaulted, and adorned with round stained glass windows. Large murals depicting scenes from the crucifixion narrative line the walls. The priests lead the service from a tall chancel at the front of the sanctuary. Most of us who had been waiting in line had to sit in 10 pews near the back of the sanctuary. The pews nearest to the front were roped off and reserved for those who had attended catechism class.

The service began quickly once everyone was seated. The priests' procession was accompanied by singing from a choir located behind us in a balcony. We engaged in a liturgy of singing, scripture reading, greeting, and prayer. I noted during the songs that very few men and only a small percentage of the women sang along. This may have been due to the printed bulletin, wherein most of the songs were misprinted; the lyrics were close, but different enough to impede confident singing. The congregational responses in the liturgies were also delivered tentatively because, again, the printed words were inconsistent with the words used by the priests.

The first portion of the service was brief, and Father Felix's homily began at 11:05. Several issues compromised the ability of the homily to stimulate the spirit. The first had to do with sound. Although Father Felix wore a cordless head mic, the volume was low. Worse, the sanctuary was essentially an echo chamber. It was difficult to distinguish Father Felix's words in the midst of competing sounds such as coughs, turning pages, and crying babies. Crying babies, in fact, effectively drowned out all other sounds at several points during the service.

Related to the sound problems at St. John's, Father Felix mumbled and used a limited range of English. As I noted above, St. John's also has several Spanish-language services, and it may be that Father Felix is more comfortable delivering the homilies in Spanish.[14] The passage he read describes a parable told by Jesus about a landowner who leases his vineyards to murderous tenants.[15] He read the sermon haltingly, often pausing to find his place in his written notes. He leaned on the podium and failed to make much eye contact with the congregation.

To the extent that it could be heard, the content of the homily was also hard to follow. Since the parable describes a murder spree, it was difficult to understand why Father Felix said "This reading is very beautiful" several times.

It was also difficult to understand what the parable had to do with peace. And yet, Father Felix told us, "Peace is important. We need peace. Look around you, and you will see violence, bad actions. . . . You turn on the TV,[16] and you see problems all around the world. We need peace in the world. And we need peace in our church, as well."

By 11:10 the congregation was restless. Several individuals seated near me were looking away from Father Felix, several yawned, and a cacophony of coughing, crying babies, and bulletin rustling grew increasingly loud. The homily ended with a mixed metaphor: "Do you produce fruits? What kind of a fruit are you?" At 11:15, the homily ended. The next 25 minutes of the service were devoted to the Eucharist, offerings, and benediction. At no point did I observe signs of intensified collective emotions. Contrary to what the crowded space had led me to expect, St. John's service is best described as emotionally draining.

The focus group meeting at St. John's led me to think that the congregation experiences significant effervescence and solidarity together, but they achieve these in rituals other than Sunday Mass. Ana, a married woman in her 30s, described the ethnic solidarity she experiences at the church:

> St. John's is a place for many to come who are Mexican. We feel like we belong because we see, "here are many like me." We have same traditions, and same things that we believe. It is a family away from our family.

St. John's provides a special venue through which immigrants from Mexico who live in the area can enact solidarity rituals they associate with their first home. They repeat common symbols and engage in common movements in each other's presence, and this provides familial feelings that can be more difficult to attain with non-Mexican-Americans in their region.[17] The familial feeling at St. John's is facilitated, at least partially, by opportunities to hear and speak their mother tongue. Ana explained:

> There are two Catholic churches in our town that hold Spanish Mass. For people who only speak Spanish, this is very important for them. So they come and they are with their family, and they take Mass, and they can hear and speak in Spanish.

Ana's comments support the notion that participants at St. John's are emotionally motivated into each other's presence by strong feelings of ethnic solidarity.

Other comments in the focus group confirmed my impression that the Sunday service itself is not the key ritual in this regard. Jonathan, a single man in his 20s, compared his experiences in St. John's services with those in a local evangelical church that he also attends on occasion:

> I also go to [a local evangelical church]. There, the music is playing all the time, and it gives me strong feelings. Here, I have difficulty hearing what the priest is saying. Because of the way sound is in [the sanctuary], it is difficult to hear his words on Sundays. So they tell you, do this, don't do that, but it is difficult to understand all that they mean.

Ana followed Jonathan's comment by saying that she usually feels "relaxed" during St. John's services. When she said this, I looked to see Jonathan's response. He smiled and shrugged in a way that indicated grudging agreement. Both agreed that being with their church family is a "calming" experience. I interpret their comments as indications that they are comforted by the solidarity that comes with gathering together. They experience positive emotions together, as well, but there is little evidence that Sunday Mass is the key ritual in this regard.

Ritual Stratification at St. John's

As noted earlier, IR dynamics are recursive and overlapping. St. John's ritual is no exception, and a combination of defective dynamics impeded the spirit's arrival. A glaring problem was that their ritual technologies failed to promote mutual focus on a common object. When trying to sing together, no one was confident about the lyrics because the bulletin was full of misprints. During the homily, many appeared to have trouble understanding what Father Felix was saying because the physical space doesn't conduct sound well. Unsuccessful management of resources impeded intersubjectivity.[18]

These problems might derail an IR of any type. Intersubjectivity is necessary for effervescence, and is more fundamentally important than copresence. As discussed at the beginning of this chapter, a degree of intersubjectivity is possible over the phone or during a conference call; lack of copresence simply limits the heights the interaction can reach. Consider, though, copresence without intersubjectivity. A crowd of strangers with no common activity or reason for gathering invites an overall drop in EE. For example, passengers on crowded airplanes and elevators will often consider their copassengers to be impediments to their own comfort (especially if they are accustomed to ample personal space). They may achieve moments of intersubjectivity related to their common goal of arriving at their destination, but their baseline response to crowdedness is often distaste. St. John's failed to achieve a significant degree of intersubjectivity, and that failure severely threatened their IR.

Still, the congregation already possessed a high level of intersubjectivity when they were waiting outside. What happened? Were there additional reasons for why they lost it so quickly? The concept of ritual deference provides reasons to think that particular properties of copresence inside the church doors helped nullify the positive emotional effects that bodily density was promoting outside.

IR theory stipulates that "asymmetrical" or "one-way" deference rituals often mitigate positive IR outcomes (Collins 1975, 73–74, 100, 157, 179; 2004, 116). Common examples include subjects before a monarch, soldiers before higher-ranking officers, and employees before their bosses (100). In such rituals, the superordinant becomes a sacred object. The subordinate must carefully manage the symbolic implications of his actions so as to not profane the status of his superior (Goffman 1967, 57). The design of asymmetrical deference rituals strongly jeopardizes shared emotions between the two parties. The superordinate is supposed to feel honored, and the subordinate is supposed to feel fortunate to be in the superordinate's presence.

For centuries, a central feature of Roman Catholicism has been deference toward the priests on the part of the laity:

> Priests are clearly marked off from laity, both by costumes and ritually segregated spaces in the church; only priests can handle the holy implements; not only is there an inner zone of physical sacred objects, but the vestments and to an extent even the body of the priest is made into a sacred object (Collins 2010, 7).

Roman Catholic rituals certainly can and often do capture the spirit. There is no reason to think that Catholic parishioners cannot achieve a shared and intense emotional state in the presence of their sacred symbols, which typically include the priest who is understood as God's agent. Hierarchy itself can be sacralized, gaining emotional resonance and legitimacy through effective IRs. In Chapter 1, for example, I noticed that the Islamic Center members gained emotional energy from the symbol of "submission to Allah," and we can consider a range of other examples as in the military and some families. In the context of America in the early 21st century, though, asymmetrical deference to priests in Catholic rituals introduces a heightened experience of subordination to congregants who are more accustomed to ritual egalitarianism and symmetrical deference when outside the confines of the church.

Collins argues that since roughly the middle of the 20th century, America has experienced "a status revolution . . . in which the decline of old-fashioned deference and demeanor was a central part" (1975, 163). This "evaporation" of a deference culture "can be characterized as a general leveling effect on manners and customs, and a trend toward informality and familiarity in deference rituals" (187).[19] Although subtler forms remain, elaborate forms of asymmetrical deference have increasingly been understood by Americans as somewhat archaic. Rather, the dominant norm is ritualized symmetrical deference. In the workplace, for instance, the boss might refer to employees as "team members" or "associates." A police officer about to penalize a speeder might refer to the subordinate as "sir" or "ma'am." It is widely considered distasteful to flaunt one's higher status.

Roman Catholic rituals are among the few occasions in contemporary American life where heightened asymmetrical deference remains normal. With this in mind, consider St. John's 10:30 service and how the nature of our copresence shifted as we entered the doors of the church. For the most part, I had observed egalitarian mini-IRs outside. The congregation had appeared to be having a great deal of fun as they laughed, danced, bought ice cream, showed affection, and so on. It is possible that those at the end of the line mildly resented those of us near the front, but they appeared to be having a comparably good time.

When we passed through the church doors, several symbols indicated a rapid transformation of the ritual space. The first was a sign that read, "Do not commit crimes! You are on camera at all times." Next to it, there was another sign that read in English and Spanish, "God will talk to you today. But not your cell. Turn off your phone!!" A third sign read, "No gum in church. Show respect to God." We then travelled past a font of holy water that most parishioners used to make the sign of the cross. Passing by all of these symbols, we learned that (1) we were under surveillance, (2) we were entering a space in which "respect" meant altering normal behaviors, and (3) the space we were entering was sacred.

Reaching the main sanctuary, those of us who had not attended Sunday School discovered the consequence: we had to sit in the rear portion of the sanctuary. Ropes formed a physical barrier that prohibited us from sitting close to the action. Some of us had waited 30 minutes or more outside the church doors, and the result was cramming into a few rows near the back. From that position, we watched the Sunday School attendees take their seats near the front. Next, we watched the priests travel to the front of the sanctuary in a sacred procession filled with incense and holy song. Later, we watched Father Felix ascend to the tall chancel.

In *Interaction Ritual Chains*, Collins writes that emotional intensity varies from person to person within an IR, and each individual's degree of participation helps establish their ritual status.[20] St. John's service suggests, further, that ritual status is related to the arrangement of bodies in the physical space. Those of us in the back received the clear message that we had not earned close access to sacred objects such as the priest and Eucharist. The Sunday

School attendees also were distanced from sacred objects, though, because the chancel was high above their heads. As a result, Father Felix was difficult to see and hear. The orientation of our bodies accentuated a message that was equally clear from the symbols placed around the sanctuary: in this space, you are expected to show deference.

It is not new information that Roman Catholic rituals commonly emphasize rank and authority, and this tendency is not necessarily incompatible with the spirit. Such rituals can provide intense experiences of sanctity and awe. Indeed, although I did not observe it during or after the service, it is likely that some members of St. John's gained EE from the ritualized stratification. Especially the priests, but perhaps also some of the more active and long-term members of the parish, likely have experienced IR chains over time which give symbolic strength and power to the Church's structure. To the extent that they do get energized by the hierarchy, though, their experience contrasts with what's normative in the dominant U.S. culture, and this helps explain St. John's overall lack of enthusiasm. Ritualized rank and authority tends to be a jarring or uncomfortable experience in the contemporary U.S.

The legacy of Protestantism is probably a key factor in promoting the ritual egalitarianism that has become more normal. Collins points out, "The proliferation of sacred objects in Catholic worship, and the resulting differentiation in religious rank enacted by differential access to various sacred objects, was replaced by the tendency towards leveling and egalitarianism in Protestant congregations" (2010, 8). The effects of this "leveling and egalitarianism" are evident in contemporary U.S. culture. In light of this, Jonathan's comments (also shown above) are unsurprising:

> I also go to [a local evangelical church] sometimes. There, the music is playing all the time, and it gives me strong feelings. Here, I have difficulty hearing what the priest is saying. Because of the way sound is in [the sanctuary], it is difficult to hear his words on Sundays. So they tell you, do this, don't do that, but it is difficult to understand all that they mean.

Although he had grown up Catholic, Jonathan sounded as though he might have been entertaining a shift to an evangelical affiliation. If he does, or if he switches to a charismatic Catholic congregation, it will likely be related to fatigue from regularly experiencing the emotional drain of ritualized asymmetrical deference.

CONCLUSION

As discussed at the top of this chapter, physical copresence is not absolutely necessary to hold an IR. Since Bell's invention of the telephone in the 19th century, revolutionary technologies have made distanced IRs possible. The inferiority of these IRs is suggested, though, by inherent constraints on emotional intensity. Lack of physical consequence and risk prevents distanced IRs from being part of the action; no matter how heated they become, they cannot culminate in a kiss or a fistfight. Still, although not as crucial as intersubjectivity, the management of bodily copresence nonetheless has important consequences on the spirit.

To help summarize its complex properties, I will briefly review the management of copresence in the six organizations from the qualitative sample. First, Congregation Shalom provided qualitative evidence, supportive of the USCLS findings, that copresence is best understood as a continuous variable. When I first entered their service, the sanctuary was sparsely populated and low energy. During the course of their service, bodies gradually accumulated until, three hours in, the ritual was standing room only. At that point, consistent with the bodily density hypothesis, Congregation Shalom's ritual had become ecstatic. Two additional strategies helped maximize the positive effects of copresence. First, mini-IRs were normal and accepted. Without distracting attention from the main event, mini-IRs brought small groups of friends physically close, stimulating the overall effervescence of the ritual. Second, copresence was largely egalitarian. Members felt free to move about the room at their whim. Rabbis regularly crossed the plane from "stage" to "audience." During the most intense moments of their ritual, participants freely danced, shuckled, and bowed in a charismatic collective celebration. Congregation Shalom showed that overall density, density in subsets (mini-IRs), and ritual egalitarianism are all resources that organizations can use to foster effervescence.

Perhaps more than any ritual in the sample, the Islamic Center demonstrated the importance of considering the particular orientation of bodies within a ritual space. Their Jum'ah ritual was sparsely populated throughout. At first, the passive postures and roving eyes of the few bodies in the room suggested that the low density was indeed inhibiting the spirit. During the final moments of the service, however, something remarkable happened: they drew on a resource from their tradition to mandate a reorganization of bodies. In order to perform the collective raka'ah sequence, the men left their isolated islands of space and formed a long shoulder-to-shoulder line at the front of the room. Instantly, ritual properties like physical contact, trust, and rhythmic entrainment were activated, and the ritual ended with a buzz of fresh EE. The men of the Islamic Center demonstrated that bodily density, rather than simple copresence, is the key to more intense group emotions.

Copresence at Promised Land and First Baptist will be considered in Chapter 4. Promised Land's congregation illustrated, again, that the impact of density is conditioned by other factors. Although their sanctuary was not literally crowded, the congregation stimulated feelings of bodily density through their management of sound. Live music from a loud organ and the enthusiastic sounds of a call-and-response sermon filled the space and conveyed action. Additionally, similar to the Islamic Center, the choice to adjust the orientation of bodies promoted a stirring climax to the ritual. We joined hands and swayed while singing, and the physical dynamic ensured feelings of intersubjectivity and togetherness. Like Congregation Shalom's charismatic ritual, Promised Land fostered an egalitarian copresence by allowing each other to move, dance, sing, and shout as each saw fit.[21] Overall, Promised Land demonstrated that sound, orientation of bodies, and ritual egalitarianism all condition the effects of copresence.

In contrast to Promised Land, First Baptist Church did not exploit the full benefits of its resource of high bodily density. When I first entered the sanctuary, a "buzz" exuded from a large gathering of people engaged in pre-ritual mini-IRs. They were happy to be in each other's presence. Despite this, benefits of copresence dropped off significantly as the service progressed. As argued in Chapter 2, this drain was related to the individualistic quality of their shared symbols. Since their goal is a one-on-one mystical experience with God, other people in the room become distractions. The sounds, smells, and movement of other bodies just get in the way. The nature of a religious organization's collective symbols conditions the effects of copresence.

The Buddhist Meditation Center discussed in this chapter has much in common with First Baptist. Like First Baptist, the Meditation Center is a high-SES religious organization whose members seek individualized religious experiences via their central ritual. By focusing on copresence at the Meditation Center, two primary explanations emerged for why people gather in public to engage in an essentially private activity. Much like members of boxing gyms, study groups, and artist retreats, they seek moral pressure and symbolic empowerment to support their solitary practice.

Finally, St. John's Catholic Church demonstrated that, in tandem with other IR dynamics, the benefits of copresence can be diminished by physicalized asymmetrical deference. This was evident once we had crossed the threshold of the front door of their church. Outside, bodies were jammed close in equality and mutual enjoyment. Once inside, we quickly learned that we were under surveillance and needed to play by the authority's rules. Additionally, Sunday School attendees had their devotion to the organization rewarded with relatively close access to the organization's sacred symbols, while free riders and newcomers were punished with physical distance. Once in our assigned seats, we regarded the sacred symbols looming ahead and above us. Unable to sufficiently hear or see the action, who knows what people nearby were thinking and feeling? By their expressions, and by the focus group's comments afterwards, it had little to do with the spirit. In the contemporary U.S., asymmetrical deference can be a tough sell.

Bodily copresence, though, is not as crucial as intersubjectivity. This sensation that other people understand and share one's ideas and feelings is a necessary condition for experiencing the spirit. Chapter 4 will revisit the rituals held at two Baptist churches, one black and one white. It should already be evident from Chapter 2 that the black church, Promised Land, more successfully stimulated shared thoughts and feelings than did First Baptist. Peering more closely at the details of their respective services will allow a more precise explanation for their divergent outcomes.

NOTES

1. Emoticons and internet slang like "LOL," "LMAO," and "SMH" are blunt efforts to resurrect nonverbal emotional cues into the interaction.

2. Estimates of the number of U.S. adult Buddhists range from 500,000 to 4 million. By all estimates, Buddhists make up less than 2% of the U.S. population (Coleman 2001; Smith 2002; Wuthnow and Cadge 2004). Buster Smith's (2007) data indicate that Vajrayana Buddhists make up approximately 14% of all American Buddhist organizations. Organizations with Tibetan roots make up approximately 5% of all American Buddhist organizations.

3. Anne Cottrell Spencer (2014) points out that terms like "convert Buddhist" and "conversion," frequently used by scholars in relation to American Buddhism, is a misapplication since Buddhism requires no such shifting of allegiance. I retain the terminology here because the members themselves used it when we spoke.

4. According to Wave 3 of the *Baylor Religion Survey* (2011), 12.4% (213/1714) of Americans practice "mindfulness meditation." This percentage includes non-Buddhist forms of meditation, however. Tibetan Buddhist meditation, in particular, is much less common at .8% (15/1714).

5. Connie is the Center's only paid employee. Otherwise, it is entirely maintained by volunteers.

6. Durkheim's definition of religion leaves out belief in the supernatural, and he argued that this allowed him to incorporate Buddhism and other nontheistic religions (1912, 28–30, 44). Stark and Finke (2000, 90) assert that it was unnecessary to avoid gods in the definition, since popular Buddhism has always been "rich in supernatural beings." At the Meditation Center, gods were included in the text of the chants but were entirely absent from members' explanations of what they were doing.

7. The center offers free public instruction in meditation to all newcomers. This is provided by some two dozen members who take turns as designated instructor. Members are strongly encouraged to serve as instructors, and doing so gives them a greater sense of investment in the organization and its symbols.

8. An oft-stated goal of Buddhist meditation is to eradicate the falsely dualistic notion of the self and experience the unity of all things. Nonetheless, the focus group at the Meditation Center, along with much of the contemporary Buddhist literature on meditation, characterize the practice in terms of individual-level enlightenment and self-improvement, a pattern also seen in many of the "New Buddhist" congregations surveyed by Coleman (2001, 20–21). From the perspective of some in the tradition, this could be considered a problematic trend. Consider, for example, the following warning about "spiritual materialism" from Trungpa Rinpoche, one of the key figures in the spread of Tibetan Buddhism in the U.S.: "There are numerous sidetracks which lead to a distorted, ego-centered version of spirituality; we can deceive ourselves into thinking we are developing spiritually when instead we are strengthening our egocentricity through spiritual techniques. This fundamental distortion may be referred to as spiritual materialism" (Trungpa 1973, 3).

9. Compare Terry's comments with those of Wendell and Addie in Chapter 2. Addie, for instance, always has an "expectation" on Sunday mornings that Promised Land's service will be "Spirit-filled" and bring "joy and happiness."

10. On this point, also see Coleman (2001, 14–15).

11. This transformation is related to the style of ritual: Latino Catholics are much more likely than non-Latino Catholics to practice charismatic styles of worship (54% vs. 12%). Close to half of Latino Catholics have attended services in which participants have spoken in tongues, prophesied, or prayed for miracles. The ritual examined here, however, was not charismatic.

12. In his study of line-joining rules, Gibson (2008, 211) observes, "A waiting line forms when there is some sought-after good (broadly construed) to be dispensed." We can add, from an IR perspective, that a line naturally choreographs a heightened experience of copresence, much as the shift to a horizontal line for raka'ah increased bodily density at the Islamic Center, as described in Chapter 1.

13. Their participation in these activities added to my expectation of a spirited service. I discuss the energizing effect of pre-ritual rituals in the analysis of Promised Land Baptist Church in Chapter 2.

14. This suggests an avenue for future research on multilingual religious organizations. To what extent do collective emotions depend on high proficiency with the language used during the service?

15. Matthew 21: 33–43. The parable tells of a landowner who planted a vineyard, leased it to tenants, and went on a journey. Twice, the landowner sent servants to collect the vineyard's produce, and both times the tenants beat and killed the landowner's servants. Finally, the landowner sent his son to collect the produce, and the tenants killed the son. Jesus' listeners (priests and elders) thought the appropriate response of the landowner would be swift justice. Jesus responded by telling them that the Kingdom of God would be taken from them and given to people who will produce its fruit.

16. See Chapter 5 regarding the sample's frequent discussions of "media," especially "TV," as either a negative force in itself or a venue for observing the terrors of contemporary life.

17. Further, consistent with the barriers hypothesis, prior research suggests that encounters with nativistic hostilities spur solidarity among Latino immigrants (Bean and Tienda 1987; Porter and Washington 1993).

18. I do not think that this was *primarily* an issue of inadequate material resources. The next chapter will consider more closely the issue of how ritual resources are managed. There, I compare an organization that underutilizes its substantial ritual resources (First Baptist) with an organization that maximizes the emotional value of its relatively meager resources (Promised Land). Rich or poor, organizations have to exercise ingenuity in managing resources to maximize effervescence. St. John's misprinted bulletin may have resulted from having an insufficient volunteer base, and they may not have had sufficient funds to update their sound system. These sorts of problems, though, are not necessarily insurmountable from an IR perspective.

19. This historical process is examined in detail in Collins 1975, 187–216.

20. The key passage:

> Where is the individual located as the IR takes place? There is a continuum from persons who are on the fringes of the group, just barely members, barely participating; others nearer the core; at the center is the sociometric star, the person who is always most intensely involved in the ritual interaction. This person is the Durkheimian participant of the highest degree, and experiencing the strongest effects of ritual membership: emotional energy, moral solidarity, attachment to group symbols. At the other end, there is the Durkheimian nonmember, who receives no emotional energy, no moral solidarity, and no symbolic attachments. This is the dimension of central/peripheral participation. (2004, 116)

21. From another perspective, freedom of physical expression could be understood as a factor that *introduces* stratification. For some participants, resentment toward charismatic "energy stars" might drain EE: "Who does he think he is? Why does he have flaunt his spirituality by incessantly raising his hands and jumping up and down?" This sort of response would most likely be a consequence of IR chains. We might expect that the resentful individual has become accustomed to less expressive religious IRs, such as those in which individualized communion with God has been the consistent goal, wherein noise from other people is considered a distraction. Religious rituals that are oriented to the collective experience, however, are likely to flourish overall to the extent that members are allowed some autonomy in their physical movement.

Chapter Four

Intersubjectivity

The concept of intersubjectivity, a focus of much attention in microsociology and phenomenology, refers to the sensation that one is not alone in one's thoughts and feelings, that other people actually share them. We can think of it as collective consciousness at the microlevel, as "bubbles of subjective reality" inflate and include others during successful IRs (Collins 1975, 113). Virtually everyone experiences something at least close to this at least occasionally. Best friends might feel they're always "on the same page," colleagues might get into a great "flow" when working together on projects, or an audience to a horror movie might express a collective gasp. Intersubjectivity involves shared perspective and emotional empathy, as expressed by a husband interviewed in Candace Clark's *Misery and Company*: "My wife and I were definitely on the same wavelength during that time when I was sick. We saw things together, as if we were one person" (1997, 17).

Shared ritual practices are the means by which we drum up (often literally) this sensation. The individual moves and make sounds, signaling to others the contents of her consciousness. She also "reads" the movements and sounds of others, seeking confirmation that her own signals have been understood. When the ritual is working, the sending and receiving of signals feels like a natural flow, a give-and-take rhythm to which one can simply submit (Csikszentmihalyi 2008).

Practices that fail to reach this state, though, can feel terrible. If my signals cannot be understood by others, then I am decisively alone, and any sensations of truth, morality, and identity are imperiled. To have a self-concept, for example, I need to be able to think about myself as an object of another's perception. If I cannot imagine the other's subjective world, there is no "me" to be perceived (Taylor 1989). Likewise, I cannot feel bound to rules of logic

95

or goodness, because nothing becomes sacred when my own consciousness is all that I have to work with.

This chapter returns to the two Baptist rituals considered in Chapter 2 for a close examination of how their practices either propelled or hindered an experience of intersubjectivity and, in turn, an experience of the spirit. First, I want to highlight a few key concepts, borrowed and updated from IR theory, that will help guide the analysis.

INTERSUBJECTIVITY IN INTERACTION RITUAL THEORY

As was the case with copresence and indeed all of the IR dynamics, intersubjectivity is best conceived not as an either/or variable, but as a continuum of perception that ranges from *low to high* or, alternately, *far away* to *close*. In certain lonely moments, as we might imagine of, say, the thoughts of a wallflower during a party, intersubjectivity can feel extremely low, even mythical. At other times, as during mundane interactions with coworkers or clients, intersubjectivity is more like an ongoing negotiation, working out by degree the extent to which separate individuals' various thoughts and emotions can more or less align. During and shortly after the most successful IRs, though, the gulf between you and me feels narrowed or even bridged, as interactants perceive that they were thinking and feeling the same sorts of things during a given ritual moment.

The concept of intersubjectivity unites two IR dynamics: mutual focus of attention and shared mood. All of the IR dynamics are interrelated, but these two are so entwined as to require co-consideration. Both are facilitated by sacred objects. The tribes members in Durkheim's work gathered around sacred objects, concentrated on the objects, moved around the objects, and attended to the objects with the same agreed-upon behaviors. The sacred objects were perceived as exerting power over them, so that improper behavior around or toward the objects was immediately felt as a shame-worthy violation. Similarly, Goffman's (1959) interactants felt and responded to the power of the situation. Interactants nurtured IRs by behaving according to largely unacknowledged yet agreed-upon sets of rules. Again, improper behavior—especially threats to self-presentation—could be immediately sensed, the typical results of which were repair efforts, shame, and/or punishment.[1] Sacred objects and social situations impress themselves upon us, as if from the outside, reinforcing the experience of identity, morality, and reality as objective fact.

Intersubjectivity is fostered not just by attending *to* each other, but by attending to objects *with* each other. There are good reasons for interactants to attribute power to such objects. As Karen Cerulo and other sociologists have emphasized, nonhuman entities routinely impact what goes on in social interactions, often in ways that become quite obvious upon reflection (Cerulo 2009; Cerulo and Barra 2008; Latour 2005; Law 1992). Doorbells, ringing phones, and barking dogs, for example, shift situational dynamics and prompt humans' responsive actions. Material objects such as food/drink, drugs, and weapons can all drastically shape how situations are perceived.[2] Likewise, sounds, smells, mental images, or concepts can compel attention and alter moods. Numerous "priming" studies suggest that a wide variety of sensory inputs can trigger responsive actions and emotions, often at a level below our conscious awareness (McGraw and Krátký 2017). Religious artifacts, in particular, are among the most common examples used by cognitive social scientists to show that different objects shape consciousness in different ways.[3]

A given sacred object may even have different meanings attached to it by different people who are attending to it, as when God concepts vary from consciousness to consciousness among people attending the same religious ritual (Froese and Bader 2010, 52–55). This variation between participants in what a shared object of attention *means* does not have to derail a ritual, though. What matters, from a Durkheimian perspective, is that everyone feels strongly that the object demands their respect and exerts force over them. When this occurs, they can begin to gain some certainty that the *experiences* of the different people who are gathered are in fact *a single, shared experience*.

Although interrelated, mutual focus and shared mood may be present in different proportions. It is possible to achieve a higher level of mutual focus than shared mood during a given ritual moment. For instance, two fans at a Super Bowl party might root for opposing teams. At the climax of the game, their attention would be glued to the TV screen, each holding his breath and tracing the path of the football into the wide receiver's outstretched hands. Their moods would diverge radically, though, upon seeing the wide receiver juggle and then drop the ball. It is also possible to achieve a shared mood while focusing on different objects. Two preschoolers can be very happy and content playing together, even while focusing on completely different imaginary universes, for example one playing "house" and the other playing "Superman." Intersubjectivity is highest, though, when the attention is mutually focused *and* the mood is shared. The most emotionally rewarding moments will come when both football fans celebrate the dropped pass, or when the preschoolers decide to have Superman come home for dinner.

Mutual focus of attention and shared mood are facilitated by two sub-dynamics: mutual monitoring and rhythmic entrainment. Again, these sub-dynamics are so entwined as to require co-consideration. Mutual monitoring means that interactants are "watching" each other, often peripherally, for cues on how to respond to the shared object of attention. As they do so, they are able to approximate each other's gestures and get caught up in each other's physical and vocal rhythms. When the interactants are attuned, they experience a satisfying synchronicity. Collins (2004, 48) writes, "As the persons become more tightly focused on their common activity, more aware of what each other is doing and feeling, and more aware of each other's awareness, they experience their shared emotion more intensely, as it comes to dominate their awareness."[4] Mutual monitoring and rhythmic entrainment are necessary to allow separate individuals to feel like a unit. Athletes sense each other's rhythms to coalesce as a team, much like musicians respond to each other's rhythms to coalesce as a band.

Figure 4.1 illustrates the core dynamics and subdynamics involved in intersubjectivity. In the most successful IRs, (1) focus of attention and (2) shared mood will both increase as they are facilitated by (3) mutual monitoring, (4) rhythmic entrainment, and (5) their reciprocal influence.

Work by ethnomethodologists and microsociologists confirms this drive for interactional synchronicity. In many cases, the research method is conversational analysis. In moment-by-moment detail, often down to microseconds, variables like rhythm, response time, pauses, and volume are used to break down conversations in terms of other variables such as synchronicity and flow (e.g., Gregory et al. 1993; Katz 1999; Scheff 1990; Schegloff 1992). Goffman (1959, 1967) describes ways in which interactants monitor each other for subtle cues regarding the management of the self. Successful IRs in Goffman's research involve careful "face-work" which protects the sacred object of the self from profanation. Without mutual monitoring, interactants would have no idea if and when it is necessary to "save face."

Jack Katz (1999) examines video recordings from an amusement park fun house to demonstrate the contagion of laughter at the microlevel. Visitors to the fun house's distorted mirrors tend not to laugh at their own distorted im-

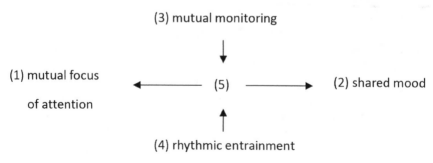

Figure 4.1.   Intersubjectivity

ages, at least not deeply, until family members come and join them. Parents will pick up their small children to align their sightlines, an effort to literally *see together* the same image in the mirror. Gazing in the same direction, their shared movements and patterns of vocalization boost confidence that they are seeing the same distortions. Laughing at this moment is an embodied demonstration of achieved intersubjectivity. Once the laughers mutually recognize the image as "funny," they shift from "doing" to being "done by" laughter as the "spirit of laughter" takes over the occasion (92).

Without moments of felt intersubjectivity, individuals would never gain the sensation of being swept up in something beyond themselves. Each would define the situation in his own way, respond to it according to his whims, and learn whatever "truth" he wanted to have learned.[5] When intersubjective moments do occur, though, interactants are able to gain access to "truth" that is "out there." They are thus able to check the correspondence between their own personal grasp of identity, morality, and reality and the identity, morality, and reality that they felt in the presence of their group and its sacred symbols. Social theorists such as Joas (2000) and Froese (2016) have argued that this ability to transcend the individual consciousness makes moral purpose and shared values possible.

Chapter 2 compared rituals in black and white Baptist churches to distinguish different types of social solidarity. Their solidarities differed in symbolic content: Promised Land worked to rejuvenate collective sacred symbols during a protracted struggle against violent enemies, whereas First Baptist promoted symbols of individualized spiritual enlightenment. The rituals clearly produced contrasting outputs of effervescence. High effervescence was evident at Promised Land in participants' clapping, enthusiastic singing, shouting, alert postures, and visible and audible engagement with the sermon. Low effervescence was evident at First Baptist in participants' bulletin rustling, sedated singing, inattention to the activities on stage, yawns, and exits from the sanctuary. Promised Land's ritual generated an extended period of jubilation; First Baptist's gave rise to malaise and fast exits.

The organizations' contrasting outputs of effervescence, though, were not due only to the collectivistic vs. individualistic content of their solidarity symbols. Promised Land also was more proficient at managing the ritual dynamics. As noted in Chapter 2, for example, Promised Land more successfully evoked barriers to outsiders. This dynamic is particularly effective at generating intersubjectivity, especially insofar as the barriers convey a sense of *threat*. Perceived threats raise the stakes of an occasion, and magnify everyone's attention to each other's intersubjective signals (Collins 2012). Promised Land's congregation, especially their pastor, conveyed dire circumstances to each other. When they raised issues like gang violence, Satan, or natural disasters, the congregation became more alert to each other and to their common experiences and fears. First Baptist, by contrast, emphasized the pleasure they take in each other's company, and the comfort provided by their common faith. While such expressions at First Baptist definitely serve as solidarity-building rituals, they convey the opposite of threat and thus make no use of a resource that could have ramped up intersubjective communication.

Promised Land more successfully focused the congregation's attention and cultivated a shared mood. We can now return to this comparison of Baptist rituals to examine how the nuts and bolts of their respective practices led to very different levels of intersubjectivity and collective effervescence. I concentrate on the organizations' uses of technology, techniques, sacred objects, and time to focus attention and mood.

FIRST BAPTIST CHURCH:
A BRIEF AND RELAXING MORNING

In several respects, First Baptist appeared to have potent IR resources. Their sanctuary, for instance, is impressive. A large stained-glass ceiling hovers above the space, and stained-glass windows adorn the walls behind their high balconies. A broad, tall stage reaches across the front of the sanctuary, with a choir loft behind. The stage holds a grand piano and conga drum to the audience's left, and a massive pipe organ to the right. At center stage is a large wooden pulpit. Overall, the sanctuary appears clean and inviting and suggests a sacred space set aside for ritual.

The danger of a spacious sanctuary is that it can feel empty, but this was not a problem at First Baptist when I observed.[6] When I first entered the space, I was immediately struck by the sounds of voices and laughter. These blended into a low roar as the space filled with people. I heard several "good mornings" close by.[7] An assistant pastor and his wife were making rounds in the pews, and warmly introduced themselves to a family of newcomers who sat in the pew next to mine. Friendly interaction was taking place in all directions. Physical copresence was not lacking, nor were baseline feelings of membership solidarity.

Compared with Promised Land, First Baptist possessed advantages in their material resources and ritual technology. They did not, however, take full advantage of the benefits of those resources. One example is their massive pipe organ, which was silent throughout the service. After the service, I discovered why. As mentioned in Chapter 2, First Baptist was making organized efforts to appeal to youths and young adults. Members told me that they rarely use

[handwritten margin note: Bodily copresence]

the pipe organ now because they feel that it is a potential turn-off to young visitors who are presumed to want a "contemporary" experience with which they can "relate." First Baptist is not alone in this perception. American Christians, particularly conservative Protestants, often debate the value of "traditional" vs. "contemporary" forms of worship music (Dawn 1995, 2003; Warren 1995; Webber 1985). In this ongoing debate, the pipe organ is often treated as the epitome of traditional music.

Whether First Baptist members are correct that most young Americans desire a "contemporary" worship experience, or whether young Americans are consistently repelled by pipe organs, remain open questions.[8] Regardless, comparison with the ritual impact of Promised Land's music suggests that First Baptist's strategy misfired. Promised Land's digital organ dominated their service with sound, compelling speakers and singers to vocalize loudly enough to be heard. It filled Promised Land's sparsely populated sanctuary with an aura of action. By contrast, very few congregants sang with enthusiasm at First Baptist. Many were silent, passively watching the music director and choir. Those who were singing mostly did so at low volume. The music was led by a talented worship director and sounded well-prepared, crisp, and melodious, but it did not catalyze enthusiastic participation or a shared mood. As we murmured through the hymns, it was hard to ignore the prominent and silent pipe organ. Did the regular attendees simply ignore it? I wondered how many viewed it as a reminder of former practices that no longer suffice, or possibly as a symbol of an organizational identity crisis. Even if First Baptist's concerns were proven valid, and playing the pipe organ would indeed make them seem old-fashioned, it almost certainly would have promoted a sense of awe. The instrument is designed to overpower and convey the sacred, and this is precisely what seemed to be missing from their worship.

[margin note: How much is due to culture]

First Baptist missed another opportunity by severely limiting its greeting time, as mentioned in this book's Introduction. This ritual technique is common in many types of religious organizations, but it varies in execution.[9] One element that varies is the risk involved for participants. By introducing a period of time devoted to mingling, the congregation risks the embarrassment of members who refuse or are refused from mini-IRs, and thus are left alone feeling irrelevant, shamefaced, or even bitter. Perhaps to avoid such consequences, and also to ensure prompt closure of the service, First Baptist's greeting time lasted less than two minutes. I do not think the brevity of the greeting time was due to a lack of interest in talking with each other; as mentioned above, I observed significant friendly interaction before the service. Because the greeting time was so short, however, there was little hope of developing "little pockets of shared mentality" with other members (Collins 2004, 52). Instead, the greeting time felt like empty ceremony. As

[margin note: So much like most interactions]

such, it suggested that intersubjectivity in worship is not a prominent goal of the organization. The ritual technique as practiced, then, drained EE during an important early moment of the ritual. Perhaps this helps explain why nearby exchanges during the greeting time were extremely brief. "Good morning" in this context was less of an invitation and more of a bitter pill. Interactants seemed to varying degrees embarrassed, uninterested, or desirous of escape, all ironic consequences of a period that may have been kept brief in order to limit social risk.

A second way in which First Baptist appeared to underutilize an IR resource had to do with how they attended to their primary sacred object. Evangelical Protestants, and Baptists in particular, are a "people of the book" (Ammerman 1987; Boone 1989; Jeffrey 1996). Conversation with First Baptist members confirmed the centrality of the Bible in their organization, as when a young woman named Cherith stressed the importance of "digging into the Bible" on her own.[10] During the morning service we engaged in a responsive reading of Psalm 107, sang songs with biblical references, and the pastor read three Bible verses aloud during the sermon.

Despite the sacred *status* of the Bible at First Baptist, or possibly because of it, the *focus* on the Bible during the sermon felt perfunctory. The pastor read three short verses in support of his claim that Christians need to rest. Each verse described an occasion when Jesus removed himself from crowds to engage in rest and solitude. Pastor Craig abruptly moved on from each verse to relevant contemporary anecdotes and practical advice. His style was "topical," a homiletic style that focuses on a topic of relevance to congregants' lives, as opposed to "expository," a style that analyzes a passage of scripture and its context in detail.[11] Very little of the sermon was devoted to discussing the passages, themselves, but extended time was devoted to the advice and anecdotes. At First Baptist, the topical frame of the sermon distracted focus from their foremost sacred object. I would not generalize from this example that expository sermons are always more engaging to congregations (proponents of the topical style assert that the opposite is the case). However, I observed a restless congregation during First Baptist's service, and failure to give sustained and serious attention to the sacred object stands out as a contributing factor. Brief attention to the sacred object limited the organization's opportunities to reach intersubjectivity.[12]

The final example of First Baptist's failure to focus attention and establish a shared mood had to do with their use of time. First Baptist was remarkably punctual, beginning exactly at 10:30 and ending exactly at 11:30. Their precise management of time conveyed careful planning, and the worship staff was consistently ready to hit their cues and eliminate "dead air." The Meditation Center, examined in Chapter 3, also finished quickly. The brevity

[handwritten marginalia: "wrong focus?"]

of the Meditation Center's and First Baptist's rituals appears to be related in both cases to the individualistic emphasis of their solidarity symbols. If the collective is peripheral to the organization's vision, there is less impetus to spend significant time together. In terms of focusing attention and capturing a shared mood, First Baptist's brevity communicated a lack of importance. Indicative of this, one of First Baptist's congregants confided to me (away from the focus group) that, for he and his wife, the short services are part of the church's appeal: "For one thing, we're both football fans and I know that I won't miss any games in the afternoon. It's perfect during the fall."[13]

In sum, First Baptist had low barriers to outsiders (see Chapter 2), under-utilized ritual technology and techniques, wavered in attention to their sacred object, and rushed through a short service. These dynamics appeared to impede intersubjectivity, a necessary condition for the spirit's arrival.

PROMISED LAND: A LONG AND INTENSE IR

In contrast to First Baptist, my first impression of Promised Land was that they might have an initial disadvantage with respect to effervescence. When I first entered the quiet sanctuary, no more than a dozen individuals had taken spots in the pews. This suggested a potential problem related to bodily density since the sanctuary appeared large enough for at least 500 participants. Within a span of 10 minutes, though, the quiet space transformed into a low roar of interaction as Sunday School was dismissed and the 10:45 starting time neared.

Sounds from a digital organ commenced the ritual. Played by a large man with a beard, the organ may have been the most important technology used during the ritual. It launched the service, punctuated the prayers, guided the singing, and filled the room with sound and emotion during transitions. The organ was louder than all other sounds in the sanctuary, and reliably focused the group's attention. The organ also made the space feel more crowded than it actually was. Roughly 100 participants occupied the pews 10 minutes into the service, with 30 or so late arrivals by the end of the service. The organ's volume forced people to increase the volume of their own singing and talking, the cumulative effect of which was to convey to participants a sense of being part of the action.[14] Although the sanctuary might have felt emptier in different circumstances, the organ helped secure feelings of crowdedness. It was a simple ritual technology that was thoroughly implemented to maximize effervescence.

Promised Land also advanced intersubjectivity by implementing additional ritual techniques common in black Protestant churches.[15] Interactive movement was one such technique. This book's introductory chapter described one such event, when four older women gathered at the front of the stage to lead the singing. All four women smiled, clapped, and moved to the music, but the oldest and smallest woman playfully marched her way into the first and second pews, making eye contact and trading huge smiles with the pews' occupants. Her twitchy avant-garde dance moves and transgression of an invisible threshold had an energizing effect not only on the occupants of the first two rows, but on the whole congregation. By modeling movements and sounds, the women made themselves available for mutual monitoring and rhythmic entrainment. By crossing an invisible threshold between "performers" and "audience," the oldest woman's actions symbolically rejected ritual stratification and implied that energy like hers was available to all.

The call-and-response preaching also helped focus attention and mood, making the sermon feel less like a one-way lecture and more like an enthusiastic exchange. This interactional technique exemplifies how rhythmic entrainment progressively escalates emotional intensity. Nelson's (1996) ethnography of an African Methodist Episcopal church in South Carolina highlights how the black Protestant "resource" of call-and-response builds emotional intensity through positive feedback circuits: "[Pastors] are able to evoke a response from the congregation. This response increases the intensity and quality of the performer's actions, which in turn evoke a greater congregational response. . . . The overall trajectory . . . is one of oscillating movement toward higher levels of intensity and participation" (392). A parallel can be found in one-on-one interactions. Consider a conversation in which the listener nods and utters verbal affirmations versus one in which the listener is completely neutral. In most cases, the first scenario would boost the speaker's confidence and encourage her to continue. The second scenario likely would drain the speaker's confidence, and send her searching for either a new topic or a new conversation partner.

Pastor Dave's EE was able to flourish through constant verbal affirmation from the congregation that they were hearing and supporting his words. Although the content of the congregation's responses seems less important than their rhythmic function, the words are, for the most part, explicitly affirmative. The Hebrew word "Amen" is usually translated in English as "truly" or "I agree." Other common utterances include "keep going," "that's right," "preach it," and "mm-hm."[16] From the congregants' perspective, the call-and-response technique also helps ensure that they don't lose their mutual focus of attention. Even if one starts to drift or daydream, it is likely to be a short hiatus since anyone at any time might shout an affirmation/wake-up call.

The greeting time was another device that promoted intersubjectivity. In contrast to First Baptist, Promised Land's greeting time was more risky for participants because it was longer (about 10 minutes). However, the congregation deftly nurtured this ritual moment. The choir and pastors advanced into the pews. Some individuals crossed the room to meet friends, collecting energy from mini-IRs as they traveled. Two individuals sitting in the pew behind me, clearly friends, laughed and talked for the entire span of time. As a visitor, I was given little opportunity to feel shamefaced since at least 10 people shook my hand, smiled, and in two cases initiated conversation.

Another effective technique was the promotion of physical contact. There were three occasions during the service when touching was built into the ritual. The first was during the greeting, when hugs, shoulder-clasps, and handshakes proliferated. The second was during the supplicatory prayer. At the invitation of the pastor, 40 congregants approached the front and held hands in a large semicircle while the pastor prayed for a long list of health concerns, financial problems, and family troubles. The pastor cried toward the end of the prayer, noting that "in Heaven, every day will be Sunday." The third occasion for physical contact was in the climax of the service, described in Chapter 2, when everyone held hands and sang "Amazing Grace." These moments encouraged feelings of trust and solidarity not only with those in immediate contact, but with the entire congregation. Holding hands made us feel like a single physical unit.[17] The singing and swaying also induced rhythmic entrainment.

The final strategy to focus attention and mood was Promised Land's management of time. Around the time that many 10:45 services around town were dismissing, Promised Land's pastor approached the pulpit and began to preach. The service was close to three hours long in total, conveying the ritual's importance and ensuring sufficient time to achieve effervescence. The length also added ritual familiarity and sense of accomplishment to participants' list of emotional benefits. The contrast with First Baptist is quite revealing, and is examined in more detail below.

There can be no doubt that Promised Land collectively effervesced. Even as an outsider, it was difficult to avoid the feeling that all in the room were united in a collective spirit. This was particularly palpable in the climax of the ritual when we all held hands, sang, and swayed in rhythm.

CONCLUSION

First Baptist's resources and ritual technology are more sophisticated than Promised Land's. Resources such as a cordless headset microphone, an expensive sound system, and a large paid worship staff ensure a smooth performance with few delays. First Baptist's service generated lower levels of collective effervescence, though, and this suggests that resources and technology can actually impede effervescence if their primary impact is to shorten the ritual and/or avoid any appearance of human error. Further, when underutilized or not utilized at all, as in the case of First Baptist's pipe organ, impressive resources can suggest a fractured identity and ambiguous organizational goals. Promised Land did not have equal material resources, but they thoroughly incorporated the interactional resources that were available. The best example was their sustained use of a modest digital organ that filled the sanctuary with volume and emotion. The black Protestant tradition in America provides Promised Land with several other ritual techniques that they fully exploited. These included interactive and rhythmic movement, call-and-response preaching, a lengthy greeting time, and frequent physical contact.

Although the primary sacred object at First Baptist was clearly the Bible, the pastor's style was to use that object as a launching point for stories and applications aimed at edifying individuals' daily lives. In this case, the choice seemed to have the ironic effect of *diverting* attention from the sacred object, which helps explain the low emotional intensity of the ritual. By contrast at Promised Land, the sacred object of the cross (discussed in Chapter 2) was called upon by the pastor as a rallying cry, the only effective weapon against local gangs, their symbols, their violence, and the broader sinful culture the gangs draw upon.

Finally, First Baptist's one-hour service presents a notable contrast with Promised Land's nearly-three-hour service. This book's field work and statistical analysis both indicate that service length influences intersubjectivity. Statistical analysis of the USCLS shows that longer services correlate with higher levels of effervescence and symbolic solidarity.[18] This trend continued in the field work. First Baptist's service length would have earned a score of 1, while Promised Land would have earned a score of 4. They represent the extreme values of the variable's range, making them a good contrast for observational analysis. Congregation Shalom, discussed in Chapter 1, engaged in sacred rituals all day on Shabbat, and the ritual I observed lasted slightly longer than Promised Land's. Supporting the quantitative findings, Promised Land and Congregation Shalom held what were clearly the most effervescent rituals in the qualitative sample.

There are at least a few different reasons for this relationship. First, emotional entrainment takes time to develop. This is a simple issue of probability. Increasing the total time spent together automatically increases the opportunity for at least some of that time to be spent in emotional connection. Second, members of voluntary organizations are likely to anticipate rewards that correspond with their investments of time; these expectations tend to become self-fulfilling prophecies as members either seize or ignore opportunities to feel the spirit. For those who devote significant amounts of their time to their organization's rituals, the "sunk costs" of their time investments are likely to create optimistic expectations about the EE "payoff" available in the organization's rituals, helping them "lean in" to the occasion. Third, increased familiarity with an organization's practices and symbols increases members' proficiency with those practices and symbols. Fourth, the effects are reciprocal: organizations who have emotionally invigorating rituals will be less inclined to depart and go home.

Contrary to what the two congregations' differential in service length might lead one to expect, however, the basic worship schedule in the two churches was quite similar in terms of the number of events. As Table 4.1 reveals, the determining factor in their different service lengths was not *how many* events took place, but the *duration of each event*, as well as the *duration of transitions* between each event. Promised Land exceeded First Baptist on both counts.

Promised Land's members stretch the duration of each event because they look forward to services that are "Spirit-filled." As Promised Land's pastor informed me, their services always last at least two hours, and often go longer if the congregation "feels the Spirit move." He repeated this idea during the portion of the sermon devoted to announcements. Regarding the timing of an upcoming evening prayer meeting, he announced, "If the Spirit tells us to cut

Table 4.1. Order of Worship at Promised Land and First Baptist

Promised Land: 15 events in 3 hours	*First Baptist: 12 events in 1 hour*
• Organ prelude	• Recorded piano prelude
• Procession	• Procession
• Congregational singing	• Announcements
• Greeting time	• Greeting time
• Choir singing	• Congregational singing
• Prayer	• Responsive reading
• Introduction of visitors	• Congregational singing
• Congregational singing	• Offering [a]
• Announcements	• Sermon
• Offering #1	• Altar call
• Prayer of supplication	• Introduction of new members
• Offering #2	• Closing prayer/benediction
• Sermon	
• Congregational singing	
• Closing prayer	

[a] First Baptist's offering took as long as the combined duration of Promised Land's two offerings because First Baptist's congregation was much larger. Promised Land's offerings are listed separately in this table, but could arguably have been collapsed. This alternate coding would have reduced Promised Land's number of events to 14, even closer to First Baptist's.

it off after 30 minutes, that's what we'll do. If the Spirit says to go longer, that's what we'll do." Promised Land's members expect greater emotional rewards if they nurture the events of the ritual, whereas First Baptist's members prioritize ending on time. The members' different expectations of event duration condition their emotional availability and engagement with the ritual.

Duration of transitions also played an important part, as Promised Land held extended transitions between events, whereas First Baptist "hit all their cues" to rapidly move from event to event. The effect of these contrasting approaches was counterintuitive since long transitions present a risk of dissipated attention and intersubjectivity. Minimizing the time of transitions, by contrast, is a more cautious strategy which aims to accommodate short attention spans. In the broader context of the congregations' rituals, however, the effects were opposite. Promised Land's long transitions provided time to pause and "gather steam" in a larger ritual movement toward an energy climax. Although a hiatus from intensity, attention was still focused by the ongoing emotional engagement of the improvising organist. First Baptist's ritual structure indicated no movement toward an energy climax, but rather discrete events strung together without an apparent narrative logic.[19] The congregations' contrasting ritual structures are rendered in Figure 4.2. The direction of the lines indicate rising, falling, or stagnant energy.[20]

As with their contrasting management of time, contrasting management of ritual resources and techniques led to different levels of intersubjectivity. At Promised Land, this impressed upon the interactants the sensation that something unique and powerful was taking place. Promised Land came together and shared an emotional experience which stimulated shared identity, morality, and goals. First Baptist, as discussed in Chapter 2, gathered together in order to foster individual-level religious experiences. For this reason, it is unsurprising that First Baptist underutilized resources that could have promoted intersubjectivity, which is simply not emphasized as part of their ritual ideology. With technical adjustments, First Baptist could experience higher levels of intersubjectivity on a more regular basis on Sunday mornings. If this happened more often and to a greater degree, it is doubtful that they would be in such a hurry to leave each other's company.

Religious groups who want to encounter the spirit must be savvy about how the arrangement and execution of their rituals promote or impede sensations of intersubjectivity. Even choices that seem relatively trivial can powerfully influence the alignment of participants' thoughts and feelings and thus their impression of supernatural force. In this sense, the spirit is picky. Chapter 5 looks at how the spirit's pickiness also extends outward, beyond the organization itself. Specifically, the spirit responds to how those who would invoke it characterize and imagine those *outside* their circle. When this

Promised Land's Three-Hour Ritual

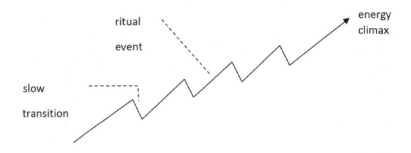

First Baptist's One-Hour Ritual

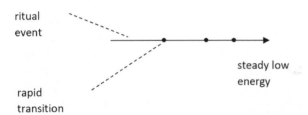

Figure 4.2. Structures of Promised Land's and First Baptist's Rituals

characterization flatters or welcomes, the spirit tends to remain in slumber. When this characterization demonizes or shuns, though, the spirit is aroused.

NOTES

1. In countless scenes in the contemporary U.S., especially among children and young adults, unanticipated silences or aberrant comments inspire one interactant to sing or exclaim "awkward!" The interactant knows the situation has been violated, but is not willing or able to articulate what rule has been broken. "Awkward!" is an alarm to the group that they quickly need to either repair the IR or perhaps even discipline or punish the offending party.

2. Collins (2004) examines the use of nicotine and caffeine in IRs, arguing that how users interpret the physical effects of these substances depends on the social context of the drug-taking rituals. Similarly, Becker (1963) shows how the ability to "get high" on marijuana depends on social rituals wherein users instruct each other how to perceive the drug's effects and interpret them as enjoyable. Anthropological research likewise illustrates how substances such as cocaine, *yagé*, and betel nuts bring focus to social (often explicitly religious) rituals across a wide variety of world cultures (Goodman and Lovejoy 1995). Based on such studies, the collective use of drugs appears to function in most cases as a means to focus attention and entrain emotions, with rich variety in the particular quality of focus and mood as social context varies. Alcohol is certainly one of the most common, serving as a sacred object that has the power to charge up emotional intensity, frequently used as a device to distinguish carousing insiders from prudish outsiders.

3. Krátký (2012), for example, analyzes a mantra chant ritual in the Hindu Gaudiya Vaishnava tradition. He shows how the substitution of one sort of sacred object for another in a given practice can drastically alter both the performance and effect of that practice. Devotees have traditionally used prayer beads as external memory devices, keeping count of the number of chants they have performed throughout the day. When switching from prayer beads to a more efficient mechanical clicker, it became *easier* to track how many times they had performed the chant, which also meant that the chanting practice occupied less space in the practitioner's moment-to-moment consciousness throughout the day—a consequence exactly opposed to that which is intended by the practice of chanting a mantra.

4. Rock star Bruce Springsteen, whose profession requires him to routinely generate effervescence in large crowds, once summed up the basic role of rhythmic entrainment as follows: "If you get their asses moving, their spirits will follow" (Sandford 1999, 177).

5. As discussed in Chapter 1, this pertains to the main problem that Durkheim (1912) was trying to solve. When the epistemological starting point is the individual, skepticism tends to follow because it is impossible to connect individuals' distinct perceptions of the world to a shared underlying reality (Hume 1777; Rorty 1979). The other common approach is to assume that each individual possesses a Kantian a priori grasp of fundamental truths. However, if the starting point for human knowledge is not the individual consciousness, but instead a social experience of perceived intersubjectivity, it becomes possible to see how truth could be experienced by the individual as a verifiable reality.

6. First Baptist Church has a large sanctuary that can seat about 1200. According to a bulletin posted on First Baptist's website, the average number of worshipers during the month when I attended was 399, suggesting a density score of about .33. Based on the USCLS data, this is about average (see Table A.2 in Appendix A). Considering that the big balcony was mostly empty, the ground floor pews actually felt significantly more crowded than 33%.

7. "Good morning" is an IR tool that can be used for diverse purposes. It is one of the most common sounds heard in sanctuaries on Sunday mornings. It is particularly useful during unformatted portions of the ritual (especially before and after) in which

individuals roam around the space looking for appealing interactions. If an individual wants to initiate an IR or join one already in progress, "good morning" is a useful way to "put out feelers" and test the others' willingness to interact. Interactions are inherently risky exchanges of emotional goods, and subtle variation of intonation in the respondent's "good morning" informs the sensitive initiator whether or not to continue to pursue the IR. If an IR begins but becomes emotionally draining, or if the formatted portion of the larger IR is about to begin, the mini-IR can also be abruptly cut off with a crisp "good morning." The subtle management of this IR tool highlights the relevance of mutual monitoring and shared moods to social solidarity.

8. Christian theologian Robert Webber argues in *The Younger Evangelicals* (2002) that the assumption is demonstrably false. During his tenure (1968–2007) as professor at the fervently evangelical Wheaton College, he observed that young evangelicals increasingly have been seeking more "traditional" forms of worship as a way to stimulate a firmer sense of identity and connection with the past in a fragmented postmodern culture. Saddleback Church's Rick Warren, by contrast, writes that the pipe organ is a 19th-century instrument that is "out of date" since no one listens to organs on the radio (1995, 290).

9. This variation is usually evident at the level of religious tradition, and is one way in which tradition structures the focus of attention. Catholics and Episcopalians "pass the peace," ensuring physical contact. Black Protestants at Promised Land traveled around the sanctuary and interacted for 10 minutes. First Baptist, like many predominantly white Protestant congregations, allotted less than two minutes for participants to turn, briefly introduce themselves, and possibly shake hands.

10. Also recall First Baptist's numerous references to the importance of hearing and reading "God's Word" in Chapter 2.

11. Expository preaching is considered closely in Haskell et al. (2008) and in Christian literature such as Robinson (2001) and Stott (1982). A Christian book on topical preaching is Allen (1992).

12. First Baptist's missed opportunity is hardly inevitable for evangelical churches. The focus on the Bible during the sermon generated little emotional engagement or rhythmic entrainment, but evangelical organizations who recognize the need for it can take steps to invigorate their focus. This may help explain the popularity of Small Group Bible Studies, a key interest in recent research on evangelicals (Bielo 2009; Dougherty and Whitehead 2011; Wuthnow 1994). As Dougherty and Whitehead found, evangelicals who take part in Small Groups report a greater sense of belonging, attend church more, and give more. Small Group Bible Studies can build participants' enthusiasm for their sacred object and their churches by emphasizing that biblical interpretation is a difficult challenge that mutual encouragement and collective effort can help accomplish.

13. For many Americans, the ritual of watching professional football on Sundays can itself be considered sacred. In Chapter 2, based on discussions with Promised Land's congregants, I introduced the notion of "pre-ritual rituals," warm-ups that prime congregants to experience the spirit in the main ritual. Watching football and eating lunch both can be considered common variants of *post-ritual rituals*, the anticipation of which can have a powerful effect on the main worship ritual. An acutely

funny illustration of how anticipation of *lunch* can crash a Sunday morning church service can be found in Lyle Lovett's 1992 song, "Church."

In this research, lunch was a routine consideration. Would the focus group members be too hungry to concentrate on our discussion, for example, after a morning church service? Bringing food to the focus groups was a ritual technique that helped us all focus. Congregations like Congregation Shalom keep the post-ritual ritual within the temporal frame of sacredness by holding congregational potlucks, picnics, and the like. In order for the anticipation of post-ritual rituals to have a positive effect on the main ritual, Sabbatarianism may be a key organizational resource. Provision of food is another, and different kinds of lunch rituals will focus attention in different ways. The post-ritual ritual is a promising avenue for future IR research. Returning to the point I'm making in the main text, though, when ritual practices are advertised as "always ending on time," they can imply that the individual's "personal time" is more valuable than the collective's sacred time, and that individual participants likely could be gaining more EE from other competing rituals.

14. See Collins (2004, 55) for a discussion of the priority of sound in IRs.

15. These include, for example, shouting, singing, dancing, call-and-response preaching, and narratives of deliverance (Ahlstrom 1972; DuBois 1904; Lincoln and Mamiya 1990; Nelson 2005).

16. Another common congregational response that is quite fascinating to consider is a simple "well. . . ." This response, which mostly seems to fulfill a rhythmic function, does not exactly affirm what the preacher has just said, but rather expresses patient optimism about what he will say next. It almost suggests a verbal pause performed by the congregation on behalf of the preacher.

17. Feeling like a single physical unit tends to promote emotional unity, and is a property of copresence. Katz (1999) provides an example in his chapter "An Episode of Whining." The chapter describes a whining preschooler who refuses to cooperate with her teacher's instructions to assemble several blocks into a larger cube. The teacher decides to gently use her own hands to guide the child's hands to the appropriate blocks. They gaze in the same direction and accomplish the same movements, and the child's mood quickly changes to pleased cooperation. Ehrenreich (1997, 2006) hypothesizes that physical synchronicity of movements feels pleasing because it is a naturally selected form of human behavior that, in prehistory, helped human groups mimic a "large animal" to scare off predators.

18. See Figure A.3 and the surrounding discussion in Appendix A.

19. First Baptist's altar call did hold potential for stimulating an emotional climax. Altar calls are common in conservative Christian congregations, especially among Baptists. They originated in 19th-century revivalist movements and are associated with famous evangelists such as Charles Finney and Billy Graham (Cox 1995; Finke and Stark 2005; Cross 1950). They can be extraordinary, life-changing IRs. Typically, the congregation sings hymns or praise songs while the pastor urges individuals to "come to the altar" and commit themselves to faith in Jesus, to formal membership in the church, and/or renewed vigor in their "personal walk." However, First Baptist's understated altar call never conveyed the urgency or fever of a revival.

20. These structures can be compared with the structure of dramatic performances, other rituals that depend on shared attention and emotion. Shakespeare's and Sophocles' plays, for example, often have a dramatic arc involving action that rises toward a climax. Between scenes of rising action, the playwrights often inserted choruses or comic interludes that gave the audience an emotional pause before the next incident of conflict. Promised Land had a comparable structure as it allowed several opportunities to pause and gather steam as the ritual steadily built to an emotional climax.

Chapter Five

Barriers to Outsiders

Religious organizations of all types gain solidarity by clearly delineating who does and does not belong. Barriers to outsiders are the cues people use to help everyone make this distinction. These cues take a variety of different forms. For instance, there are actual physical barriers such as fences and turned backs, and there are also more symbolic barriers such as inside jokes and creeds. The basic principle that exclusivity unites insiders figures prominently in several of sociology's most influential theories. Related concepts include outgrouping (Sumner 1906), cultural capital (Bourdieu 1984), social boundaries (Lamont 1992; Sahlins 1989), tension (Stark and Bainbridge 1987; Stark and Finke 2000), subcultural identity (Smith et al. 1998), and symbolic boundaries (Gans 1974; Lamont 2000; Lamont and Molnar 2002). As Simmel (1922) and Coser (1956) argued, external conflict is functional for groups and organizations.[1] We can add that it entices the spirit.

Barriers vary according to their *size* and *consequence*. By "size," I mean the percentage of the population whom the barriers exclude. For example, a group of Americans in a public setting talking about their recent participation in a popular pastime like watching the Oscars would present only a small barrier to outsiders; many or most other people nearby are likely to have shared the experience and would be able to join in if they so desired. If the conversation were to turn to, say, a mutual passion for dog fighting or genital piercings, the size of their ritual barriers would increase significantly.[2] Barriers vary in size in religious rituals, as well. The largest barriers are built by extremists who preach damnation for everyone except themselves, as in the hate-filled funeral protests conducted by Westboro Baptist Church. At the other extreme, many congregations pride themselves on being "open to all," as in Unitarian Universalist congregations and (in this research) the Meditation Center from Chapter 3. Pluralistic invitations of this sort are no doubt sincere in most cases, but they have natural limits. The barrier is small but still consequential because expressions of bigotry and extremism will inevitably prompt moral sanctions. An open-minded organization defines itself in opposition to closed-mindedness.

"Consequence" of barriers refers to the intensity with which the group intends punishment on those who trespass. If a circle of smokers is joined by a nonsmoker, they might tease the newcomer or try to cajole her into joining them. In most cases, however, the social consequences for her trespass will be minimal. If, on the other hand, a smoker were to light up at the wrong occasion—in a library, for instance—punitive emotions would run high among the nonsmokers in the room. The consequence would be more intense for the smoker in the library.

Small and inconsequential barriers draw on tacit public agreement that IRs are most enjoyable when uninterrupted. Interactants need to be given room to develop an interactional rhythm and flow, and most people know it can be inconsiderate or mildly risky to impose oneself into a preexisting rhythm and flow. Traversing small barriers usually carries relatively minor consequences, if any.

In the most intense IRs, those which produce the strongest group feelings and the most potent group symbols, barriers tend to be large and highly consequential. We know not to interrupt a couple during sex, for instance. Traversing this barrier would normally demolish the IR, and would threaten future IRs between the mutually humiliated parties. Also, we know that it is a serious offense to disrespect a religious organization's sacred objects. Blasphemers risk damnation, as do those who threaten the organization's safety or way of life. Powerful rituals are enclosed rituals, and violators get punished.

The concept of barriers is critical in IR theory because it links solidarity and conflict. These concepts are complementary. As Collins (2012, 2) points out:

> Conflict theory is not the opposite of a theory of human ideals, social cooperation, and solidarity. We don't have a sentimental good theory of human beings on one hand and a cynical conflict theory on the other. It's all part of the same theory. . . . Polarization is the dark shadow of the highest levels of successful interaction ritual.

Human nature, by this reasoning, is neither good nor bad. Rather, conflict of a certain kind produces solidarity and solidarity of a certain kind produces conflict. This insight has profound implications for comprehending the origin and progression of all sorts of antagonisms, small- or large-scale. Opposing sides in social conflicts draw on the same fundamental motivations: love and fellowship.

In this chapter, I return to the analysis of the Islamic Center's and Congregation Shalom's rituals to compare the ways they construct and manage barriers to outsiders. The basic hypothesis is that clearly defined boundaries will stimulate the spirit. As previous chapters attest, the interplay of IR dynamics is complex. A single dynamic usually does not wholly account for the ritual's outcomes; rather, the dynamics condition each other's influence and take precedence over each other in ways that only qualitative research can untangle. As indicated in Chapter 1, Congregation Shalom's Shabbat service achieved the highest degree of effervescence in the sample, whereas most of the Islamic Center's Jum'ah service was unfocused and low-energy. The analysis pointed to Congregation Shalom's relative success at activating strategies and resources that maximized intersubjectivity and copresence. While much of the discrepancy in the organizations' ritual outcomes can be traced to those dynamics, this chapter lends support to the barriers hypothesis, as well, especially with regard to effervescence and *symbolic* solidarity.

It is crucial to note at the outset that barriers can be built from within or imposed from without. American Jews and Muslims are religious minorities who have a long history of imposed barriers. Max Weber (1922b, 492–98) referred to Jews as "a pariah people" for whom barriers from without have long been the norm and a core feature of their collective identity. The systematic murder of millions of Jews during World War II ensured that the survivors and their families would be well aware of the persistent threat of hostility from outsiders. American Muslims must regularly cope with general ignorance about their practices and beliefs, along with outright hostility and violence.[3] They experience more subtle forms of cultural disadvantage, as well. As discussed in chapter 1, for example, the fact that their holy day is on Friday rather than Saturday or Sunday makes it a challenge to even get together at the same time to pray.

Given the way that barriers are imposed on American Jews and Muslims, one might question whether it is sufficiently precise to characterize Jewish and Muslim organizations as "constructing" or "managing" barriers. As Smith et al. (1998) show, however, the key theoretical issue is not the actual amount of hostility that is directed toward a social group, but rather the group's *perception* of the same. If members of an organization tell each other they are hated, even if outsiders actually like them or don't have an opinion about them, the invented animosity can promote solidarity within the organization. Conversely, an organization oblivious to outsiders' hatred will not be able to turn it to their own advantage.

Apart from the source of the barriers, another key issue is how an organization *responds* to them. Both organizations in this chapter belong to religious traditions whose members face real marginalization and persecution in numerous forms on an ongoing basis. Both organizations accurately perceive this to be the case. However, their ritualized responses to these barriers are quite different. The Islamic Center is desperately trying to survive in an unac-commodating "Bible Belt" setting, and their response to marginalization is to seek interfaith accord. Their imam is active in their local interfaith commu-nity, they expressed no hostility toward outsiders, and the only criticisms they mentioned were directed at their own organization and tradition. Congrega-tion Shalom, by contrast, iterated enemies' atrocities and rallied around their support for Israel in its conflict with Palestine. The most frequent sentiment expressed in their Bar Mitzvah ceremony, in fact, was collective pride in the 13-year old boy's Zionism and his plan to enlist as an Israeli soldier. I argue that the organizations' respective outcomes in effervescence and symbolic solidarity are directly related to the way they did or did not utter a desire to oppose antagonists and defend their own. Solidarity and conflict are corre-spondent, not contrary.[4]

Table 5.1 summarizes the organizations' basic similarities and differences with respect to barriers.

Table 5.1.   **Barrier Work at the Islamic Center and Congregation Shalom**

Barrier work	The Islamic Center [a]	Congregation Shalom
Barriers of ritual proficiency	High	High
Barriers from without	High	High
Perception of barriers from without	High	High
Response to perceived barriers	• Criticism of own organization and tradition • Promotion of interfaith harmony	Support for Israel in its conflict with Palestine
References to atrocities	None	Two emotionally powerful references
Collective effervescence	• Moderate • Brief	• Intense • Lengthy
Membership solidarity	High	High
Symbolic solidarity	Low	High

[a] Only men were observed.

BARRIER WORK AT THE ISLAMIC CENTER: PERCEPTION AND RESPONSE

Barriers from Within

The Islamic Center evinced significant cultural and ritual barriers to outsid-ers. By my observation, none of these emanated from the organization per se. Rather, all of the barriers were due to the disparity between the tools of their religious tradition and prevailing cultural norms in the U.S. In Arabic, "Islam" means submission and obedience to Allah. Submission is considered to be an ongoing act of worship, and regulations of lifestyle serve as daily reminders of submission. These involve dietary rules, abstention from drugs and alcohol, modest dress, the wearing of hijabs by many Muslim women, and other forms of religious "strictness" (Kelley 1977; Iannaccone 1994; Stark and Bainbridge 1987). These sorts of cultural distinctives are a regular feature of Muslim communities worldwide.

Along with regulation of lifestyle, Islam involves substantial regulation of ritual. These regulations include literal barriers, as women are usually required to worship separately from men, often in the same room but shielded from the men's sight by a screen. This is one of the clearest examples of ritual stratification available in modern religious practice.[5] I will return to this practice later in this chapter.

For men and women, Islamic tradition mandates careful preparation and attention to detail in the ritual of *salat* (prayer). The requirement to pray five times per day means that Muslims must be intentional about their personal schedules. Devout practice of salat is thus a means by which Islam can permeate one's consciousness. As an American Muslim quoted in Wuthnow (2005, 59) explained, "The best Muslims don't fit the prayers into their schedules but organize their lives around the prayers." Alongside this mandate for ritual repetition, the physical movements involved in salat are typically performed in a precise sequence (*raka'ah*) with careful attention to detail. For example, kneeling is not simply getting on your knees, but based on tradition involves sitting on your left foot while extending your right foot behind while directing your eyes to your extended right index finger which should be resting in your lap.

Prior to salat, Muslims also engage in ablution, ritual cleansings of the body. Standard ablution, or *wudhu*, is detailed in the *hadiths*, reports of Muhammad's life which serve as major sources of guidance for Muslim beliefs and practices. Siddiqui (2005) lists the steps involved in Wudhu as follows:

- Wash one's hands three times from fingers to wrist (right hand, then left)
- Rinse the mouth three times
- Rinse the nose three times
- Wash the face from forehead to chin three times
- Wash the forearms from wrist to elbow three times (right then left)
- Run water through the hair from forehead to neck three times
- Wash the outside and inside of the ears three times (right then left)
- Wipe the back of the neck with the back of one's hands three times
- Wash the feet from toes to ankles three times (right then left)

The precise manner in which wudhu and salat are practiced can be daunting to the untrained. The same can be said about the heavy use of Arabic during salat.[6] In all of these areas, ritual proficiency increases through daily practice and instruction from fellow Muslims. This practice and instruction often begins in the home and continues through masjid attendance. As a college student from the Islamic Center named Fawaz explained to me, "I know how to read Arabic since my family all learned it, but I don't understand all of it. Khutba [the sermon] helps me understand what the Quran is saying in some places. Khutba helps me learn parts I don't know."

The practices involved in salat present high barriers to ritual novices, clearly designating who has and has not gathered enough of the right cultural capital to belong.[7] The ability to perform the right movements and say the right words is a sign of devotion, because only a member who had attended numerous collective salats, or possibly (although less likely) one who had devoted ample time to practice on his own, would be able to keep up. In other visits for this research, I participated as fully as possible in all of the ritual practices. At the Islamic Center, I never seriously considered participating in the raka'ah. I was an outsider, I knew it, and fumbling through the raka'ah would have only broadcasted that fact.[8]

Barriers from Without

The behavioral and ritual barriers discussed thus far are actively generated by Muslims, and can be identified as *barriers from within*. As discussed in Chapter 1, Muslims also face substantial *barriers from without*. Edgell et al. (2006) show that 26% of Americans believe Muslims "do not at all agree" with their vision of American society, while 33% would disapprove if their child chose to marry a Muslim. On a list of 10 different social demographics,[9] Muslims are the second most disagreeable to other Americans, falling behind atheists and ahead of homosexuals. Edgell et al.'s arguments suggest that moral boundaries with atheists are a means by which many Americans construct feelings of national symbolic solidarity, and a similar argument may also apply to boundaries with Muslims. For many, American identity implies faith in Jesus, and the presence of Muslims provides a contrast against which to imagine their own patriotism.

Particularly since September 2001, social context has made solidarity with other Americans a challenge for many Muslims. Subsequently, numerous Muslim organizations held rituals such as annual 9/11 candlelight vigils to help assure other Americans of their good intentions, American identity, and opposition to extremists (Wakin 2002). These challenging circumstances, to the degree that they are faced by Muslims, are unique among American religious organizations. American Muslims can be characterized as having high barriers with non-Muslims, but with the exception of the religious cultural capital described above, these barriers are mostly imposed from without. In many cases, American Muslims strive to collapse the barriers. However, the default status of American Muslims necessarily involves awareness of barriers with the predominantly Christian surrounding culture.[10]

The Islamic Center's Response to Perceived Barriers

Islamic Center members confirmed that they are well aware of their barriers from without. This was most evident in the khutba prior to the collective raka'ah sequence. During the first portion of his khutba,[11] the Islamic Center's imam, Omar, spoke of the challenges of living as a Muslim in America. In the latter portion, Omar challenged the Islamic Center's members to behave with responsibility and submission despite those challenges. Early in the khutba he said, "This is the hardest time for Muslims ever. Watch TV.[12] Everyone has difficulties with Muslims."

Rather than blaming the outsiders, however, Omar claimed that Muslim unfaithfulness has caused and exasperated the problem. For one thing, he argued, Muslims have failed to faithfully read their holy text. "The Quran is collecting dust in our houses," he said. "This is unacceptable. You are Muslims. You follow your book: the Quran." He reminded the congregation that faith comes without conditions and that Muslims are commanded to be obedient.

Omar went on to argue that Muslims have also failed to faithfully practice salat. "Nobody twists your arm to be a Muslim. You people are here today because you have a conscience. Many of us are not here. It's not convenient. Look around you. If you see someone who is missing, call them." He concluded the first section of the khutba with his main theme: "Every Muslim knows how we are treated today. It's happening because we are not following Allah."

The second half of the khutba was also a call to intensified practice, with an emphasis on personal reading of the Quran. Omar again criticized his tradition, pointing to the confusion caused by conflicting messages from "self-made imams" on the internet and elsewhere.[13] He exhorted the men to read the Quran for themselves. If possible, they should read it in its original language. "I regret that I do not read Arabic. I pray to Allah that before I die, I will have the chance to read Arabic." He concluded the khutba with a discussion about Ramadan, which was imminent. "Make Ramadan special in your life. But don't be a part-time Muslim. Whatever we do in Ramadan must continue throughout the year."

Islamic Center members perceived clear barriers with outsiders, and Omar used this perception in an effort to stimulate greater levels of involvement. This scenario is markedly similar to that expressed in Smith et al.'s (1998) study of American evangelicals, who communicate to each other that they are "embattled" by secular culture, allowing them to "thrive" as a community. However, the Islamic Center did not encourage any hostility *toward* outsiders. To the contrary, members of the focus group informed me that Omar is in fact highly proactive in interfaith activities in their local community. I was able to confirm this later by locating numerous reports of Omar's participation in interfaith events and conferences. His interest is in demonstrating that Muslims are compassionate and empathetic toward other Americans.[14]

Omar was critical of only one social group: his own. He expressed frustration with brothers who neglect to read the Quran, or who show up for khutba only during Ramadan. The barriers he promoted, then, were with insiders whose commitment levels had lapsed. His sentiments recall sociological work on organizational strictness (Iannaccone 1994; Kelley 1977) that points to the deleterious effects of "free riders" and weakly committed members in voluntary organizations. The Islamic Center actively discourages these weaker levels of commitment, and Omar directly challenged those present to contact absent members. The focus group confirmed to me that members regularly call members of the community who are absent from Jum'ah.[15] The Islamic Center does not blame outsiders for their struggles. Rather, they admonish each other to be better Muslims.

The Impact of the Islamic Center's Barrier Work on Effervescence and Solidarity

As discussed in Chapter 1, the Islamic Center's ritual did not evince a strong or consistent experience of collective effervescence.[16] This result would not support IR theory's barriers hypothesis if we were only considering the barriers that are imposed on the Islamic Center from without. Since Muslims' cultural and ritual barriers are virtually automatic in the U.S. context, it would seem as though this status would promote effervescence within their IRs. Further, it would not suffice to suggest that the Islamic Center is somehow unaware of their tradition's marginal status in America. The key, however, is their response. Other factors are involved in effervescence, but it likely would have increased heart rates and energy levels had Omar and the congregation emphasized their need to defend themselves against outside hostilities. Comparative support for this idea will follow below in the analysis of Congregation Shalom's Shabbat morning service.

The Islamic Center did appear to possess strong membership solidarity. The community is very small, but a core group of 15–20 attends regularly and knows each other well. Focus group member Antoine indicated that, although these regulars are from different nations and backgrounds, collective salat makes them feel "unified." During Ramadan the attendance numbers stay consistently around 50 as members come together nightly to break their fast. Fawaz explained, "It's a special time. All of the families are here together. We do it every night, so we really get to know each other better then." The Islamic Center's strong membership solidarity is not consistent with the hypothesis from IR theory. However, it *is* consistent with the USCLS findings.[17] Again, it appears that barriers have more to do with effervescence and symbolic solidarity, and less to do with membership solidarity. As I suggested previously, membership solidarity seems to be more of a baseline necessity that organizations require in order to survive.

Although they do experience membership solidarity, members of the Islamic Center did not confirm that they share symbolic solidarity in the form of a common goal or vision. As with the low output of effervescence, their low output of symbolic solidarity is consistent with IR theory's barriers hypothesis, and also with the quantitative findings. Their disinclination to rally against outside threats weakens their ability to boost symbolic solidarity. A focus group member named Tyler suggested another very relevant factor: the small size of their community makes it difficult to have any common goals apart from keeping the Islamic Center in operation. Based on the Islamic Center's low resource base, Tyler's assessment seems accurate. The "goal" is none other than to persist with a small resource base in an unaccommodating culture. Thus, whether an organization has a basically sufficient resource base conditions their potential for symbolic solidarity.

Taken together, the evidence suggests an addendum to IR theory: barriers to outsiders promote symbolic solidarity, in particular. There is little evidence in this research that barriers are necessary for membership solidarity.

Fractured Solidarity

As Fawaz noted, the Islamic Center's meetings during Ramadan are "a special time." He connected this specialness with the presence of "families." Jum'ah, though, is an occasion when male and female family members need to stay away from each other. The Islamic Center, then, like most other masjids, allows women and men to commingle in some social rituals but segregates them during salat.

I asked the all-male focus group why women are required to sit behind a screen during Jum'ah. Antoine explained, "Well, you know how men are.

It can be hard to pray when women are right there." Tyler added, "That's the tradition, and it works for us." In these two responses, the men appealed to tradition and what they presumed was male common sense in order to defend the segregation. Antoine's suggestion of untamable male sexuality, "you know how men are," was an effort to activate what he expected would be my own feelings of male solidarity. Since I am a man, surely I would see the common wisdom in hiding women from my view during worship. How would I, or any male, be able to focus on Allah while all the while thinking about sex with women who were kneeling and bowing nearby?

As several researchers have discussed (Mule and Barthel 1992; Predelli 2004; Read 2004; Read and Bartkowski 2000), Islam's common emphasis on a subordinate or "complementary" status for women is one way in which the tradition invariably encounters tension with modernist value systems, particularly in societies where Muslims are minorities. Although there is a noteworthy range of views within Islam regarding Muslim women's status (Aslan 2006; Predelli 2004), the power of tradition makes it difficult for even the more egalitarian-minded organizations to eradicate gender stratification during religious IRs. By comparison, American Protestants also have a wide range of views regarding the status of female members (Chaves 1999; Gallagher 2003), with more stratified views associated with biblical literalism (Hoffman and Bartkowski 2008).[18] Differing somewhat from Christianity,[19] however, separation by gender has been the predominant practice throughout most of Islam's history, continuing in recent years (Mattson 2006). Altering the ritual format and revealing women to the men's sight during salat may have even starker consequences than (Antoine's concern) the activation of male fantasies; it would symbolically threaten a long-standing ritual practice, and thus, by Durkheimian reasoning, part of the core of Muslim identity. For this reason, change would likely come slowly, if at all.

The segregation of women from men's sight during Jum'ah is a clear example of ritual stratification. The men are spatially closer to the ideological leader (the imam), the emotional leader (the muezzin), and the primary sacred object (the Quran as recited by the muezzin and imam, and as physically located on the *minbar* [pulpit]). As noted in Chapter 1, the women's screened-off section was located directly adjacent to the busy doorway. During the khutba and discussions with members, the symbolic emphasis was on Muslim *brotherhood*. Women were not expected or morally pressured to attend. Perhaps it should not be surprising, then, that I only observed one woman entering or exiting the building when visiting the Islamic Center. The structure and symbols of the ritual speak clearly to the organization's orientation: women should not expect the same degree of access to EE as men. Even as many Muslims around the world develop more egalitarian views of women's status in the home and workforce, as the symbol of the hijab wanes in many Muslim communities, and as some modern women continue to be drawn to male-dominated religions,[20] Muslims' central rituals continue to signify a fractured solidarity. This is a unique contribution that ritual analysis can contribute to the understanding of gender relations within Islam.

If Muslims were to desegregate their religious rituals, one benefit would be an increase in bodily density (physical copresence). Disadvantaged Muslim organizations such as the Islamic Center would benefit from the probable increases in effervescence and solidarity.[21] Perhaps modesty could be protected while also allowing women to be visible in the room. Women could be treated as not only welcome but crucial in collective worship. A more direct focus on invigorating women's participation in collective salat could lead to innovative ritual solutions while preserving Muslim values. A transformation of this sort, though, might depend on the extent to which the solidarity being symbolized is about *Muslim* identity as opposed to *male* identity and privilege.

BARRIER WORK AT CONGREGATION SHALOM: RALLYING AGAINST EXTERNAL THREATS

As discussed early in this chapter, American Jews have been forced to cope with persistent and serious threats from without. Like the Islamic Center, Congregation Shalom was well aware of these barriers, and referred to them on multiple occasions when I attended. Also like the Islamic Center, Congregation Shalom exhibited substantial ritual barriers from within, as I discuss below. In contrast to the Islamic Center, though, Congregation Shalom did not erect barriers with insiders by criticizing their own tradition or by ritually marginalizing female congregants. Rather, they rallied around support for a common cause: defending the nation of Israel. Combined with the high intersubjectivity and copresence described in Chapter 1, this common cause helped accelerate effervescence and solidarity to extremely high levels. Only Promised Land Baptist Church, considered in Chapters 2 and 4, compared with the emotional excitement and shared mission I observed at Congregation Shalom.

Barriers from Within

Jewish identity works into the consciousness of Conservative Jews through their observance of an extensive list of behavioral restrictions during Shabbat. The Talmud, a record of fundamental teachings from Jewish oral tradition, identifies 39 forbidden activities. As just a few examples, Jews on Shabbat are forbidden from writing anything, tearing an object in two, tying anything, lighting a fire, cooking, planting, doing laundry, building anything, or destroying anything.

In addition to restrictions such as these, Shabbat services often enact detailed practices which include speaking and reading Hebrew, wearing yarmulkes (kipas) and other head coverings, singing, shuckling, standing or sitting at designated times, covering one's eyes during a particular prayer, carrying Torah scrolls from the ark to the tabernacle to the sanctuary, along with other practices that can have the effect of making novices feel out of place.

Conservative Jews' long list of Sabbatary regulations can make their worship feel exclusive. Leaders of Congregation Shalom welcomed me to attend and were always cordial, but I was also directed to adhere to Shabbat regulations. For example, I was told not to record the focus group discussion on Saturday afternoon because that would require the use of an electronic device. As another example, I was instructed to wear a kipa before entering the sanctuary. While Jewish congregations often are very welcoming to visitors, it can be difficult for non-Jewish participants to shed the sensation that a vast gulf of history and tradition separates them from solidarity with members of the congregation.

Ritual barriers are not unique to either Muslim or Jewish rituals. At the Islamic Center and Congregation Shalom, I was in a good position to experience the exclusivity of the ritual barriers because of my relative lack of experience in those traditions. A Jewish researcher with limited experience in Protestant churches might have a similar experience when, for instance, the "blood and body of Christ" are passed around for consumption, or during an "altar call" such as the one I observed at First Baptist.[22] All organizations conduct distinct ritual practices that can automatically make the uninitiated feel some degree of exclusion. When conscious of this, organizations have a choice to (1) assimilate to their perception of what would make the "broader culture" more comfortable, (2) maintain their ritual distinctions, or (3) increase their ritual distinctions. Even those who choose (1) may not be entirely successful.[23] The logic of IR theory suggests, however, that those who choose (2) and (3) will be best positioned to host the spirit.

Barriers from Without

I have already referred a few times to the fierce barriers from without that Jews have faced throughout their history. From ancient empires in Assyria, Persia, Greece, and Rome; to medieval Europe, tsarist Russia, the French Third Republic, the Third Reich, and the Soviet Union; to America in the 21st century (where, as mentioned above, Jews are the most frequent victims of all religion hate crimes as reported by the FBI), Jews have been reviled, physically abused, subjected to pogroms, insulted, raped, tortured, murdered, and more (Cohen 1994; Levin 2001; Mann 1986, 1993; Morris 2001).

Throughout these abuses, "Israel" has symbolized God's promise of refuge. After many centuries of Diaspora, the nation-state of Israel was formed in 1948 as a haven for Jews from around the world. For many Jews, mention of "Israel" stirs deep emotions of love, loyalty, and pride. As stated in the introduction to this chapter, solidarity and conflict are correspondent, not contrary. Consistent with this, the modern state of Israel has engaged in violent conflict with surrounding territories since its inception. The Israeli-Palestinian conflict remains one of the most divisive issues in our era, and countless failed efforts to achieve peaceful resolution leave the impression that it will continue indefinitely.

Congregation Shalom's Response to Perceived Barriers

Rabbi Duane was the most polished and commanding speaker of all of the organizations in the sample. He is tall with white hair and has a deep, resonant voice. His 15-minute sermon contained moments of erudition, levity, and sadness.[24] Although he couldn't have known this, his sermon seemed tailored to fit my research question.

The subject of Rabbi Duane's sermon was how Jews should treat their enemies, based on a passage from Deuteronomy in which Israeli law is established regarding conquered armies and the spoils of war.[25] He swiftly shifted to the contemporary world and Islamic terrorism. He read aloud transcripts of two phone calls between passengers on United Flight 93 and their family members prior to the plane's crash in Pennsylvania. In doing so, Rabbi Duane enabled the audience to make an immediate emotional connection to the atrocious nature of the terrorists' attack. He posed the question, "How should we respond to such a thing?" His answer was complex and ambiguous. Bloodlust is to be avoided; however, there is sometimes just cause for fighting "evil" and "evildoers." He stated, for instance, that "We are commanded not to kill. But we are also commanded not to *be* killed." The primary impact of Rabbi Duane's sermon was to activate feelings of empathy toward victims with whom we identify (fellow Americans), and feelings of the need to defend ourselves against evildoers (Muslim terrorists).

Rabbi Duane's message can be summarized as: (1) evil is real, (2) defending ourselves against evil is important, and (3) sober justice is virtuous. Based on what I had observed in the Bar Mitzvah proceedings prior to the sermon, Rabbi Duane's message was consistent with the congregation's overall Zionist orientation. This orientation was explicit as members of the congregation spoke of their feelings about Michael, the 13-year old boy who was being honored. As his mother explained with pride, Michael "was a Zionist before he even knew what that meant." Later, a rabbi who had worked closely with Michael commented, "His dream is to be the prime minister of Israel," to which the congregation laughed appreciatively. As both Michael and his parents commented with pride, Michael planned to "join the Israeli army" when he was old enough.

Congregation Shalom possesses deep emotions related to the nation of Israel. Israel symbolizes their collective identity and their sense of what is true and good. Support for Israel also drives their morality. These good feelings are accelerated by their perception that the sacred land is threatened and must be vigorously defended.

The Impact of Congregation Shalom's Barrier Work on Effervescence and Solidarity

As stated above, Congregation Shalom held the most effervescent service in the sample. I observed tears, laughter, dancing, hugging, alert body language, and enthusiastic singing. Focus group members explained that their service left them feeling "uplifted." Because IR dynamics are interrelated in theory and practice, it is not always feasible to isolate the impact of one particular ritual dynamic by controlling for all the others. However, we can assess whether the outcomes are consistent with the hypotheses. At Congregation Shalom, direct reference to a real and imminent threat appeared to instantly stimulate feelings of excitement, togetherness, and common cause. Rabbi Duane communicated through the 9/11 phone texts that the threat is not simply something happening in a distant part of the world; Muslim terrorists attack people just like us, Americans trying to travel from one part of the country to another. He skillfully made the threat feel personal and immediate. His rhetoric made it feel natural and sensible to *do* something about the threat, especially if this could be done with sobriety and therefore without becoming bloodthirsty like our enemies.

Congregation Shalom possesses strong symbolic solidarity in their common support of Israel. The organization also is in a position of considerable power and influence. I asked the focus group about Congregation Shalom's relationship with the local community. A retired high school teacher named Mary responded, "Well, we have a former [political position of substantial influence] here, as well as several [political positions of lesser influence]."[26] Sam, a man in his 50s, added, "There are a lot of powerful people in this congregation. And a lot of money." Other comments by focus group members, as well as my own observation of clothes, accoutrements, and car models confirmed a high socioeconomic status among members. As an organization, as well, their campus and reported donations evinced substantial financial resources. I note these observations because it is unlikely that Congregation Shalom's symbolic solidarity only has symbolic effects. Politicians and the affluent are in a better position than most of the population to exert power in support of a particular cause. Members of Congregation Shalom gain EE from the congregation's sacred symbols, and this is likely to impact interaction ritual chains that extend outside the congregation, as in business, politics, and other spheres of influence.

CONCLUSION

In Randall Collins' 2011 American Sociological Association Presidential Address, he extended his conflict theory by outlining the "time dynamics of conflict." Part of what escalates intergroup conflict over time is the feedback loop of solidarity and conflict. Strong solidarity feelings make members more sensitive to threats to that solidarity, and they also improve members' ability to organize to protect their borders; external conflict stimulates solidarity by focusing attention on a common enemy that everyone feels the same about (anger and fear). As the solidarity-conflict feedback loop operates within opposing organizations, their mutual conflict escalates.

Collins added to the model an additional feedback loop that further escalates conflict over time: the "atrocities-polarization loop." He defines and elaborates on atrocities as follows:

> Atrocities are actions by the opponent that we perceive as especially hurtful and evil, a combination of physical and moral offense that we found outrageous. Atrocities generate righteous anger, an especially Durkheimian emotion, bringing about the imperative feeling that we must punish the perpetrators, not just for ourselves, but as a matter of principle (2012, 2).

Atrocities are accelerated by "ideological polarization," which he describes as follows:

> Polarization is an intensification of the Durkheimian process of identifying the group with good, and evil as what is outside the boundary of the group. . . . The enemy is evil, unprincipled, stupid, ugly, ridiculous, cowardly, and weak, negative in every respect. Our side becomes increasingly perceived as good, principled, intelligent, brave, and all the other virtues (5).

Atrocities increase ideological polarization, and ideological polarization increases the likelihood of further atrocities. The atrocities-polarization loop escalates conflict. Because the enemy is bad and because we visualize the atrocities he will commit in the future, he deserves what we will do to him. Further, because he is stupid, cowardly, and weak, we can be confident that our smart, courageous, and strong forces will be victorious over his. Of course, this works in both directions, which helps explain why some conflicts seem to persist indefinitely. Figure 5.1 models the atrocities-polarization process.

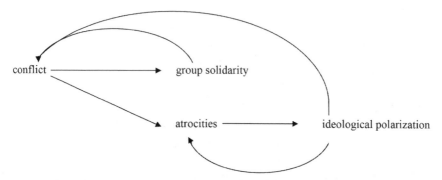

Figure 5.1.   Solidarity, Conflict, and the Atrocities-Polarization Feedback Loop
Reproduced with permission of the publisher from p. 4 of "C-Escalation and D-Escalation: A Theory of the Time-Dynamics of Conflict," American Sociological Review 77(1):1-20, by Randall Collins. ©2012 by SAGE Publications.

At the Islamic Center, there was no mention of atrocities by enemies of Islam. Omar did comment that "Everyone has difficulties with Muslims," but he did not depict these difficulties as unjust, enraging, or terrifying. Instead, he suggested to his congregation that if American Muslims were more devout, the barriers from without would decline. Whether or not Omar's prognosis was accurate is not pertinent. The point is that he did not repeat atrocities, did not promote polarization, and failed to generate strong symbolic solidarity. As Collins (2012, 15) puts it, during de-escalation of conflicts, all of the IR dynamics "go into reverse." Barriers with outsiders did not promote symbolic solidarity within the Islamic Center, nor did solidarity within the Islamic Center provide an emotional charge for further conflicts with outsiders. I indicated earlier that the Islamic Center's lack of symbolic solidarity is likely related to its marginalization in the U.S. (within "the Bible Belt," in particular) and its poor material base. Even if Omar *did* want to promote conflict with non-Muslims,[27] such efforts would likely be weak unless he were able to generate external financial support.

In contrast to the Islamic Center, Congregation Shalom repeated atrocities that stirred our emotions (the 9/11 transcripts), gave moral support to a conflict (celebrating Michael's desire to fight in the Israeli army), and performed an intense ritual that demonstrated strong symbolic solidarity. Their moral support for Israel was accompanied by the material means to do something about it. The organization possessed substantial financial resources, contained "a lot of powerful people," and was in a position to sacrifice at least one young soldier to the Israeli-Palestinian conflict.

NOTES

1. Coser's *The Functions of Social Conflict* (1956) draws on Simmel's *Conflict and the Web of Group Affiliations* (1922) to argue that social conflict promotes functionality in groups and societies. Although Coser's work assumes an overall functionalist framework that is inconsistent with the assumption of conflict in IR theory, several of Coser's specific arguments are perfectly compatible. The most relevant ideas are that conflict binds groups together (33–38), increases groups' internal cohesion (87–95), and defines group structures (95–104).

2. The more that a culture constructs an activity as deviant, the larger the barriers are likely to be for the daring few who promote or engage the activity. Deviant sexual rituals, for instance, induce large barriers that increase participants' experience of antinomian pleasure in their execution (Becker 1963; Collins 2004, 223–57).

3. Consider the outraged protests surrounding Muslims' attempts to build masjids in the decade following the World Trade Center attacks. The Ground Zero mosque is the most famous example. See O'Brien (2011) for a journalistic account of a heated conflict in response to efforts to build a masjid in Murfreesboro, Tennessee. Muslims are also regular targets of religion-based hate crimes in the U.S., although Jews continue to be the most frequent victims. Together, Jews and Muslims are by far the primary victims of hate crimes based on religion in the U.S. In 2010, for example, hate crimes against people in these two traditions comprised about 80% of the religion hate crimes tallied by the FBI (U.S. Department of Justice 2010).

4. Observations regarding these organizations' management of external conflict are not meant to be stereotyped to rituals that I did not observe, or to any trends in their broader traditions. There is enormous variety within both Islam and Judaism.

5. The following description from the Muslim apologist Abdul A'la Maududi depicts salat as a highly egalitarian ritual. Note, though, the complete absence of women from this description of ritual "fraternity":

"When possible, prayers must be performed in congregation, especially the Friday prayer. This serves to bind the Muslims together on the basis of love and mutual understanding. It arouses a tremendous sense of unity within them, and builds them into a national fraternity. All Muslims pray in one congregation and this gives them a deep feeling of brotherhood. Salat is also a symbol of equality, for the poor and the rich, the low and the high, the rulers and the ruled, the educated and the uneducated, the black and the white, all stand in one row and prostrate before the same One God (1977, 101)."

6. For a similar phenomenon in Christian worship, consider the use of Latin in some Catholic services and the archaic King James translation in a wide variety of Christian traditions. In addition to boosting cultural barriers, using unfamiliar or highly formal language helps convey a set-apart, sacred status for the occasion.

7. For some extremely devout Muslims, symbols of this cultural capital, or "religious capital" (Stark and Finke 2000), even become physically embodied in a prayer callus on the forehead. Front-and-center in face-to-face interaction, this *zebibah* serves as a constant reminder to others of the devout person's regular practice of pressing his head against hard surfaces during salat.

8. This would have posed a methodological problem. Especially since the number of participants was small, and because my proficiency with raka'ah is novice at best, my participation could have skewed the results. In the other participant observations, larger numbers and greater personal familiarity with the practices allowed me to blend in more.

9. These include: atheists, homosexuals, conservative Christians, recent immigrants, Hispanics, Jews, Asian Americans, African Americans, and white Americans.

10. This shared barrier from without also may be a source of accord between different Islamic traditions in the U.S. The Islamic Center is Sunni, but members of the focus group adamantly emphasized their solidarity with all Muslims.

11. Muslim organizations often present the khutba as two separate sermons. The first is longer, whereas the second is brief and prompts salat.

12. Compare this comment with Father Felix's mention of TV at St. John's in Chapter 3. In both cases, the speakers referenced television in order to remind their listeners of immanent evil and danger. In neither case did the speakers elaborate how TV communicates these threats; perhaps they meant the atrocities constantly repeated in news shows. Consider also Pastor Craig's sermon at First Baptist (Chapter 2), where relief from social media consumption was considered consistent with Christ-like behavior. So many references to media in this study's small sample suggest that "the media" is a poignant symbol for American religious organizations.

13. His observation is consistent with Reza Aslan's (2006) summary of Islam's historical and ongoing conflicts over designating legitimate sources of religious authority. Aslan argues that the rise of the internet has contributed to a decline in the authority of the Ulama, the loose community of elite clerics and scholars who historically have had the most influence over Muslim orthodoxy and orthopraxy. Online, anyone who calls himself an imam can, to some extent, function as such. This not only makes allegiance to radical ideas more likely, but it also exacerbates the confusion over identifying legitimate sources of authority.

14. This type of response may be common not just in Muslim organizations, but in any religious group who is perceived as too "foreign" in the predominantly Christian context of the U.S. Chen (2002) studied a California Buddhist temple whose members were mostly Taiwanese immigrants. The temple experienced tension with local community members who had unfounded fears of a "religious cult" performing animal sacrifices. Chen shows how, in response, the temple is highly active in local interfaith events and conspicuously displays an American flag on its campus.

15. An addendum that can be applied to strictness theory is that strictness is often enforced in a gentle or gracious manner. The focus group indicated their sensitivity to the difficulty of scheduling Jum'ah into hectic daily lives. A focus group member named Antoine explained the process of checking up on members as follows:

"If you look around and see someone's not there, we call and see how they're doing. 'Everything alright, man? How you holdin' up?' And that feels good. I was gone from the last three Jum'ahs, and one of my brothers called me. It feels good to know we're looking out for each other. It's a cold world out there, and no one seems to know each other. But I know these guys and we look out for each other."

16. Recall that the Islamic Center did, however, achieve a few moments of moderate effervescence by drawing on the resource of raka'ah and rearranging the location and orientation of bodies within the room. Their barriers involving raka'ah proficiency assisted in making this process feel special, thus helping to stimulate effervescence.

17. See Figures A.6 and A.7.

18. Hoffman and Bartkowski also argue that biblical literalism empowers conservative Christian women by allowing them to appeal to "God's Word," and not a male intermediary, in discussions of biblical interpretation. However, their *need* to appeal to a higher authority than men further illustrates their default subordinate status in conservative congregations.

19. See Stark (1996).

20. As Davidman (1991) shows, some otherwise very modern women opt for religious subordination in order to find "tradition in a rootless world."

21. In supplementary analysis of USCLS data, I examined whether the gender distribution within congregations has a relationship with effervescence or solidarity. This approach unfortunately cannot tell us anything about whether the women in these congregations are segregated during worship, but it nonetheless conveys a general sense of how more or less involvement from women can affect a congregation's rituals.

The USCLS sample contains one all-female Methodist congregation (who report above-average scores on effervescence and both types of solidarity), and no all-male congregations. Consistent with other research on religion and gender, women are *much* more highly represented in U.S. congregations, with 317/324 congregations (98%) reporting majority female memberships. Bivariate analysis indicates that higher proportions of women slightly improve congregations' effervescence scores, but this relationship becomes nonsignificant in multivariate models. The percentage of women in a congregation bears no significant relationship with symbolic solidarity in bivariate or multivariate models. However, the percentage of women appears to *strongly* shape a congregation's membership solidarity, with a robust positive relationship at both bivariate and multivariate levels of analysis. In short, the USCLS data indicate that congregations with more involvement from women are likely to experience somewhat more effervescence in worship, and substantially higher levels of membership solidarity.

22. Chafets (2007) and Pinsky (2006) provide funny and illuminating accounts of Jewish journalists writing about their experimental forays into evangelical subcultures.

23. Consider evangelical megachurches, who typically design their rituals with the aim of anticipating and serving broad consumer demand (Chaves 2006; Thumma and Travis 2007; Warren 1995). This strategy has been productive over the last three decades, and Thumma and Travis show that if all American megachurch members were combined into a single tradition, they would represent the third largest religious tradition in the country (1). Thumma and Travis also point out, though, that the megachurch strategy has earned numerous critics who consider megachurch rituals strange or even threatening.

24. Pastor Dave at Promised Land Baptist Church (Chapters 2 and 4) was also a charismatic speaker, and I consider Congregation Shalom and Promised Land to have held the most effervescent rituals in the sample. The impact of preaching style on ritual outcomes is mostly an issue of focus of attention and shared emotions (intersubjectivity).

25. Here is one excerpt:

> When you go out to war against your enemies, and the Lord your God delivers them into your hand, and you take them captive, and you see among the captives a beautiful woman, and desire her and would take her for your wife, then you shall bring her home to your house, and she shall shave her head and trim her nails. She shall put off the clothes of her captivity, remain in your house, and mourn her father and her mother a full month; after that you may go in to her and be her husband, and she shall be your wife. And it shall be, if you have no delight in her, then you shall set her free, but you certainly shall not sell her for money; you shall not treat her brutally, because you have humbled her (Deuteronomy 21: 10–14).

26. The specific political positions are withheld to preserve the organization's anonymity.

27. Omar never gave any such impression, either in personal conversation or during his khutba.

Conclusion

Religion, it is safe to say, is complex and multifaceted. Rather than trying to grasp or express the entire phenomenon all at once, sociologists of religion use analytical categories that distill it into its different facets, the different "dimensions of religiosity" (Stark and Glock 1968). These typically include *practice, belief, identity,* and *experience.*[1]

This book has focused on the dimension of religiosity that Émile Durkheim considered foundational to all the rest: practice. A prevailing assumption in popular and scholarly discourse on religion is that practices are the consequences of underlying belief systems. This book proposes flipping that formula. Without ritual practices and the emotional force they alone can generate, we would be incapable of religious beliefs, identities, or experiences. Further, the little details of ritual practice have profound consequences for how congregations and individuals imagine and engage with the world around them. These insights have far-reaching implications for theory and research on religion.

This chapter considers a number of related areas of investigation in the sociology of religion, and proposes ways to link these with research on religious interaction rituals. A section on the dimension of *beliefs* will consider Max Weber's views on the origin and purpose of religion, along with contemporary research that extends Weber's insights regarding images of God. A section on *identity* will consider the rational choice theory of religion. Rational choice theory strongly emphasizes beliefs, but its most influential arguments—regarding organizational strictness and the church-sect cycle—ultimately pertain more to religious identity. Finally, a section on *experience* will focus on ideas from William James, along with, again, more recent research that has extended his insights in new directions. This chapter's final section will focus on the broader issue of social conflict. Before considering

each dimension separately, it will be helpful to articulate a big-picture model
of how they fit together based on this book's theory of rituals.

RITUAL PRACTICE AND THE PRODUCTION OF HUMANS, FUNCTIONAL RELIGIOUSNESS, AND RELIGION

Here is a model for how religious rituals transform individuals and cultures:

First, we are creatures who *ritualize*. Prior to human reason, prior to morals
and civilization, prior to myths and ideologies, we are animals with distinctive sorts of adaptive behaviors. Specifically, when we get together, we have
a unique collective ability to coordinate our sounds and movements in a way
that generates a shared feeling, a force that we cannot feel when we're alone.
Practitioners frequently interpret this feeling as a religious *experience*. The
most important thing about this feeling is that it feels coercive, authoritative,
and undeniably *real*.

When we succeed at achieving it, this feeling does several things for us and
to us. Most fundamentally, the feeling of force turns us into humans, because
it gives us the sensation necessary to share, as we do, a small set of universal
laws for reasoning together, which allow us to be mutually intelligible to
each other, and which philosophers call "the categories of the understanding."
These frameworks for rational thought, of which Durkheim identified six, ultimately refer to social relationships. The first of these is *classification*, as the
force generated in ritual compels us to respect an absolute moral distinction
between things sacred and profane. We also pick up the categories of *force*,
and of *causality*, because our shared practices around sacred objects instigate
an effect that we can feel—an intense emotional encounter that transforms
our consciousnesses and even, at times, our physical surroundings. We learn
to think in terms of *totality* because the force allows us to see that there is a
world of things outside the individual consciousness; we come to see society
as a "whole" that encompasses the discrete elements (individuals) within it,
and we can only feel this whole because of effervescent rituals. Last, the categories of *time* and *space* depend on moral forces that compel us to be in the
right place at the right time, sacralizing some moments and locations while
treating others as merely mundane.

These frameworks for thinking that make it possible for us to reason together also make it possible for us to moralize together, to designate right
and wrong according to collective, more objective standards rather than
individuals' subjective egoistic preferences. We become able to realize that
desecrations of the sacred are absolutely unallowable and even worthy of

punishment. We correctly sense that human civilization depends on the creation and recreation of a moral society, which means respecting sacred things.

So far, the model I am describing deals with the *foundations* of human knowledge and morality. In other words, it deals with epistemology rather than the sociology of knowledge. In this foundational sense, rituals make us *functionally* religious—"religious" in a Durkheimian sense—because the feeling of coercive sacred force jolts us out of individual perception and into a larger moral and rational universe that we call society. Atheists and agnostics are "religious" in this sense, too.[2] Any claim to truth or moral authority ultimately depends on a special awareness of a power that is compelling enough to override the individual's own moment-to-moment perceptions and preferences.

Moving past this universal framework for thought, though, we are confronted with the obvious fact that humans do not all think the same things. The sociology of knowledge begins with the observation that *different groups create different sacred objects*, and different sets of rules for how to respect them. The fact that we all create sacred objects gives us the ability to think in the fundamental ways that humans think. The fact that different groups create different sacred objects leads to all of the diversity of human thought across cultures.

Thus, in addition to making all of us "*religious*," the feeling of force produced in rituals also leads most of us to *religions*. I mean *religions* here in a substantive sense: participation and membership in officially religious organizations, assent to prescribed doctrines regarding the supernatural, and adherence to attendant norms of piety that develop over time in specific cultures. A culture's stock of sacred symbols multiplies as they expand their repertoire of rituals, as do their sets of rules for showing due reverence to the symbols. When "priests" are designated to run the cult, the priests tend to expand the objects and rules into elaborate religions, if the cult survives long enough. Cults that survive a long time expand into religious traditions.

A given culture's stock of sacred objects, and the words and pictures that signify the objects, are equivalent to Durkheim's "collective representations." The representations are ideas and *beliefs*, and a great deal of sociological scholarship since Durkheim has been devoted to ascertaining their various consequences. This "idealist" approach has been quite valuable, and much of the research cited in this book, as well as the present study itself, confirms that ideas certainly have consequences of their own. For example, we find that they circulate back to the ritual and influence its practices, as when individualism inspires shorter services.

Collective representations also serve as the basis of *identity*. By backing away from the usual focus on the ideas themselves, and instead seeking their origins in ritual practices, we can learn to recognize the energies that bind us to some and repel us from others.[3] Since the same practices that make us human and rational and civil also give rise to our culturally specific sacred symbols, threats to these symbols can feel like threats to one's basic sense of reality, and to all that is pure and good. Ironically, though, *my* group gains a better sense of how exactly to identify ourselves by actively distinguishing our own sacred symbols from other groups' sacred symbols, especially in highly pluralistic contexts, and this is easiest to accomplish when we denigrate *their* symbols. After all, no member of their group would do such a thing; my disrespect certifies my distinct identity. Thus, barriers to outsiders become a routine and important feature of my group's practices, as if saying to each other, "To stay really clear about who we are and why we are special, let's always be sure to define ourselves in opposition to those who are clearly *not* us, and who are not as special." Forging a religious identity relies more on negation than affirmation. The more we negate *them*, the more we become recognizable to ourselves.

In sum, then, ritual practices are responsible for human morality and civilization in the broadest sense, but also for the particular rules, ideologies, and identities that make up a given culture, including its alliances and conflicts. Religious practice generates a religious experience. Religious beliefs are retrospective attempts to conceptualize and preserve both the practice and the experience. Religious identity is the feeling of allegiance to symbols made sacred in one's own collective practices, consequentially propelling the individual toward her own group's rituals while repelling her from others'.

We can now consider beliefs, identity, and experience in turn. There are several promising openings to synthesize arguments and let different research traditions inform each other.

RELIGIOUS BELIEFS

Religious beliefs are collective representations of one's group, sacred symbols in the form of articulable assertions about reality. Any *allegiance* to a particular belief depends entirely on an experience of emotional force emanating from shared practices. Beyond this, though, higher levels of *certainty* or *confidence* in the belief depend on the intensity and frequency of one's participation in successful IRs that treat the belief as sacred.

Max Weber and the Naturalistic Origins of Religion

Weber's *Sociology of Religion* (1922b) in many ways appears to challenge the basic assertions of Durkheim's theory of religion. Most notably, Weber understands religion as a phenomenon that is fundamentally about *beliefs*. Also, compared with Durkheim, Weber wrote much less about rituals per se. When he did consider "rites," his interest was mostly in how they are instituted and controlled by cults of priests, how these priests thereby seize power and status, and how the cults evolve over time into major religious traditions which, in turn, shape cultures and economies. Religious beliefs have sometimes altered the course of history, as in Weber's famous argument that Reformation doctrines regarding predestination and vocation opened the door to the world-transforming forces of rational capitalism (Weber 1904). Weber's entire method is based on analysis of concepts, "ideal types," and how these concepts determine different trajectories for humans' actions.

Like Durkheim, though, Weber also offers a naturalistic explanation of the origins of religion, and it points to ecstatic rituals. Weber does this at the very beginning of *The Sociology of Religion,* and it is here—in the earliest pages of the book—that the usual dividing line between the two theorists becomes much fuzzier. It is also true that, two chapters later, Weber writes that it is a "tremendous exaggeration" to attribute all religion to totemism (434). Weber was mostly interested in totemism insofar as it influences cultural taboos regarding trade and kinship. But the fact that Weber downplays the role of totemism does not mean that his theory of religion is entirely at odds with Durkheim's. Consider the following arguments expressed by Weber in the eight paragraphs that open *The Sociology of Religion* (399–402).

- In the book's first two paragraphs, Weber asserts that he will not try to define religion. Rather, we must examine religious behaviors (i.e., practices) and seek to understand their meaning to people who perform them.
- The third paragraph states that the most "elementary" forms of religious behavior are motivated by this-worldly concerns. Weber proceeds to describe religious rituals,[4] which rationalistically try to secure some sort of benefit for those who enact them.
- The fourth and fifth paragraphs introduce his concept of "charisma," an "extraordinary power" which only certain people and objects possess. He notes that charisma is understood as part of the essence of these people and objects, although sometimes "dormant" charisma needs to be "evoked" by certain practices. His description of charisma thus has substantial overlap with Durkheim's descriptions of "sacred" objects and persons, although Weber takes a weaker position regarding whether practice is always necessary to produce this power (while still acknowledging that practice often does produce this power).
- In the sixth paragraph, then, Weber considers how people explain charismatic power. To what do they attribute it? It is here that Weber introduces

the idea of "spirit." His arguments here are obviously relevant to the current project, and are worth quoting in full:

> A process of abstraction, which only appears to be simple, has usually already been carried out in the most primitive instances of religious behavior which we examine. Already crystallized is the notion that certain beings are concealed "behind" and responsible for the activity of the charismatically endowed natural objects, artifacts, animals, or persons. This is the belief in spirits. At the outset, "spirit" is neither soul, demon, nor god, but something indeterminate, material yet invisible, nonpersonal and yet somehow endowed with volition. By entering into a concrete object, spirit endows the latter with its distinctive power. The spirit may depart from its host or vessel, leaving the latter inoperative and causing the magician's charisma to fail. In other cases, the spirit may diminish into nothingness, or it may enter into another person or thing (401).

Here, Weber claims that charisma is attributed to "spirit" and "spirits." Further, the spirit seemingly can come and go, causing charisma to fail when it departs.
• How would people recognize, though, whether the magician's charisma has become inoperative? This becomes clear in the book's 7th and 8th paragraphs, where Weber compares magicians' and laities' respective abilities to access charisma. How is charisma accessed?

> [The magician] has turned into an "enterprise" the distinctive subjective condition that notably represents or mediates charisma, namely ecstasy.... [E]cstasy occurs in a social form, the orgy, which is the primordial form of communal religious association (401).

Remarkably, Weber here identifies the "condition" that "mediates" charisma, and it is the same condition that mediates the sacred in Durkheim's work: ecstatic ritual. Weber goes on to explain that drugs, alcohol, and especially music are key ingredients of "the magician's art."

After these initial arguments regarding the elementary forms of religious life, Weber proceeds to unfold a theory of the emergence of souls, gods, and eventually major world religions. Without a doubt, these later developments are Weber's primary interest, in contrast to Durkheim whose obsession with the naturalistic origins of religion is obvious throughout *The Elementary Forms*. Weber returns to discussions of rites and spirits at various points, but he is mostly concerned with the consequences of various religious *beliefs*, especially insofar as they promote or discourage the emergence of rational capitalism.

What we ultimately find, then, is that although Durkheim and Weber had rather different research agendas in the sociology of religion, and although they had different views on the significance of totemism per se, their positions on the experiential origins of religion are really quite similar. Humans experience a power or force when they engage in ecstatic practices, and then attribute the force to spirits and—as a later historical development—to gods.

The two theorists' perspectives on the consequential nature of religious beliefs are also quite similar. Along with Weber, Durkheim considered religious beliefs, or "collective representations," to have major consequences of their own. For example, Durkheim (1897) famously argued that a Protestant belief in individualism was responsible for high suicide rates in dominantly Protestant societies. Likewise, for Durkheim, the belief that an object is taboo, or that a given person is a deviant, will affect how people engage with that object or person. But Protestants would not be individualists, objects would not be taboo, and persons would not be deviant unless ritual practices and the resulting emotional certainty had established such convictions as fact.

Unfortunately for Durkheim's legacy, though, he declined to recognize the influence of one particular type of religious belief that Weber definitely did not overlook, and which appears to be more consequential than any other: individuals' and cultures' images of God.

Images of God

"Images of God," or "God concepts," are humans' subjective, symbolic impressions of God's nature and personality. They function as foundational ontologies and basic theologies that impact how humans interpret and respond to the world around them.[5]

Images of God get at the core of what religion subjectively "means" to people, and as such are a quintessential Weberian theme. The idea that different ways of conceiving God fashion different sorts of cultures frames much of his work on religion. In fact, in *The Sociology of Religion*, Weber begins to consider the origins and consequences of different God concepts only one paragraph after the paragraphs I summarized above regarding religion's origins (402). He writes, for example, that gods might be more or less personified, or associated with different forces of nature (e.g., with death, birth, or fire). They might be male or female, deceitful or trustworthy, strong or weak, etc. They can be hero gods who bring success in battle, fertility gods who bless wombs and harvests, gods who can be coerced or cajoled through sacrifice, and so on, as the theme persists throughout his book.

To Weber, all of these concepts matter, but one image of God in particular severely shifted the course of human history: the Hebrews' innovation of One True God who rules over all of creation, and whose moral laws apply to all humans everywhere.[6] Through the efforts of Hebrew prophets and, later,

Christian missionaries, this conception of an all-seeing, all-powerful God prepared the ground for universalistic ethics, which to Weber were a necessary condition for the eruption of rational capitalism (also see Bendix 1960; Collins 1986; Weber 1917–1919, and Weber 1923).

A Weberian focus on God concepts resurfaced in American social science in the early 1960s, and ever since researchers have completed hundreds of studies that collectively attest to the conclusion that one's mental picture of "God" is immensely consequential. The psychologist Bernard Spilka and his colleagues (1964) launched much of the empirical work that would follow by asking 500 people to respond to the question, "What does God mean to you?" Analysis of their responses yielded about 10 factors that summarize major patterns in how individuals describe God.[7] Subsequently, numerous studies have shown strong independent relationships between images of God and an impressive range of other attitudes, behaviors, and ideologies.

The effects are wide-ranging, with, for example, "authoritarian"[8] images of God predicting punitive ideologies about justice (Bader et al. 2010), intolerance toward gays and lesbians (Froese et al. 2008), and a general lack of trust in other people (Mencken et al. 2009). Thompson and Froese (2017) show that authoritarian God concepts override even one's political party affiliation in shaping opinions about the death penalty, fighting terrorism, and U.S. military policy. More "loving" images of God, by contrast, correlate with marital happiness (Greeley 1996), support for environmental causes (Greeley 1993), civic engagement (Mencken and Fitz 2013), and a long list of mental health benefits (Bradshaw et al. 2008; Ellison et al. 2014: Sharp 2010; Stroope et al. 2013). Whitehead (2012) demonstrates that God's imagined gender has powerful consequences, as well, and that construing God as a "he" makes patriarchal gender ideologies more likely.

Throughout this sizable body of scholarship, Émile Durkheim's name hardly ever comes up. Given his iconic status in the discipline, the omission seems odd. But there is a good reason for it: Durkheim claimed that the study of gods is tangential to the sociology of religion. Rodney Stark has drawn much attention to Durkheim's claim, citing an early-career review of a book by Herbert Spencer in which Durkheim states that the idea of God is "no more than a minor accident" in the historical progress of religion (Durkheim 1886, 19; Stark 2001a, 2003).

This statement by Durkheim seems to border on the ridiculous. And yet, he was hardly a lazy thinker, and it is important to keep in mind the academic context in which he was writing. Durkheim was working to establish sociology as a viable discipline with a unique field of investigation. He had already argued that "social facts"—inescapable collective forces—are the proper domain for sociologists. Social scientists cannot study God, but they can study the social forces that compel certain behaviors, including moral behaviors. These forces are found not only in theistic religions, but also in nontheistic religions such as Taoism and some versions of Buddhism, and even in purely secular social movements. Durkheim's great discovery, already evident in his early work although not fully worked out, was that these social forces are none other than ritual practices that generate sacred feelings. Stark's great discovery regarding God concepts' impacts on cultures should also be kept in context: a century of scholarship in which sociologists, influenced by Durkheim, were far too hesitant to focus closely on the social significance of gods.

This chasm between Durkheimian theory and Weberian/Starkian research on God images is totally unnecessary. In fact, Durkheim's theory of religion provides God image research with the missing link. What is needed is an adjustment in our conception of where these images come from. Sociologists have produced much fascinating work on image of God *outcomes*, but often leave the search for their *sources* up to psychologists of religion. Psychologists of religion, in turn, have most often drawn upon either "object relations theory" or "attachment theory" to explain how God concepts develop. Both of these theories point to early childhood, when parents bequeath God images through processes such as modeling, socialization, and style of discipline (Rizzuto 1974; Kirkpatrick 1992; Meissner 1984; Vergote et al. 1969). The images which develop in childhood can be amended, though, as the child leaves the home and meets new people, for example if he goes to college, gets married, or converts to a new religion (Meissner 1984; St. Clair 2004; Vergote 1969). In other words, psychologists of religion have been demonstrating for decades that images of God depend on *social interactions*, on *interaction rituals*.

Images of God, then, are symbols made sacred through ritual practice. As such, the part they should play in Durkheim's theory of religion becomes more apparent. Initially, images of God are literal images—the totems. When the totems are internalized by individuals, they become God *concepts*, Weberian meanings that direct the individuals' actions. Given their well-documented, powerful independent influence on a wide range of other attitudes, behaviors, and beliefs, they are even the preeminent sacred symbols of religious life. No other religious belief has been shown to wield such widespread and consistent influence on humans' subjective experience of the world. They are the most important symbolic content in most religions worldwide, and yet this is not to say that they are the foundational essence of what religion is. Rather, they are second-order phenomena, collective representations made sacred through the first-order phenomenon of feeling the spirit. Stark acknowledges that ritual is important in boosting an "individual's confidence in religious explanations"

(2001b; 177–78), but this falls short of Durkheim's point that without ritual effervescence, we would not feel supernatural power, and so would never believe or have confidence in any gods at all.

RELIGIOUS IDENTITY

Religious identity, like religious belief, is based on the collective representations of one's group. These two dimensions of religiosity are closely entwined. Symbolic solidarity is recognizable in shared ways of talking, including the repetition of words and phrases that define reality. Allegiance to a particular religious tradition means allegiance to my people and their version of reality, both of which depend on the emotional bonds produced in ritual.

Rational Choices and Organizational Strictness

Rational choice theory is widely applied in the sociology of religion. Stark and Bainbridge (1987) initiated much of this work by building a formal, deductive theory of religion based on a few main assumptions. Citing its use in exchange theory, learning theory, and microeconomics, they state the fundamental axiom as follows: "Humans seek what they perceive to be rewards and avoid what they perceive to be costs" (27).[9] At an elemental level, they argue, religion is a means by which humans promote their own interests. Building on this, they propose that humans seek explanations of how to obtain rewards and avoid costs. Religion, they argue, is a system of general explanations of existence that are based on supernatural assumptions (39). As a key example, religions often provide explanations of what will happen once we die. It is a "rational" choice to pay costs in the form of personal sacrifices and other forms of devotion if one has cause to believe that paying these costs will secure rewards such as eternal life. Devoting oneself to a religion is also "rational" from the perspective of a person's psychological well-being, especially if the religion's general explanations provide a degree of comfort in the face of mortality. As another example, mentioned above, Stark (2001b) argues that it is a rational choice to devote oneself to One True God who is rational, responsive, dependable, powerful, and who demands an exclusive exchange relationship.

The rational choice theory of religion explicitly posits individual-level beliefs as the foundation of what it means to be religious (Stark and Finke 2000, 92). However, its most influential and well-supported arguments actually pertain more to religious identity, not at the level of the individual, but at the level of organizations. For example, Stark's "One True God" argument helps explain the rapid historical growth of Christian organizations; this type of God will hold the greatest appeal to the most people, and thus will have a strong "market niche" in "religious economies." Organizational research in the rational choice school focuses largely on organizations' tension within broader cultures, the church-sect cycle, and organizational vitality (Iannaccone 1994; Stark and Finke 2000; Finke and Stark 2005). All of these arguments are about religious affiliation, or what is usually meant by "religious identity." Even for those who claim to be "spiritual but not religious" or "believing but not belonging," they are claiming an identity via a *rejection* of formal religious affiliation (Davie 1994; Hout and Fischer 2002).

Rational choice theory has considerable overlap with IR theory (Baker 2010; Barone 2007; Collins 2004). Rational choice theory's insistence on "methodological individualism" is obviously at odds with IR theory's insistence on the causal efficacy of the social situation, but the two theories nonetheless paint a similar picture of individual-level motivations: humans seek to maximize their rewards and minimize their costs.

One of the biggest challenges in rational choice theory, though, is determining what exactly represents "increased value" to actors. Which *kind* of reward needs to be maximized? As originally applied in economics, the answer to this question was easy: money. Individuals want to improve their financial assets and minimize their financial debts. When applying the theory to religious motivations, though, it becomes obvious that other sources of value are also involved, and often will even override financial motivations (as when someone donates their wealth to a religious cause).

Interaction ritual theory offers a solution to the problem of determining value in rational choice theory, and the solution can be generalized to all types of IRs: Individuals constantly pursue emotional energy. Rituals that boost EE are highly valuable, and rituals that deplete EE take something of great value away.[10] *Emotional energy calculation* is the primary factor that determines the tradition, denomination, and house of worship with which individuals will choose to identify.[11] This has many implications for rational choice research. For example, on the "demand side" of religious economies, microlevel analysis could focus on the IR chains that prime individuals to seek EE in certain types of organizations rather than others. On the "supply side," researchers could consider the extent to which leaders' proficiency with the IR dynamics shapes their product and ability to win customers.

Interaction ritual theory is also pertinent to rational choice arguments regarding organizational strictness. Iannaccone's (1994) argument is that "strictness"—organizational rules for practice (e.g., regarding clothes, diet, leisure time, or sexuality) by which the devout express their separate and distinctive religious lifestyles—strengthens organizations by discouraging the resource-wasting involvement of "free riders." As an organization's costs of membership increase, the average level of commitment in a congregation will automatically trend upward (Baker 2010). This is very close to the idea that barriers to outsiders stimulate organizational solidarity. In this project, I considered different types of barriers that stimulate solidarity in different ways. Strictness is one type of barrier, specifically involving congregational rules and proscriptions. Expectations of ritual proficiency, as at the Islamic Center and the Meditation Center, work in the same fashion; they either weed out novices or inspire them to work hard and fast to become experts.[12] Those who neglect mastery of the practices and thus free ride indefinitely will not be able to secure enough cultural capital to experience the heights of emotional intensity achieved by their congregations. Many of these will leave of their own accord and seek EE maximization elsewhere. Those who stay, though, will weaken their congregation's level of solidarity. Congregations for whom free riders do not sound an alarm will grow weaker with time. Congregations who are able to perceive and communicate to each other a resulting weakening of spirit will find ways, subtle or not, to let the free riders know that they are no longer welcome (Nelson 2005).

Symbolic Boundaries and Subcultural Identity

The barriers hypothesis is also relevant to comparable religious identity research outside of rational choice theory, including research on "symbolic boundaries" and "subcultural identity." As was the case with strictness theory, these concepts overlap significantly with the barriers hypothesis, but nonetheless have different emphases.

"Symbolic boundaries" are a common focus in studies of religion (Draper and Park 2010; Edgell et al. 2006; Lamont 2000; Park and Baker 2007). Symbolic boundaries are "the lines that include and define some people, groups, and things while excluding others . . . expressed through normative interdictions (taboos), cultural attitudes and practices, and patterns of likes and dislikes" (Lamont et al. 2015, 850). The concept of symbolic boundaries is quite broad, as it summarizes similar findings from a range of different social science disciplines (Lamont and Molnar 2002). Barriers to outsiders, organizational strictness, and subcultural identity can all be subsumed under the large conceptual umbrella of symbolic boundaries.

Also comparable to the barriers hypothesis, Smith et al.'s (1998) subcultural identity theory proposes that subcultures thrive when they respond to perceived embattlement from hostile outsiders. They propose the following regarding a religion's "strength":

> In a pluralistic society, those religious groups will be relatively stronger which better possess and employ the cultural tools needed to create both clear distinc-

tion from and significant engagement and tension with other relevant outgroups, short of becoming genuinely countercultural (118–19).

Again, this is quite similar to strictness, barriers, and boundaries. Smith and colleagues point out that their theory is complementary to rational choice theory, but rephrased in the language of cultural sociology which the authors consider more tasteful than the economic verbiage typical of rational choice research (118). Subcultural identity theory adds an important emphasis, though, which is that embattlement must be accompanied by engagement with relevant outgroups in order to strengthen religious organizations. It is not enough to *be embattled*; rather, congregations must successfully *communicate embattlement* to each other. In order to do this, they will need effective ritual practices that convey this picture of reality, which may or may not have anything to do with the actual viewpoints or intentions of outsiders.

Barriers to outsiders, like the other concepts just described, refer to identity formation by means of exclusion. The difference is that barriers, themselves, are posited as a basic element of IR practice; the concept draws attention to people actively communicating exclusivity as part of their larger effort to collectively effervesce. The current research has shown that there are many different types of barriers that can help achieve this goal. Barriers can be built from within or imposed from without; in either case the important thing is that the congregation perceives and communicates them. They can be physical or purely symbolic. They can involve expectations of ritual proficiency, or the recitation of atrocities committed by a perceived enemy. In some cases, the enemy's identity might be cloaked by reference to an idea, such as the idea of "diversity," or reference to a mythological being such as "Satan." Rational choice theory's concept of organizational strictness expresses one of the many mechanisms by which barriers promote solidarity. Subcultural identity theory draws attention to the need for perception of and engagement with outgroups. "Symbolic boundaries" is a more general way to refer to all of these arguments.

Organizational Vitality vs. Size of Tradition

Reflecting back on the findings from Chapters 2 and 4, it seems a little strange that First Baptist and St. John's, the two organizations from the sample who belong to two of the *most* popular American religious traditions,[13] were among the *least* successful at capturing the spirit. How could this be? Does this contradict the idea that those most adept at capturing the spirit will be the most influential organizations? If the pursuit of EE is such a basic human drive, why are so many Americans drawn to evangelical and Catholic churches?

It is important to recall that it would be a methodological sin to use this study's qualitative observations to make inferences about their broader religious traditions. To do so convincingly, a much larger sample would be needed. Any ritual in the current sample could be an aberration of trends in its larger tradition. Still, if we allow the conjecture that these rituals accurately represent at least some trends in their broader traditions, a few explanations help solve the seeming discrepancy.

First, it is only an irony, not a logical inconsistency, that organizations within more culturally prominent American religious traditions often have lower levels of vitality than those in more culturally marginal traditions. *Vitality* and *size* are distinct concepts. In fact, IR theory suggests that we should expect a generally *inverse* relationship between a tradition's size and vitality, as long as their rituals can muster sufficient levels of bodily copresence. This is because higher barriers (often experienced in smaller traditions) are expected to promote the spirit, and lower barriers (often experienced in larger traditions) are expected to impede it. Complicating the issue, it is the perception of barriers that matters more than their actual size, so prominent and influential traditions can nonetheless thrive as long as they are adept at imagining outgroups and enemies (Smith et al. 1998).

It turns out that an inverse relationship between prominence and vitality is actually a well-documented historical pattern in religious traditions. This "sect-church cycle" has been observed by numerous scholars, including Weber (1922b), Niebuhr (1929), Troeltsch (1932), and Johnson (1963). "Sect" and "church," in these cases, are theoretical concepts meant to summarize how much tension a religious organization experiences with the culture that surrounds them. The sect-church cycle was perhaps best documented in recent years in Finke and Stark's *The Churching of America* (2005). This populist rendering of American religious history makes the case that the "upstart sects" (especially Baptists and Methodists) came to dominate the American religious market at the expense of the rich and powerful "mainline churches" (especially Episcopalians and Congregationalists) *because of* rather than *in spite of* the upstarts' marginalized status. Put briefly, the small "sects" who initially experienced a greater level of tension with the surrounding culture were forced to innovate, work overtime, and emphasize otherworldly rewards in order to win adherents. For those sects who were able to survive an initial period of high tension, these attributes helped them grow into "churches" with relatively uncontroversial practices and beliefs.

The sect-church cycle can be understood as an organization-level secularization theory. As their number of adherents grows, as leaders and members begin to sense their potential for power and influence, religious organizations inevitably water down their distinctiveness and compromise early principles that many feel they have outgrown. Internal conflict over perceived compromise coupled with an increasingly bland "product" weakens the organization, and its members find that their passions have dulled. The sect has become a church. Inevitably, some of the members will object to the worldly direction their tradition is taking and appeal to their earlier high-tension principles. These prophetic figures will often part ways with the tradition and start a new sect, initiating the cycle all over again.

Evangelicals, in particular, haven't exactly avoided cultural tension in recent decades, evident for example in ongoing debates over abortion, gay rights, and the teaching of evolution in public schools. As suggested in Chapter 2, though, the time may be fast approaching when the evangelical tradition as a whole is better understood as a "church" than a "sect." Religious traditions are ambitious analytical constructs rather than monolithic categories, and different evangelical organizations will continue to occupy different points on the tension spectrum. More research is needed, though, to test church-sect theory's implicit hypothesis that a growing proportion of evangelical denominations and congregations are better characterized as inoffensive, moderate, relatively world-affirming, and short on vitality. First Baptist's avoidance of barriers, along with their low effervescence, is consistent with this hypothesis. In short, First Baptist is more representative of a moderate and church-like direction for evangelicalism than of the tradition's often-controversial sectarian past. Evangelical Protestants, in other words, may not be embattled and thriving indefinitely.

There is a second explanation, though, for the discrepancy between organizational and traditional vitality that was evident at times in this research: organizations' main worship services are not always their main source of effervescence. This research was limited to organizations' main gatherings, such as Mass and Jum'ah, but these are not the only rituals in which members participate. For example, research on evangelical churches shows the growing prevalence of Small Groups (Bielo 2009; Dougherty and Whitehead 2011; Whitehead 2010; Wuthnow 1994). Bible study groups, prayer teams, men's groups, etc. also hold IRs, and these can be analyzed much as I've done here (Inbody 2015). These types of activities provide alternate opportunities for effervescence and solidarity, and in many cases they may even serve as members' primary source of EE.[14] Support for this interpretation was evident among the Muslims in this study as they discussed their Ramadan celebrations. As Fawaz explained, the nightly breaking of the fast (called the "iftar") is a peak moment of solidarity for the Islamic Center, as it is for countless Muslim organizations worldwide (Aslan 2006). Perhaps not incidentally, Ramadan is a time when the female members become more equal co-participants in the ritual. Such alternate sources of EE may be one reason why the Islamic Center continues to meet despite low-effervescence Jum'ah services. Comparable to the Islamic Center, St. John's fostered more membership solidarity during the IR anticipating their Mass than during the Mass itself, and the focus group described a range of solidarity-building parish activities. Promised Land and First Baptist hold Sunday School and other community events, as does the Meditation Center (e.g., Zen archery classes and new member training).

These sorts of relatively informal religious IRs will more often capture the spirit than the more formal rituals held on Sunday mornings, Saturday mornings, and Friday afternoons. Informal rituals should make it easier to ease into effervescence because they provide more opportunities for "backstage interaction" (Collins 2004; Goffman 1959), and thus more opportunities to build intersubjectivity and barriers to outsiders. On the other hand, though, informality is likely to weaken rituals' ability to convey sacredness, thus decreasing the likelihood that an informal IR will stand out as a peak identity-forming emotional experience. In general, we should expect the spirit to arrive more *often* in informal gatherings like iftar and Bible studies, but more *intensely* when it arrives in more formal gatherings like Jum'ah and Sunday morning worship.

RELIGIOUS EXPERIENCES

Religious experiences are felt encounters with the supernatural, whether experienced in isolation or with one's group. When in isolation, the individual accesses the spirit through solitary practices recommended or modeled by one's group, including solitary contemplation of their sacred symbols.

In the Introduction, I defined spirit as "a feeling of the supernatural." By this definition, capturing the spirit is itself a religious experience. The same cannot always be said of collective effervescence, though. In IR theory, effervescence can result from entirely secular rituals, as well as from religious ones. Although one could argue, as I do here, that collective effervescence always has functionally "religious" qualities, it really should only be considered a "(substantively) religious experience" when participants deem or understand it as such (Taves 2009).

What are we to make, though, of perceived encounters with the supernatural that take place outside the bounds of a ritual, when an individual is all alone? Even just asking the question in this way cuts against the grain of much research on religious experience, which, starting with William James' *The Varieties of Religious Experience* (1902), typically takes as its analytical starting point the perspective of a solitary individual who is having the experience. To James, this individual-level experience was even the essence of religion, which he defined as "the feelings, acts, and experiences of individual men *in their solitude*, so far as they apprehend themselves to stand in relation to whatever they may consider the divine" (39; my italics). Defining religion in this way was a choice motivated by James' analytical priorities, limiting his investigation of the subject matter to what interested him most as a psychologist, and explicitly choosing to "ignore the institutional branch [of religion] entirely" (37). Unsurprisingly, Durkheim (1983) directly criticized James' anti-sociological strategy. As I have emphasized, Durkheim's theory of religion was also a theory of knowledge, and he argued that an utterly isolated individual would not be able to become certain about anything. Only through collective ritual and moral force can humans confirm individual-level perceptions. Thus, a wholly individualist view of religious experience fails to connect the experience of the individual to an underlying reality, which can only be a social reality (Rawls 1997a; 2004).[15] When considering individuals' experiences, the choice to ignore social influences is a choice to ignore the very source of individuals' constructions of reality.

Durkheim's prioritization of ritual does not mean that solitary religious experiences do not occur; they clearly do, and James' classic work on the topic is full of such examples. The point, though, is that these solitary experiences draw on the individual's prior rituals for confirmation and interpretation. In the language of IR theory, we could say that IR chains prime some individuals for solitary religious experiences, just as they prime others to believe that reports of such experiences must always be works of fiction. In this sense, solitary religious experiences depend on symbolic solidarity.

Empirical work has shown that deep immersion in a religious tradition's practices increases the likelihood of reporting a religious experience (Baker 2009, Draper and Baker 2011, Poloma and Pendleton 1989). Frequency of worship attendance positively predicts religious experiences, but frequency of prayer is a much stronger and more consistent predictor. Given that much or even most of the "prayer frequency" measured in past surveys is of the solitary rather than corporate type, this suggests the possibility that private religious practice is more efficacious of religious experiences than is corporate religious practice, and this would seem to be more supportive of James' rather than Durkheim's understanding of religious experiences. Considered from the perspective of IR theory, though, the tight connection between prayer and religious experiences simply suggests that those religious individuals who spend the most time and effort cultivating and reflecting on their tradition's sacred symbols are best positioned to experience the spirit, even when they are away from the group, itself. Although they are not physically copresent with the group during the solitary experience, they are routinely "present" with them in a different sense through their frequent practice of concentrating on and nurturing positive emotional associations with the shared sacred symbols that first gained their emotional power during collective ritual. In short, participation in collective ritual is a necessary condition for the conviction that a religious experience has occurred; the conviction becomes more likely, though, to the extent that individuals cultivate symbolic solidarity in private practices such as prayer and meditation.

THE SPIRIT OF CONFLICT

All theories ultimately depend on assumptions about the nature of reality. Interaction ritual theory is no different, and all of its hypotheses rest on an image of social life wherein the actions of individuals and groups are rooted in current or potential conflicts over scarce resources. It draws on Max Weber's (1922a) version of conflict theory, in particular, which emphasizes "legitimate domination," or how members of social groups become convinced that their groups' laws and missions are good, true, and binding. Successful legitimation gives groups strength not only in numbers but also in a shared desire to mutually commit and sacrifice, a "parochial altruism" that improves their chances of surviving conflict (Haidt 2012). Members have to believe in the group, trust its leadership, imagine it with pride, and be willing to fight for it if necessary. Their feeling that their cause is just propels their involvement. Weber's arguments, then, ultimately point to the *emotional* dynamics that drive human conflicts.

Social organizations who become proficient at generating effervescence gain an advantage over their competitors, at both collective and individual levels. At the collective level, highly spirited religious organizations can secure members' loyalties and attract new members, yielding numerous benefits such as financial gifts, human capital, and "action." These benefits tend to build on themselves exponentially, as when financial gifts are used to purchase new ritual technologies, or when a sense of action bolsters recruitment efforts. In a competitive religious economy, this also means that organizations who struggle to capture the spirit are at a disadvantage, and in danger of decline.

At the individual level, members reap the benefits of EE, and carry powerful emotional memories and symbols of their organization even after they leave each other's company. These memories and symbols can help them thrive in other situations, as well, buoying sensations such as purpose, self-confidence, and moral certainty. The individual-level outcomes of successful interaction ritual chains thus serve as transituational resources that can help members flourish. These resources can also become the basis for conflict with nonmembers, and such conflicts, in turn, stimulate still higher levels of solidarity with the organization.

From this perspective, effervescence and solidarity are not optimistic concepts that can be extracted from a pessimistic general theory. Rather, effervescence and solidarity *cause* conflict within and between groups of people. *Within* organizations, emotional energy is usually synonymous with power: the high-status stars who have more of it are often envied, and those on the fringes are often ignored, pitied, despised, or even abused. In this sense, emotions are not simply the weapons used in battle; they themselves are the resources over which people fight. This research, then, is also an effort to understand how people overcome inherent intra-organizational EE disparities during key rituals, using a wide array of subtle techniques to minimize internal conflict's deleterious consequences and build toward a spirit of unity.

The ramifications of the theory also extend to inter-organizational dynamics, the borders *between* them. To the extent that members of an organization are able to stimulate powerful emotional experiences in each other's presence, they become more collectively certain about why they are special, good, and right. This spirit of certainty flourishes when they are able to pit their own version of solidarity against that of an enemy who is clearly incapable of distinguishing right from wrong and true from false. When they tell each other that the enemy poses an imminent threat, two things are likely to happen to them: their unity will abound, and some type of battle, more or less bloody, will ensue. The spirit of unity and that of discord are, in practice, intimately bound together.

NOTES

1. Glock and Stark's original schema also included "knowledge" and "consequences" and did not include "identity," but the four dimensions I've listed are now the most common dimensions focused upon in contemporary research in the sociology of religion. "Knowledge" should not qualify as a *dimension of* religiosity, since anyone can know *about* religions regardless of how they feel about them. Nor should "consequences" be included, as this category simply acknowledges that religiosity can impact other phenomena in various ways.

2. I do not advocate calling atheists and agnostics "religious," but do so here to convey Durkheim's perspective. In most contexts, referring to atheists and agnostics as "religious" is not only confusing, but also potentially offensive. To identify as an atheist, for example, is to define oneself *against* or *in contrast to* religion (Baker and Smith 2015). Durkheim's point about *functional* religiosity, though, is that all ideologies and identities depend on the same basic ritual processes and the same

basic experience of emotional force. We sacralize different symbols, whether those symbols be "God," "France," "Rationality," "Science," etc. Rituals affixed with the label "religion" are uniquely equipped to convey sacred authority, but all rituals and ideologies, regardless of labels, nonetheless depend on sacred authority.

3. Such a process is particularly urgent in a highly pluralistic, deeply conflicted culture such as the United States. Recognizing the power of practice encourages the stance that one does not have to abandon one's own convictions in order to appreciate that the convictions of others, despicable as they may be, are due to the same basic social processes that gave rise to one's own. Durkheim faced a comparable cultural challenge in the rapidly modernizing context of the early years of France's Third Republic. In *The Division of Labor in Society,* he argued that societies with advanced divisions of labor would have to learn to depend on cultural commitments to *shared practices* rather than *shared beliefs*. To sustain such a commitment, sociologists could make a vital contribution by building up a detailed science of ritual practices, and of the self-regulated interaction orders within which they operate (Durkheim 1893; Rawls 2003).

4. Weber is also discussing "magic" rituals in these paragraphs, but it is clear from his comments that he sees the distinction between magic and religion as fairly arbitrary, pertinent to later scholarly debate rather than meaningfully distinguished by humans in search of supernatural favors. "Magic," to Weber, is a label added by scholars to "designate . . . fallacious attributions of causality as irrational" (400).

5. Some content from a previous study is reproduced in this section with permission from John Wiley & Sons, from an earlier publication in *Sociology Compass* (Draper 2017).

6. See Rodney Stark's *One True God* (2001b), which builds on Weber's argument, for what is arguably the most comprehensive and systematic contemporary sociological theory of God images.

7. A trap in this field of investigation is to continuously "refine" Spilka et al.'s original findings, repeatedly asking new samples the same question and arriving at only slightly different patterns of description. The "Four Gods" typology of Froese and Bader (2010) conveniently limits the scope of investigation to two spectra that consistently have strong correlations with other beliefs and behaviors: God's level of *engagement with* and *judgment toward* humans.

8. Using Froese and Bader's schema, the "authoritarian" concept is of a God who is highly engaged with and highly judgmental toward humans.

9. This axiom is identical with Weber's (1922a) ideal type of "instrumental rationality."

10. For many individuals, as Collins (2004,141–82) argues, "financial profit" becomes the sacred symbol that is their greatest source of EE. This explains the obsessive acquisitiveness of people who are already very rich, especially in finance industries: their prior IR chains have wired them to pursue ritual practices that focus on making more money. The goal is not to make money simply so they can buy more stuff; rather, financial acquisition becomes its own emotional reward. The concept of emotional energy helps explain "addictions" of all kinds.

11. Other related factors certainly come into play, for example socialization and coercion (consider children who are "dragged" to church by their parents, for example). These factors, though, inevitably involve EE calculations. Even a child can calculate how much EE she is likely to lose via punishment or shame if, for example, she flatly refuses to get out of bed on Sunday morning and get in the family car. EE calculations can be short- or long-term. For example: "How will this worship service affect my morning?"; "What will happen at Tuesday's prayer meeting if I skip this morning's service?"; or "If I commit to this practice routinely, will I be proud of myself years from now?"

12. New converts can learn group symbols more swiftly by practicing the religion than they can through intellectual effort alone. For example, Alex, the new Muslim convert quoted in Chapter 1, explained to me that he had learned Muslim practices very quickly. Even though he hadn't yet had enough time to consider Islamic thought in all of its complexity, he learned how to practice raka'ah and salat soon after his conversion.

13. The *Baylor Religion Survey* (2011) shows that 31% of respondents identify with evangelical denominations, and 23% of respondents identify as Catholic. Over half of all Americans, then, identify with one of these two traditions.

14. Some evangelical sources are fairly explicit about their intent to boost emotional energy and even rhythmic entrainment. Lindsay Olesberg's (2012) *The Bible Study Handbook*, to give just one example, encourages Small Groups to work together through printed pages of scripture, building group energy as they write down meaningful phrases, make connections between different passages, and identify patterns that jump out at them from the text. Interactive approaches such as this have potential to generate high levels of effervescence and solidarity.

15. Anne Rawls (1997a, 9–10) explains:

> Because [James' pragmatist philosophy] gives up the relation to underlying reality it does not link thought to reality, but only individual thought to individual action which has been posited [by pragmatists] as the only reality. . . . The creating consciousness must be socially constructed so that it can create and sustain a communicable world. Truth based on an individual creating consciousness would be not only infinitely variable, but incomplete because it would keep changing over the course of even individual lives.

Appendix A

USCLS Findings

There are several possible ways to test and extend the interaction ritual model. Although no single method is likely to be sufficient on its own, there is much to be gained from an incremental and triangulated approach. The previous chapters drew upon close-up observations and interviews culled from time spent with particular religious organizations. It is also important to consider the theory's viability at a more macrolevel, using the tools of large-scale statistical analysis.[1]

There are good reasons to be cautious when using statistics to analyze IR theory. The theory draws heavily on Goffmanesque microphenomena such as glances, frowns, and double takes. How can survey data possibly inform propositions from a theory that deals with activities like "mutual monitoring" and "rhythmic entrainment"? The crucial thing to keep in mind is that quantitative analysis is a tool, and only a tool. Statistical findings always need to be interpreted cautiously, whether the question has to do with causes of suicide, shifts in global economies, grade point averages, or anything else. Here, quantitative analysis reveals relationships between the IR dynamics and outcomes across a broad spectrum of religious organizations. Despite all the differences in these organizations' particular practices, intriguing patterns in the data suggest several paths forward for the sociology of religious IRs.

SOURCE: THE UNITED STATES
CONGREGATIONAL LIFE SURVEY

In 2001, the Presbyterian Church (U.S.A.) worked with the Hartford Institute for Religion Research to survey a diverse selection of religious groups in America. Their *United States Congregational Life Survey* (USCLS) provides unprecedented insight into a wide range of very practical issues faced by contemporary religious congregations.

To aid interpretation of the analysis that follows, a few brief remarks should be made about the design of this survey. First, the sample of congregations was selected based on a prior survey, the *General Social Survey* (GSS; 2000).[2] Respondents to the GSS who stated that they attend worship services were asked to name their congregations, and their responses allowed the survey designers to track down a random sample of 1,214 U.S. congregations. 434 congregations agreed to participate in the USCLS (a 36% response rate), and a total of 73,196 individuals within those congregations completed surveys.[3]

The second thing to note is that the USCLS is really two separate surveys. The first is a "congregational profile" completed by a leader from each of the 434 participating congregations. The congregational profile reports on factors such as the average number in attendance at services, the number of seats in their sanctuary, and how long their services tend to last. The second, the "attendee survey," was given to the above-mentioned 73,196 adult worshipers who attended services during the weekend of April 29, 2001. The attendee surveys report factors like respondents' personal characteristics (e.g., gender, income, education), their emotional states during worship with their congregation, and how much they feel a "sense of belonging" in their congregation.

Because the USCLS involves two different surveys, a methodological challenge presented itself. I wanted to consider questions from both surveys, but because they involved different units of analysis (individuals and organizations), it was initially impossible to test certain hypotheses. For example, the average length of a congregation's services is reported in the congregational profiles, but congregants' emotional reactions to their services are reported in the attendee surveys. 434 service-length measures cannot be used to predict 73,196 individuals' responses. My solution was to favor the organizational level of analysis, and I did this by aggregating the attendee surveys into an average, or rate, for each congregation. This was a choice based on the theory, especially the idea that the spirit is a collective phenomenon. Thus, the measure of collective effervescence, for example, is the average of all of a congregation's individual-level responses. Likewise, the measure of membership solidarity is the proportion of each congregation who expressed on the attendee surveys that they feel like they belong. In short, I transformed the individual-level variables into congregational rates so that the analysis compares groups rather than individuals.[4,5]

TESTING FOR SPIRIT

Over 40 years ago, Randall Collins' *Conflict Sociology* (1975) presented a general conflict theory meant to apply to all areas of social life. The applications of the theory are wide-ranging in scale, from childrearing strategies to macroeconomics. Within this broader context, Collins laid the foundations for IR theory. He derived several propositions that, conveniently for researchers, can still be used as a basis to develop and refine the theory. These propositions led to the five hypotheses that guide this chapter's analysis.

Effervescence and solidarity are the main focus, so how they are measured is extremely important. First, consider the following series of questions:

"How often do you experience the following during worship services at this congregation? (Mark one response for each: Always, Usually, Sometimes, Rarely)

- A sense of God's presence
- Awe or mystery
- Inspiration
- Joy"

This series represents different aspects of collective effervescence as defined by Émile Durkheim. Sensing that God is present involves the perception of an external force that is above and beyond the individual. A sense of awe or mystery similarly suggests an encounter with sacred power, a moment in stark contrast with everyday mundane experience. Likewise, "inspiration" calls to mind a spiritual epiphany, a special insight gained from a supernatural encounter. Finally, joy is an intensely positive emotion. Collective effervescence does not need to be pleasant, but joy nonetheless serves well as one of many possible positive indicators of the concept. Any one of these items arguably could serve, on its own, as an indicator of effervescence. But it is more informative to combine the measures into an index, synthesizing different aspects of the phenomenon being considered. Conceptual coherence would not be not sufficient to form an index, but the items show strong internal consistency in the appropriate statistical tests, as well.[6] Interaction ritual theory posits that collective effervescence takes on different emotional qualities in different situations (Collins 2004, 2010). Here, the index captures intense feelings in worship (i.e., the spirit). Each congregation, then, earned an average effervescence "score" that could potentially range from 4 to 16.[7]

Next, consider the following two items:

"Do you have a strong sense of belonging to this congregation?

- Yes, a strong sense of belonging that is growing
- Yes, a strong sense—about the same as last year
- Yes, but perhaps not as strong as in the past
- No, but I am new here
- No, and I wish I did by now

- No, but I am happy as I am
- Don't know/not applicable"

"Does this congregation have a clear vision, goals, or direction for its ministry and mission?

- I am not aware of such a vision, goals, or direction
- There are ideas but no clear vision, goals, or direction
- Yes, and I am strongly committed to them
- Yes, and I am partly committed to them
- Yes, but I am not committed to them"

These two items both depict important features of social solidarity. Most often, the concept refers to feelings of membership, and this fits very well with the question above about sense of belonging. On the other hand, the concept also denotes shared commitment to goals, as when labor unions stick together during collective bargaining, and this fits very well with the question about shared vision/goals/direction.[8] These items, though, did not cohere well as a statistical index, so I analyzed them as separate indicators of different types of solidarity. The type associated with feelings of membership is "membership solidarity," and the type associated with feelings of shared purpose is "symbolic solidarity." As is also evident in the qualitative research discussed in the main chapters, the two types, though similar, often differ in how they relate to the other ritual dynamics.

The two USCLS questions offer multiple response options. I wanted to ensure, though, that the positive indicators of solidarity were not ambiguous. For this reason, I combined the response options listed above into simple "yes" and "no" categories. For membership solidarity, only the first two options are coded as "yes." For symbolic solidarity, only the third option is coded as "yes." Table A.1 shows the average levels of effervescence and solidarity in the sample of U.S. congregations.

On average, 39% of a congregation's members report strong commitment to the vision, goals, and direction of the congregation. Many more, 77% on

Table A.1.   Descriptive Statistics: Effervescence and Solidarity

Variable	N	Mean	SD	Min	Max
Membership solidarity	323	.77	.09	.51	1.00
Symbolic solidarity	323	.39	.16	.05	.88
Collective effervescence	323	10.99	1.02	6.83	13.6

Source—United States Congregational Life Survey (2001).

average, report a strong sense of belonging to the congregation. The two solidarity measures also differ in terms of how they're dispersed across congregations. While some congregations have as few as 5% who strongly feel symbolic solidarity, there are no congregations in the entire USCLS sample in which fewer than half of the respondents strongly feel membership solidarity. This suggests that feelings of belonging are easier for congregations to attain than symbolic consensus. It also suggests a new hypothesis for future research: in order for a voluntary organization to persist, at least half of the members need to experience membership solidarity; otherwise they will disband.

Hypothesis 1: Collective Effervescence → Social Solidarity

The most theoretically consequential hypothesis is Durkheim's idea that collective effervescence breeds social solidarity. This is the core argument in the ritual theories of Durkheim and Collins, as expressed in the following propositions from *Conflict Sociology*:

> *4.6* The stronger the emotional arousal, the more real and unquestioned the meanings of the symbols people think about during that experience.

> *4.7* The longer people are physically copresent and the more they focus their attention by stereotyped gestures and sounds, the more real and unquestioned are the meanings of the symbols people think about during that experience.

> *4.8* The more the conditions for strong ritual experiences are met, providing they do not produce mutual antagonism or asymmetrical threat-deference arousals, the greater the interpersonal attachment and feeling of security (153–54).

Notice the causal direction implied by these propositions. In Propositions 4.6 and 4.7, emotional arousal *begets* the confidence we have in symbols and ideas. The more common assumption runs in the opposite direction. With respect to Proposition 4.8, as well, the usual logic is reversed. It is not that we relish doing things with people with whom we feel secure; rather, we will feel secure with certain people if we can find a way to relish doing things with them.

To test this hypothesis, I broke up the sample into equally sized thirds based on the congregations' reported levels of effervescence.[9] Then, I determined the average proportion experiencing each type of solidarity within each of the three subsets. Figure A.1 illustrates the relationship between effervescence and both types of solidarity.

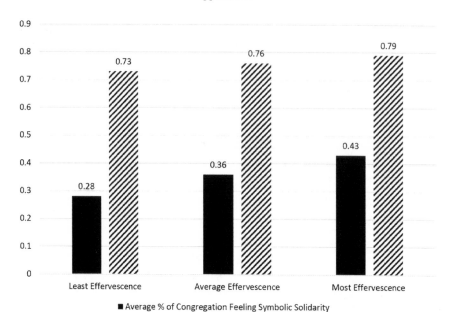

Figure A.1. **Average Proportion Feeling Social Solidarity (per-congregation average)**
Source—United States Congregational Life Survey (2001).

Although the increases in membership solidarity are small, the results support the hypothesis. With respect to symbolic solidarity, the results are even clearer: the proportion of a congregation feeling symbolic solidarity depends heavily on the degree to which they experience effervescence together during worship. Crucially, both patterns remain robust in well-controlled multivariate models (Draper 2014).[10,11] Consistently and clearly, effervescence boosts solidarity. This finding provides, for the first time, broad statistical evidence in support of Durkheim's classic hypothesis.

Hypothesis 2: Bodily Density → Collective Effervescence

4.2 The greater the number of human beings who are physically copresent, the more intense the emotional arousal. (153)

4.6, 4.7, and *4.8* [above.]

Hypothesis 2 introduces the dynamic of bodily copresence. As discussed in the Introduction and Chapter 3, copresence needs to be thought of as a continuous rather than dichotomous variable. The relationship between the "number of human beings who are physically copresent" and "emotional arousal" will depend on a third variable, the size of the space which contains the ritual. The resulting feeling of "crowdedness" or "bodily density" changes the situation's level of "action."

I combined three different questions from the congregational profiles to measure the average bodily density in each congregation's worship services. The first asks, "So far this year, what is your best estimate of average weekly attendance at worship services for this congregation? If you have more than one worship service, record the average attendance for all services combined." As the phrasing suggests, it is necessary to divide this measure by the number of services that each congregation holds in a typical week. The quotient is the average weekly per-service attendance. The USCLS also asks a question about seating capacity: "What is the approximate seating capacity of the space where your largest service is held?" This item served as the denominator in the equation:

bodily density = average number in attendance ÷ seating capacity

Although this variable is only an approximation, it gives a good sense of the relative crowdedness of each organization's rituals. Further, we can begin to see how bodily density varies across the spectrum of religious organizations in the U.S. Table A.2 shows a summary of the average number in attendance among the USCLS congregations, and also the average bodily density. The average congregation in the sample has about 76 people in attendance in their typical worship service. The smallest congregation has roughly seven attendees in each service, but only two other congregations in the sample average fewer than 10. At the high end, one church averages 1667 attendees, but this is by far the highest number reported. Only three other congregations average higher than 500 in attendance (660, 668, and 980), and a large majority (272/323 congregations) average fewer than 200. Regarding bodily density, the average congregation in the sample is typically about 30% full during services. At the low end, 27/323 congregations are less than 10% full on average. At the high end, one congregation reports that it is regularly filled beyond capacity at 136%, but apart from this outlier the highest bodily density is 92%.

Table A.2. Descriptive Statistics: Average Attendance and Bodily Density

Variable	N	Mean	SD	Min	Max
Average Attendance	323	76.48	66.62	6.66	1666.66
Bodily Density	323	.30	.17	.02	1.36

Source—United States Congregational Life Survey (2001).

When looking at the initial bivariate correlations, I was surprised to find that bodily density has a *negative* relationship with effervescence (-.206**). I thought there might be more to the story, though, because (a) the relationship becomes nonsignificant once other factors are controlled in multivariate models, and (b) bodily density has a *positive* relationship with both types of social solidarity in multivariate models. Digging further, I discovered in supplementary regressions that the relationship between density and effervescence is negative until socioeconomic status (SES) is added to the model as a control variable. This suggested the possibility that SES might be a latent factor in the negative bivariate relationship between bodily density and effervescence.

To explore this possibility more, I analyzed the effervescence model again with an interaction effect between SES and bodily density.[12] Based on a standardized measure that combines education and income, I examined the impact of density on effervescence among congregations with average levels of SES, congregations who are one standard deviation below average in SES (relatively poor), and one standard deviation above average in SES (relatively rich).

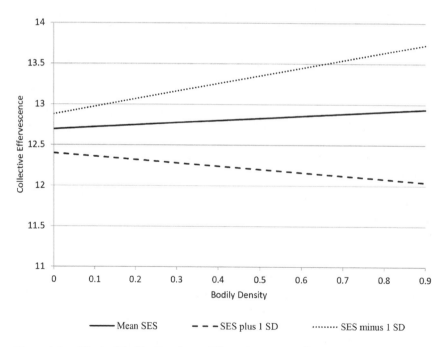

Figure A.2.   Effect of Bodily Density on Effervescence, Conditioned by SES
Source—United States Congregational Life Survey (2001).

As Figure A.2 illustrates, SES conditions how bodily density affects effervescence. For those in the low and average SES categories, bodily density tends to increase effervescence. For those in the highest SES categories, though, bodily density strongly *diminishes* effervescence. Based on these findings, closeness of bodies tends to intensify group emotions, unless those bodies mostly belong to members of the upper class.

Hypothesis 3: Longer Rituals → Collective Effervescence

4.1 The longer human beings are physically copresent, the more likely automatic, mutually reinforcing nonverbal sequences are to appear, and the stronger the level of emotional arousal.

4.3 The greater the common focus of attention among physically copresent human beings, the more likely they are to experience a common emotional arousal or mood. (153)

4.6, *4.7*, and *4.8* [above.]

How long should a ritual last? Intersubjectivity probably does not happen instantly, but rather takes time to gain momentum. Likewise, a ritual that ends too early would likely cause participants to feel as though they've been cheated out of the EE boost they anticipated when they first chose to attend. Baseball fans do not yearn for rainouts. On the other hand, though, we know of no IRs that continue indefinitely. It seems likely that each IR would carry an optimal termination point, based on the participants' prior experiences in similar IRs, beyond which focus of attention and emotional intensity will rapidly deteriorate. Additionally, even fairly brief IRs will likely feel too long when other dynamics are weak, as when a shared focus of attention is not achieved.[13]

With the USCLS data, it is possible to gain a sense of the influence of time on the ritual. Average service length, or duration, is taken from the congregational profile, with the response options "up to 1 hour," "1–1.5 hours," "1.5–2 hours," and "2 or more hours."

Figure A.3 supports hypothesis 3 and shows that longer services are associated with higher levels of effervescence. Like bodily density, the service length measure takes no account of anything that is actually said or done during the services—the content of the IR. What we're seeing, then, is a general principle that congregations who gather together for worship increase their chances of capturing the spirit when they remain in each other's presence for a relatively long time.

Beyond the fact that it takes time for participants to establish a sense of intersubjectivity, how else can this tendency be explained? One likely factor

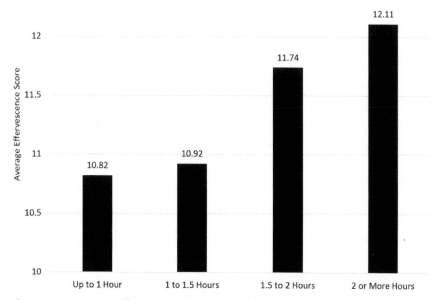

Figure A.3. Average Effervescence Score Based on Average Service Length
Source—United States Congregational Life Survey (2001).

is a desire on the part of ritual participants to feel as though their invest-ment of time will be compensated with emotional rewards. Rational choice scholars (for example, see Iannaccone 1994) might argue that, particularly in voluntary organizations such as churches, participants' "sunk costs" (time) lead to optimistic interpretations of their "payoffs" (emotional energy). Voluntary time investments promote positive summaries of the experience, whereas anyone who becomes skeptical about such benefits usually can just stop attending.

A second explanation is that extending the duration of services enhances participants' familiarity with their organization's sacred symbols, thereby incrementally expanding these symbols' emotional poignancy. Organizations use a variety of "ritual resources" to focus attention and establish moods, and some of these resources appear to gain strength through repetition. Many evangelical Protestant churches, for example, sing "praise songs" together. These songs usually are simple, brief choruses, often projected on a screen above the stage, often focusing on a single theme such as God's might or Christ's sacrifice. Each repetition of the chorus is an opportunity to gather even more EE. Similarly, the call-and-response preaching style so characteristic of black Protestant churches uses rhythm and repetition, often repeating a key phrase for emphasis, likewise allowing EE to "gather steam" and build on itself as the sermon progresses. Repetition is a valuable ritual resource, and congregations whose worship schedule allows temporal space for this technique put themselves at an advantage.

Of course, remaining at a ritual for too long can also foster negative emotions, and there is likely a point of diminishing returns. However, I did not find evidence for a diminishing returns hypothesis in the USCLS data. I looked for, but did not find, a "curvilinear" relationship between service length and effervescence. Rather, effervescence grows with each incremental increase in service length, with the biggest jump occurring between the third and final time categories. It looks as though effervescence just keeps growing as more time is added to a service. This trajectory should be interpreted cautiously, though, since the USCLS survey item does not provide a response option for services that stretch to 2.5 hours and beyond. A good direction for future IR research would be to build on this excellent survey item from the USCLS by measuring the length of rituals with greater precision and a longer maximum duration.

As with bodily density, the effect of service length is probably more complex than a straightforward positive relationship. Although there is more to discover, a basic rule is evident here: longer services tend to be more emotionally invigorating.

Hypothesis 4: High Organizational Attendance Rates → Collective Effervescence

4.4 The more that people use stereotyped sequences of gestures and sounds, the greater the common focus of attention.

4.5 The more that people use stereotyped sequences of gestures and sounds, the more likely they are to experience a common mood. (153)

4.3, 4.6, 4.7, and *4.8* [above.]

Survey data on worship attendance cannot ascertain the extent to which congregations use stereotyped sequences of gestures and sounds in their rituals. It is theoretically possible (although extremely unlikely based on experience) that a congregation will do and say something different with each other each time they meet, or that the congregants will always fail to get caught up in each other's patterns of expression. It seems much more likely, though, that a congregation's repeated experience and deepened familiarity with their favored symbols and practices would enable them to more easily achieve a shared focus and mood together. Organizations wherein a high percentage of members attend services frequently would likely experience high levels of ritual proficiency and group conformity. As they prove proficient, it is likely that they would want to repeat the ritual, thus further honing their proficiency.

The organizational rate of attendance at worship services is measured by asking how often individual respondents attend services at their congregation. Options include "This is my first time," "hardly ever," "less than once a month," "once a month," "2–3 times a month," "usually every week," and "more than once a week." Responses are aggregated to create a mean rate of attendance for each congregation.

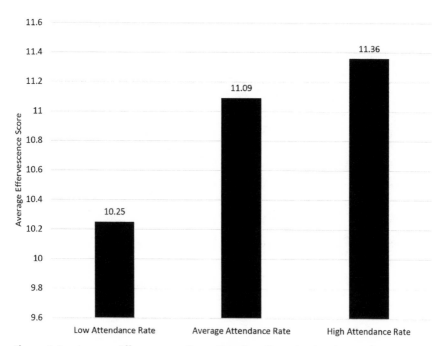

Figure A.4. **Average Effervescence Score Based on Organizational Attendance Rates**
Source—United States Congregational Life Survey (2001).

As shown in Figure A.4, the relationship is positive, with the biggest jump in effervescence scores occurring between the low and middle attendance categories. Religious organizations with high levels of attendance are more adept at reaching high levels of effervescence. Their experiences together can also be addictive, and this serves as a reminder that the IR model is recursive. When IRs succeed at stimulating EE, participants will be motivated to return repeatedly to replenish their personal supply. Based on this evidence, the rates at which interactants repeatedly return to an organization's IRs should be understood as a central factor determining IR outcomes.

Regularity of participation in an organization's rituals may be the best available quantitative measure of IR "chains" (Collins 2004), as high attendance rates enhance the organization's ability to reach a shared focus of attention together, and bond members together through a long-term series of invigorating IRs. Multivariate models with interaction effects reveal that the combination of high attendance and high effervescence has a powerful impact on social solidarity (see Figure A.5; only symbolic solidarity is shown here, but the effects are similar for membership solidarity).

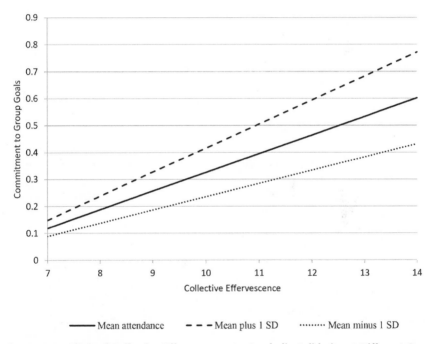

Figure A.5. **Effect of Collective Effervescence on Symbolic Solidarity at Different Organizational Attendance Rates**
Source—United States Congregational Life Survey (2001).

Hypothesis 5: Barriers to Outsiders → Collective Effervescence

Barriers to outsiders come in several different forms. Simple physical barriers, for example, such as closed doors or turned backs, help establish an internal focus for an IR. Other barriers are more symbolic, as when organizations denounce each other's values, sacred objects, or behaviors. In Collins' conflict theory, symbolic and ideological barriers permit organizations to minimize internal conflicts and redirect animosity toward nonmembers. He argues, "A strong church needs its devil, and any organizational leader can enhance his power by making sure there are visible enemies or competitors against whom minor conflict can be quickly escalated when internal stresses become more serious" (1975, 306). The following propositions predict how barriers to outsiders will impact effervescence and solidarity:

4.6, 4.7, and *4.8* [above.]

10.6 The more that members of an organization are aware of danger and hostility from another organization, the more loyalty to the organization (provided that there is not already greater hostility between groups *within* the organization).

10.61 The more exclusively an organization recruits from a cultural group (ethnic, racial, class) that is in conflict with another cultural group, and the more an organization emphasizes ceremonial tests of cultural similarity for membership, the greater the loyalty to the organization. (305)

The USCLS contains good measures of two different types of barriers. First, we can consider congregations' *behavioral proscriptions*, also known as forms of religious "strictness." The congregational profile asks, "Does your congregation or denomination have any special rules or prohibitions regarding the following?" The listed behaviors include smoking, drinking alcohol, dancing, personal appearance, and gambling. By stigmatizing these behaviors, certain organizations make clear which kinds of people do and do not belong within their ranks.

Initial analysis did not show a clear relationship between the number of proscriptions and congregations' effervescence scores. There is no discernable difference in effervescence between organizations who prohibit 1, 2, 3, 4, or all 5 of the behaviors. Figure A.6, though, reveals that congregations with *none* of the prohibitions report, by far, the lowest levels of effervescence. The average congregational effervescence score in the full sample is 10.99. Those with zero prohibitions are the only type of congregation in this analysis with an average effervescence score (10.44) that is below the average for the full sample. This provides initial support for the barriers hypothesis.

A second type of barrier has to do with *openness to diversity*. The USCLS asks respondents, "Which of the following aspects of this congregation do you personally most value?" Respondents were instructed to select up to three responses from a list of 14 different options.[14] One of these options is "openness to social diversity." The phrase itself is somewhat ambiguous, and

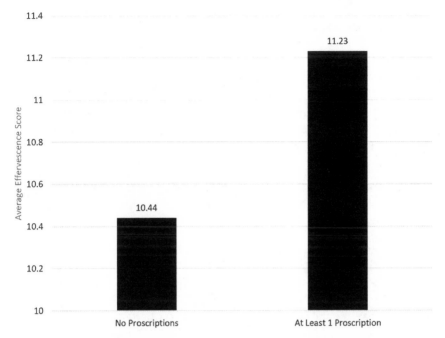

Figure A.6. Average Effervescence Score Based on Number of Proscriptions
Source—United States Congregational Life Survey (2001).

there is no sure way to know which type of diversity respondents may have had in mind. Beyond this, it is entirely possible that congregations who claim to "value" diversity might not actually be very demographically diverse; moreover, these congregations might very well erect other barriers that have little to do with how they think about "diversity." Keeping these caveats in mind, though, it is quite revealing to consider the effervescence scores in organizations wherein a high percentage of respondents selected this option, as shown in Figure A.7.

Openness to diversity has a strong negative relationship with effervescence, and this turns out to be the strongest predictor in the entire model.[15] This evidence does not show that diversity per se compromises effervescence, but it does support the conclusion that those congregations who are least enthusiastic about expanding their cultural boundaries are also the congregations who are best positioned for effervescence. As I argue in Chapter 5, barriers to outsiders is one of the most complex IR dynamics to assess, mainly because there are so many different types of barriers. Still, the USCLS data is persuasive: the spirit privileges groups who exclude.

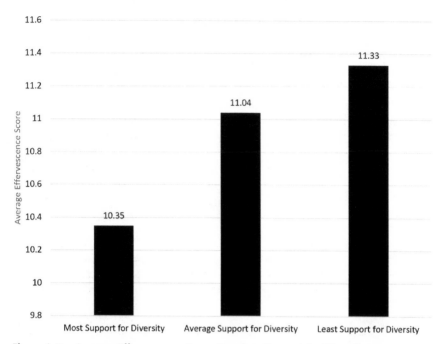

Figure A.7. Average Effervescence Score Based on Support for Diversity
Source—United States Congregational Life Survey (2001).

CONCLUSION

The USCLS contains rare and valuable measures of organizational efferves-cence and solidarity, but these can be refined further in new surveys. The data set has a weaker capacity for assessment of barriers to outsiders and in-tersubjectivity, dynamics which are complicated to measure because they are so multifaceted. There are many ways an organization can erect barriers, and there are many strategies that an organization can use to promote intersubjec-tivity. Still, quantitative analysis can benefit this area of research to the extent that it controls for the different strategies as well as possible, and emphasizes probabilistic rather than deterministic effects.

Microlevel observation must remain the primary method for continuing to develop this theory. Statistical analysis can only be considered supple-mentary. As shown here, it can also suggest new directions for analysis. The evidence from the USCLS strongly supports Durkheim's and Collins' foun-dational proposition that collective effervescence catalyzes social solidarity, an idea with powerful implications for understanding how humans become certain of their identities, moralities, and truths. The results shed light on several other propositions, as well, and inspired the observational research reported in this book.

NOTES

1. Some content from a previous study is reproduced here with permission from John Wiley & Sons, from an earlier publication in *The Journal for the Scientific Study of Religion* (Draper 2014).

2. Conducted by the University of Chicago's *National Opinion Research Center*, the GSS is one of the most reliable and frequently analyzed data sets in the social sciences, second only to the U.S. Census (National Opinion Research Center 2014).

3. The sample is a diverse collection of religious traditions, including black Protestants (7 congregations), Jews (5), Mormons (3), and Buddhists (2), all of whom are often overlooked in the sociology of religion in the U.S. Traditions with relatively high numbers—mainline Protestants (136), evangelical Protestants (93), and Catholics (74)—are also represented, and comprise most of the current sample. Such a diverse sample of congregational data is rare and quite valuable in empirical research on religion.

4. Due to missing data, several congregations were removed from analysis through listwise deletion. 324 congregations remain in the final combined sample.

5. All analyses incorporate weights that accompany the USCLS data.

6. Factor analysis indicates that the four measures load on a common factor with loading scores above .64. Added into an index, they have a Cronbach's alpha score of .77.

7. For each of the four questions, "rarely" = 1, "sometimes" = 2, "usually" = 3, and "always" = 4.

8. Shared commitment to goals is closely related to two other outcomes in the IR model—sacred objects and standards of morality—and captures a more prolonged form of group identification. Shared commitment to the organization's goals is a shared commitment to the organization's sacred symbols, and these are able to reinvoke feelings of membership and morality even in the absence of the group.

9. Lowest third: 6.83→10.86 (108 congregations); Middle: 10.87→11.53 (108); Highest: 11.54→13.6 (108).

10. Multivariate regression models allow researchers to compare the relative effects of different independent variables on a single dependent variable. Among other advantages, this technique helps minimize spurious findings by statistically "controlling" for a range of different influential factors. The other independent variables in my models include measures of IR dynamics and standard controls in sociological research on religion: average socioeconomic status (SES), % white, % married, average age, bodily density, congregation size, length of service, organizational attendance rates, index of behavioral proscriptions, and religious tradition.

11. The effervescence index was also broken into its component parts ("awe," "inspiration," "sense of God's presence," and "joy") so that each item could be assessed

individually. Again, the results consistently and clearly support Durkheim's model. Regardless of which measures I included in the model, effervescence always has a robust and statistically significant relationship with solidarity.

12. Researchers can measure "interaction effects" by considering the impact of a particular independent variable when a different independent variable is fixed at certain values. In this case, I considered the impact of bodily density on collective effervescence when socioeconomic status is fixed at low, average, or high levels. Figure A.2 shows results from the full multivariate model, with the interaction effect included.

13. This is perhaps the central challenge faced by teachers, for example. For 45-60 minutes, can the teacher entice a classroom of students to share his interest and passion regarding content with which the students have little or no experience? To the extent that the students think the class goes on "too long," the teacher has failed the challenge.

14. These include: "wider community care or social justice emphasis"; "reaching those who do not attend church"; "traditional style of worship or music"; "contemporary style of worship or music"; "sharing in Holy Communion, Eucharist, Lord's Supper"; "social activities or meeting new people"; "sermons, preaching, or homilies"; "Bible study or prayer groups, other discussion groups"; "ministry for children or youth"; "prayer ministry for one another"; "practical care for one another in times of need"; "the congregation's school or pre-school"; "openness to social diversity"; and "adult church-school or Sabbath-school class."

15. In multivariate regression using any and all combinations of predictor variables included in this chapter, standardized coefficients are the highest, by far, for this measure.

Appendix B

Focus Group
Questions and Characteristics

SET QUESTIONS FOR FOCUS GROUPS

1. Are you a member of [religious organization]?
2. How many years have you been attending [religious organization]?
3. During a typical week, how many times do you attend worship services at [religious organization]?
4. Would you say that today's service was a typical service for [religious organization]?
5. [How so/why not]?
6. Did any aspects of today's service stand out to you as, for any reason, particularly memorable?
7. [If "yes"] Why does that stand out to you?
8. What is/are your favorite part(s) of a typical service at [religious organization]?
9. How would you describe your mood after today's service was complete?
10. How would you describe your mood before today's service had begun?
11. How would you describe your mood during today's service?
12. Did you learn anything new in today's service?
13. [If "yes"] Please tell me about what you learned.
14. To what extent do you think people [in this organization] experience a sense of belonging?
15. To what extent does this congregation share a common goal or vision?
16. Describe [religious organization's] relationship with your local community.
17. What other activities, other than worship services, do you take part in with [religious organization]?

FOCUS GROUP CHARACTERISTICS

Table B.1. Characteristics of the Focus Groups

Organization	Gender	Approximate Age	Marital Status
Congregation Shalom			
	female	50s	Widow
	male	30s	Married
	male	50s	Widower
	female	60s	Married
	female	60s	Married
The Islamic Center			
	male	20s	Single
	male	30s	Single
	male	50s	Married
	male	20s	Single
Promised Land Baptist			
	female	70s	Married
	male	40s	Married
	female	60s	Married
	female	40s	Single
	female	30s	Single
	female	40s	Married
First Baptist			
	male	50s	Married
	female	50s	Married
	female	20s	Married
	male	50s	Married
	female	60s	Married
The Meditation Center			
	male	30s	Single
	male	40s	Single
	female	20s	Single
	female	30s	Married
	male	30s	Single
	female	30s	Single
St. John's Catholic Church			
	female	30s	Married
	male	20s	Single
	female	70s	Widow
	female	40s	Married

References

Ahlstrom, Sydney E. 1972. *The Religious History of the American People.* New Haven: Yale University Press.

Allen, Ronald. 1992. *Preaching the Topical Sermon.* Louisville: Westminster/John Knox Press.

Ammerman, Nancy. 1987. *Bible Believers: Fundamentalists in the Modern World.* New Brunswick: Rutgers University Press.

———. 1995. *Baptist Battles: Social Change and Religious Conflict in the Southern Baptist Convention.* New Brunswick: Rutgers University Press.

———. 1997. *Congregation and Community.* New Brunswick: Rutgers University Press.

Anderson, Elijah. 1999. *The Code of the Street: Decency, Violence, and the Moral Life of the Inner City.* New York: Norton.

Aslan, Reza. 2006. *No God but God: The Origins, Evolution, and Future of Islam.* New York: Random House.

Aveni, Adrian. 1977. "The Not-So-Lonely Crowd: Friendship Groups in Collective Behavior." *Sociometry* 40(1): 96–99.

Bader, Christopher, Scott Desmond, F. Carson Mencken, and Byron Johnson. 2010. "Divine Justice: The Relationship between Images of God and Attitudes toward Criminal Punishment." *Criminal Justice Review* 35: 90–106.

Baker, Joseph. 2009. "The Variety of Religious Experiences." *Review of Religious Research* 51(1): 39–54.

———. 2010. "Social Sources of the Spirit: Connecting Rational Choice and Interactive Ritual Theories in the Study of Religion." *Sociology of Religion* 71(4): 432–56.

Baker, Joseph, and Buster Smith. 2015. *American Secularism: Cultural Contours of Nonreligious Belief Systems.* New York: New York University Press.

Barone, Carlo. 2007. "A Neo-Durkheimian Analysis of a New Religious Movement: The Case of Soka Gakkai in Italy." *Theory and Society* 36(2): 117–40.

Bean, Frank, and Marta Tienda. 1987. *The Hispanic Population of the United States.* New York: Russell Sage.

Becker, Howard. 1963. *Outsiders: Studies in the Sociology of Deviance.* New York: The Free Press.

Bell, Catherine. 1992. *Ritual Theory, Ritual Practice.* New York: Oxford University Press.

———. 1997. *Ritual: Perspectives and Dimensions.* New York: Oxford University Press.

Bellah, Robert, Richard Madsen, William Sullivan, Ann Swidler, and Steven Tipton. 1996. *Habits of the Heart: Individualism and Commitment in American Life.* New York: Harper & Row.

Bendix, Reinhard. 1960. *Max Weber: An Intellectual Portrait.* Garden City: Doubleday.

Berger, Peter. 2016. "Death, Ritual, and Effervescence." *Ultimate Ambiguities: Investigating Death and Liminality*, edited by Peter Berger and Justin Kroesen, 147–83. New York: Berghahn Books.

Bielo, James. 2009. *Words Upon the Word: An Ethnography of Evangelical Group Bible Study.* New York: NYU Press.

Bond, Gilbert. 2002. *Community, Communitas, and Cosmos.* Lanham: University Press of America.

Bonilla-Silva, Eduardo. 2003. *Racism Without Racists: Color-Blind Racism and the Persistence of Racial Inequality in the United States.* Lanham: Rowman and Littlefield.

Boone, Kathleen. 1989. *The Bible Tells Them So: The Discourse of Protestant Fundamentalism.* Albany: State University of New York Press.

Bourdieu, Pierre. 1984. *Distinction: A Social Critique of the Judgment of Taste.* Cambridge: Harvard University Press.

Bradshaw, Matt, Christopher G. Ellison, and Kevin J. Flannely. 2008. "Prayer, God Imagery, and Symptoms of Psychopathology." *Journal for the Scientific Study of Religion* 47(4): 644–59.

Bruce, Steve. 1999. *Choice and Religion: A Critique of Rational Choice Theory.* New York: Oxford University Press.

Cadge, Wendy. 2005. *Heartwood: The First Generation of Theravada Buddhism in America.* Chicago: University of Chicago Press.

Cadge, Wendy, Peggy Levitt, and David Smilde. 2011. "De-centering and Re-centering: Rethinking Concepts and Methods in the Sociological Study of Religion." *Journal for the Scientific Study of Religion* 50(3): 437–49.

Cainkar, Louise. 2002. "No Longer Invisible: Arab and Muslim Exclusion after September 11." *Middle East Report* 224: 22–29.

Caughey, John. 1984. *Imaginary Social Worlds: A Cultural Approach.* Lincoln: University of Nebraska Press.

Cerulo, Karen. 2009. "Nonhumans in Social Interaction." *Annual Review of Sociology* 35: 531–52.

Cerulo, Karen, and Andrea Barra. 2008. "In the Name of…: Legitimate Interactants in the Dialogue of Prayer." *Poetics* 36: 374–88.

Chafets, Zev. 2007. *A Match Made in Heaven: American Jews, Christian Zionists, and One Man's Exploration of the Weird and Wonderful Judeo-Evangelical Alliance.* New York: Harper Collins.

Chaves, Mark. 1999. *Ordaining Women: Culture and Conflict in Religious Organizations.* Cambridge: Harvard University Press.

———. 2004. *Congregations in America.* Cambridge: Harvard University Press.

———. 2006. "All Creatures Great and Small: Megachurches in Context." *Review of Religious Research* 47(4): 329–46.

———. 2017. *American Religion: Contemporary Trends.* Princeton: Princeton University Press.

Chen, Carolyn. 2002. "The Religious Varieties of Ethnic Presence: A Comparison between a Taiwanese Immigrant Buddhist Temple and an Evangelical Christian Church." *Sociology of Religion* 63(2): 215–38.

Chödrön, Pema. 1991. *The Wisdom of No Escape and the Path of Loving-Kindness.* Boston: Shambhala Publications.

Clark, Candace. 1997. *Misery and Company: Sympathy in Everyday Life.* Chicago: University of Chicago Press.

Cohen, Mark R. 1994. *Under Crescent and Cross: The Jews in the Middle Ages.* Princeton: Princeton University Press.

Coleman, James. 1990. *Foundations of Social Theory.* Cambridge: Harvard University Press.

Coleman, James W. 2001. *The New Buddhism: The Western Transformation of an Ancient Tradition.* New York: Oxford University Press.

Collins, Randall. 1975. *Conflict Sociology.* New York: Academic Press Inc.

———. 1986. *Weberian Sociological Theory.* Cambridge: Cambridge University Press.

———. 2004. *Interaction Ritual Chains.* Princeton: Princeton University Press.

———. 2010. "The Micro-Sociology of Religion: Religious Practices, Collective and Individual." Association of Religion Data Archives "Guiding Paper" Series. http://www.thearda.com/rrh/papers/guidingpapers/Collins.asp.

———. 2012. "C-Escalation and D-Escalation: A Theory of the Time-Dynamics of Conflict." *American Sociological Review* 77(1):1–20.

Coser, Lewis. 1956. *The Functions of Social Conflict.* New York: The Free Press.

Council on American-Islamic Relations. 2009. *The Status of Muslim Civil Rights in the United States 2009: Seeking Full Inclusion.* Washington, D.C. https://www.cair.com/images/pdf/CAIR-2009-Civil-Rights-Report.pdf

Cox, Harvey. 1995. *Fire from Heaven: The Rise of Pentecostal Spirituality and the Reshaping of Religion in the Twenty-first Century.* Cambridge: Da Capo Press.

Cross, Whitney R. (1950) 1982. *The Burned Over District: The Social and Intellectual History of Enthusiastic Religion in Western New York, 18001850.* Ithaca: Cornell University Press.

Csikszentmihalyi, Mihaly. 2008. *Flow: The Psychology of Optimal Experience.* New York: Harper Collins.

Davidman, Lynn. 1991. *Tradition in a Rootless World: Women Turn to Orthodox Judaism.* Berkeley: University of California Press.

Davidson, James, and Suzanne Fournier. 2006. "Recent Research on Catholic Parishes: A Research Note." *Review of Religious Research* 48(1): 72–78.

Davie, Grace. 1994. *Religion in Britain Since 1945: Believing Without Belonging.* Oxford: Blackwell.

Dawn, Marva. 1995. *Reaching Out Without Dumbing Down: A Theology of Worship for this Urgent Time.* Grand Rapids: William. B. Eerdmans Publishing Company.
———. 2003. *How Shall We Worship? Biblical Guidelines for the Worship Wars.* Carol Stream: Tyndale House Publishers.
Dixon, Marc, Vincent Roscigno, and Randy Hodson. 2004. "Unions, Solidarity, and Striking." *Social Forces* 83(1): 3–33.
Dougherty, Kevin D., and Andrew L. Whitehead. 2011. "A Place to Belong: Small Group Involvement in Religious Congregations." *Sociology of Religion* 72(1): 91–111.
Draper, Scott. 2014. "Effervescence and Solidarity in Religious Organizations." *Journal for the Scientific Study of Religion* 53(2): 229–48.
———. 2017. "The Preeminent Sacred Symbol: Theorizing Image of God Outcomes." *Sociology Compass* 11(10).
Draper, Scott, and Joseph Baker. 2011. "Angelic Belief as American Folk Religion." *Sociological Forum* 26(3): 623–43.
Draper, Scott, and Jerry Z. Park. 2010. "Sunday Celluloid: Visual Media and Protestant Boundaries with Secular Culture." *Sociological Spectrum* 30: 433–58.
DuBois, W.E.B. (1904) 1989. *The Souls of Black Folk.* New York: Penguin Books.
Durkheim, Émile. (1886) 1994. "Review of Part VI of the Principles of Sociology by Herbert Spencer." In *Durkheim on Religion*, edited by W.S.F. Pickering, 13–23. Atlanta: Scholars Press.
———. (1893) 1947. *The Division of Labor in Society.* Translated by George Simpson. New York: The Free Press.
———. (1897) 1951. *Suicide: A Study of Society.* Translated by John A. Spaulding and George Simpson. New York: The Free Press.
———. (1912) 1995. *The Elementary Forms of Religious Life.* Translated by Karen E. Fields. New York: The Free Press.
———. 1974. "The Determination of Moral Facts." In *Sociology and Philosophy*, translated by D.F. Pocock, 35–62. New York: The Free Press.
———. 1983. *Pragmatism and Sociology*, edited by J.C. Whitehouse. Cambridge: Cambridge University Press.
Edgell, Penny. 2012. "A Cultural Sociology of Religion: New Directions." *Annual Review of Sociology* 38: 247–65.
Edgell, Penny, Joseph Gerteis, and Douglas Hartmann. 2006. "Atheists as 'Other': Moral Boundaries and Cultural Membership in American Society." *American Sociological Review* 71: 211–34.
Ehrenreich, Barbara. 1997. *Blood Rites: Origins and History of the Passions of War.* New York: Henry Holt.
———. 2006. *Dancing in the Streets: A History of Collective Joy.* New York: Henry Holt.
Elias, Norbert. 1978. *The Development of Manners.* Vol. 1 of *The Civilizing Process.* Translated by Edmund Jephcott. New York: Urizen Books.
———. 1982. *Power and Civility.* Vol. 2 of *The Civilizing Process.* Translated by Edmund Jephcott. New York: Pantheon Books.

Ellison, Christopher G., Matt Bradshaw, Kevin J. Flannelly, and Kathleen Galek. 2014. "Prayer, Attachment to God, and Symptoms of Anxiety-Related Disorders among US Adults." *Sociology of Religion* 75(2): 209–33.

Emerson, Michael, and Christian Smith. 2000. *Divided by Faith: Evangelical Religion and the Problem of Race in America.* New York: Oxford University Press.

Feagin, Joe, and Eileen O'Brien. 2003. *White Men on Race: Power, Privilege, and the Shaping of Cultural Consciousness.* Beacon: Beacon Press.

Fine, Rabbi David J. 2002. "Women and the Minyan." Committee on Jewish Law and Standards of the Rabbinical Assembly. http://www.rabbinicalassembly.org/sites/default/files/public/halakhah/teshuvot/19912000/oh_55_1_2002.pdf.

Finke, Roger, and Rodney Stark. 2005. *The Churching of America 1776–2005: Winners and Losers in our Religious Economy.* New Brunswick: Rutgers University Press.

Freud, Sigmund. 1989. "Obsessive Actions and Religious Practices." In *The Freud Reader,* edited by Peter Gay, 429–36. New York: Norton.

Froese, Paul. 2016. *On Purpose: How We Create the Meaning of Life.* New York: Oxford University Press.

Froese, Paul, and Christopher Bader. 2010. *America's Four Gods: What We Say about God and What that Says About Us.* New York: Oxford University Press.

Froese, Paul, Christopher Bader, and Buster Smith. 2008. "Political Tolerance and God's Wrath in the United States." *Sociology of Religion* 69(1): 29–44.

Gallagher, Sally. 2003. *Evangelical Identity and Gendered Family Life.* New Brunswick: Rutgers University Press.

Gans, Herbert. 1974. *Popular Culture and High Culture: An Evaluation and Analysis of Taste.* New York: Basic Books.

Gibson, David R. 2008. "Doing Time in Space: Line-Joining Rules and Resultant Morphologies." *Sociological Forum* 23(2): 207–33.

Glock, Charles, and Rodney Stark. 1965. *Religion and Society in Tension.* Chicago: Rand McNally.

Goffman, Alice. 2014. *On the Run: Fugitive Life in an American City.* New York: Picador.

Goffman, Erving. 1959. *The Presentation of Self in Everyday Life.* Garden City: Doubleday.

———. 1963. *Behavior in Public Places: Notes on the Social Organization of Gatherings.* New York: The Free Press.

———. 1967. *Interaction Ritual.* Garden City: Doubleday.

———. 1971. *Relations in Public: Microstudies of the Public Order.* New York: Basic Books.

———. 1981. *Forms of Talk.* Philadelphia: University of Pennsylvania Press.

Goodman, Jordan, and Paul E. Lovejoy, eds. 1995. *Consuming Habits: Drugs in History and Anthropology.* New York: Routledge.

Goodwin, Jeff, James M. Jasper, and Francesca Polletta. 2007. "Emotional Dimensions of Social Movements." *The Blackwell Companion to Social Movements,* edited by David Snow, Sarah Soule, and Hanspeter Kriesi, 413–32. Malden: Blackwell.

Greeley, Andrew. 1993. "Religion and Attitudes toward the Environment." *Journal for the Scientific Study of Religion* 32:19–28.

———. 1996. *Religion as Poetry*. New Brunswick: Transaction Publishers.

Gregory, Stanford, Stephen Webster, and Gang Huang. 1993. "Voice Pitch and Amplitude Convergence as a Metric of Quality in Dyadic Interviews." *Language and Communication* 13: 195–217.

Grunfeld, Isador. 2003. *The Sabbath: A Guide to its Understanding and Observance.* Jerusalem: Feldheim Publishers.

Haidt, Jonathan. 2012. *The Righteous Mind: Why Good People are Divided by Politics and Religion.* New York: Vintage Books.

Haskell, David, Kenneth Paradis, and Stephanie Burgoyne. 2008. "Defending the Faith: Easter Sermon Reaction to Pop Culture Discourses." *Review of Religious Research* 50(2): 139–56.

Heider, Anne, and R. Stephen Warner. 2010. "Bodies in Sync: Interaction Ritual Theory Applied to Sacred Harp Singing." *Sociology of Religion* 71(1): 76–97.

Hirsch, Eric L. 1990. "Sacrifice for the Cause: Group Processes, Recruitment, and Commitment in a Student Social Movement." *American Sociological Review* 55(2): 243–54.

Hoffmann, John, and John Bartkowski. 2008. "Gender, Religious Tradition, and Biblical Literalism." *Social Forces* 86(3): 1245–72.

Hout, Michael, and Claude S. Fischer. 2002. "Why More Americans Have No Religious Preference: Politics and Generations." *American Sociological Review* 67(2): 165–90.

Hume, David. (1748) 1977. *An Enquiry Concerning Human Understanding*. Indianapolis: Hackett Publishing Company.

———. (1777) 1975. *Enquiry Concerning the Principles of Morals*. New York: Oxford University Press.

Iannaccone, Laurence R. 1994. "Why Strict Churches are Strong." *American Journal of Sociology* 99(5): 1180–1211.

Inbody, Joel. 2015. "Sensing God: Bodily Manifestations and Their Interpretation in Pentecostal Rituals and Everyday Life." *Sociology of Religion* 76(3): 337–55.

James, William. (1902) 1961. *Varieties of Religious Experience: A Study in Human Nature.* New York: Collier Macmillan.

Jeffrey, David Lyle. 1996. *People of the Book: Christian Identity and Literary Culture.* Grand Rapids: William B. Eerdmans Publishing Company.

Joas, Hans. 2000. *The Genesis of Values.* Translated by Gregory Moore. Chicago: University of Chicago Press.

Johnson, Benton. 1963. "On Church and Sect." *American Sociological Review* 28(4): 539–49.

Kant, Immanuel. (1781) 2007. *Critique of Pure Reason.* Translated by Marcus Weigelt. London: Penguin Books.

Katz, Jack. 1999. *How Emotions Work.* Chicago: University of Chicago Press.

Kelley, Dean. 1977. *Why Conservative Churches are Growing*. New York: Harper & Row.

Killian, Caitlin. 2007. "From a Community of Believers to an Islam of the Heart: 'Conspicuous' Symbols, Muslim Practices, and the Privatization of Religion in France." *Sociology of Religion* 68(3): 305–20.

Kirkpatrick, Lee A. 1992. "An Attachment-Theory Approach to the Psychology of Religion." *International Journal for the Psychology of Religion* 2: 3–28.

Krátký, Jan. 2012. "Cognition, Material Culture and Religious Ritual." *Diskus. The Journal of the British Association for the Study of Religions* 13: 49–62.

Kruger, Justin, Nicholas Epley, Jason Parker, and Zhi-Wen Ng. 2005. "Egocentrism Over Email: Can We Communicate as Well as We Think?" *Journal of Personality and Social Psychology* 89(6): 925–36.

Lamont, Michèle. 1992. *Money, Morals, and Manners: The Culture of the French and American Upper-Middle Class.* Chicago: University of Chicago Press.

———. 2000. *The Dignity of Working Men: Morality and the Boundaries of Race, Class, and Immigration.* Cambridge: Harvard University Press.

Lamont, Michèle, and Virag Molnar. 2002. "The Study of Boundaries in the Social Sciences." *Annual Review of Sociology* 28: 167–95.

Lamont, Michèle, Sabrina Pendergrass, and Mark Pachuki. 2015. "Symbolic Boundaries." In *International Encyclopedia of the Social & Behavioral Sciences,* edited by James Wright, 2nd edition, Volume 23, 850–55. Oxford: Elsevier.

Lantzer, Jason S. 2012. *Mainline Christianity: The Past and Future of America's Majority Faith.* New York: New York University Press.

Latour, Bruno. 2005. *Reassembling the Social: An Introduction to Actor-Network-Theory.* New York: Oxford University Press.

Law, John. 1992. "Notes on the Theory of Actor-Network: Ordering, Strategy, and Heterogeneity." *Systems Practice* 5(4): 379–93.

Levin, Itamar. 2001. *Locked Doors: The Seizure of Jewish Property in Arab Countries.* Westport: Praeger Publishers.

Levi-Strauss, Claude. 1958. *Structural Anthropology.* New York: Doubleday.

Lincoln, C. Eric, and Lawrence H. Mamiya. 1990. *The Black Church in the African American Experience.* Durham: Duke University Press.

Lindsay, D. Michael. 2006. "Elite Power: Social Networks within American Evangelicalism." *Sociology of Religion* 67(3): 207–27.

Lovett, Lyle. "Church." Recorded 1992. Track 2 on *Joshua Judges Ruth.* Curb/MCA. Compact Disc.

Luhrmann, Tanya M. 2012. *When God Talks Back: Understanding the American Evangelical Relationship with God.* New York: Alfred A. Knopf.

Madsen, Richard. 2009. "The Archipelago of Faith: Religious Individualism and Faith Community in America Today." *American Journal of Sociology* 114(5): 1263–1301.

Mann, Michael. 1986. *A History of Power from the Beginning to A.D. 1760.* Vol. 1 of *The Sources of Social Power.* Cambridge: Cambridge University Press.

———. 1993. *A History of Power from 1760 to 1914.* Vol. 2 of *The Sources of Social Power.* Cambridge: Cambridge University Press.

Mariner, Rabbi Rodney J. 1996. Introduction to *The Torah,* translated by The Jewish Publication Society of America, 7–13. New York: Henry Holt.

Mattson, Ingrid. 2006. "Women, Islam, and Mosques." *Encyclopedia of Women and Religion in North America*, edited by Rosemary Skinner Keller and Rosemary Radford Ruether, 615–18. Bloomington: Indiana University Press.

Maududi, Abdul A'la. 1977. *Towards Understanding Islam.* Indianapolis: Islamic Teaching Center.

McAdam, Douglas. 1986. "Recruitment to High Risk Activism: The Case of Freedom Summer." *American Journal of Sociology* 92: 64–90.

McGraw, John J., and Jan Krátký. 2017. "Ritual Ecology." *Journal of Material Culture* 22(2): 237–57.

McPhail, Clark. 1991. *The Myth of the Madding Crowd.* New York: Aldine.

Mead, George Herbert. 1934. *Mind, Self, and Society.* Chicago: University of Chicago Press.

Meissner, William W. 1984. *Psychoanalysis and Religious Experience.* New Haven: Yale University Press.

Mencken, F. Carson, Christopher Bader, and Elizabeth Embry. 2009. "In God We Trust: Images of God and Trust in the United States among the Highly Religious." *Sociological Perspectives* 52: 23–38.

Mencken, F. Carson, and Brittany Fitz. 2013. "Images of God and Community Volunteering Among Religious Adherents in the United States." *Review of Religious Research* 55(3): 491–508.

Mipham, Sakyong. 2005. *Ruling Your World: Ancient Strategies for Modern Life.* New York: Random House.

Morgan, David. 1996. *Family Connections: An Introduction to Family Studies.* Cambridge: Blackwell Publishers.

Morris, Benny. 2001. *Righteous Victims: A History of the Zionist-Arab Conflict, 1881–2001.* New York: Vintage Books.

Mujahid, Abdul Malik. 2001. "Muslims in America: Profile 2001." Cited in Wuthnow (2005). www.soundvision.com/info/yearinreview/2001/profile.shtml.

Mule, Pat, and Diane Barthel. 1992. "The Return to the Veil: Individual Autonomy vs. Social Esteem." *Sociological Forum* 7(2): 323–32.

National Opinion Research Center. 2014. "General Social Survey." http://www.norc.org/Research/Projects/Pages/general-social-survey.aspx.

Nelson, Timothy J. 1996. "Sacrifice of Praise: Emotion and Collective Participation in an African-American Worship Service." *Sociology of Religion* 57(4): 379–96.

———. 2005. *Every Time I Feel the Spirit: Religious Ritual and Experience in an African American Church.* New York: New York University Press.

Niebuhr, H. Richard. 1929. *The Social Sources of Denominationalism.* Gloucester: Peter Smith.

Numrich, Paul David. 2000. "How the Swans Came to Lake Michigan: The Social Organization of Buddhist Chicago." *Journal for the Scientific Study of Religion* 39(2): 189–203.

Oates, Joyce Carol. 1987. *On Boxing.* Garden City: Doubleday.

O'Brien, Soledad. 2011. "Unwelcome: The Muslims Next Door." CNN's *In America.*

Olaveson, Tim. 2001. "Collective Effervescence and Communitas: Processual Models of Ritual and Society in Emile Durkheim and Victor Turner." *Dialectical Anthropology* 26: 89–124.

Olesberg, Lindsay. 2012. *The Bible Study Handbook: A Comprehensive Guide to an Essential Practice.* Downers Grove: Intervarsity Press.

Pagis, Michal. 2010. "Producing Intersubjectivity in Silence: An Ethnography of Meditation Practices." *Ethnography* 11: 309–28.

Panagopoulos, Costas, and Peter L. Francia. 2008. "Trends: Labor Unions in the United States." *The Public Opinion Quarterly* 72(1): 134–59.

Park, Jerry, and Joseph Baker. 2007. "What Would Jesus Buy: American Consumption of Religious and Spiritual Material Goods." *Journal for the Scientific Study of Religion* 46(4): 501–17.

Pattillo-McCoy, Mary. 1999. *Black Picket Fences: Privilege and Peril Among the Black Middle Class.* Chicago: The University of Chicago Press.

Pew Forum on Religion and Public Life and Pew Hispanic Center. 2007. "Changing Faiths: Latinos and the Transformation of American Religion." http://religions.pewforum.org.

Pew Research Center. 2017. "New estimates show U.S. Muslim population continues to grow." http://www.pewresearch.org/fact-tank/2018/01/03/new-estimates-show-u-s-muslim-population-continues-to-grow/.

Pinsky, Mark. 2006. *A Jew among the Evangelicals: A Guide for the Perplexed.* Louisville: Westminster John Knox Press.

Polanyi, Michael. 1967. *The Tacit Dimension.* Garden City: Doubleday.

Poloma, Margaret M. 1982. *The Charismatic Movement: Is There a New Pentecost?* Boston: G.K. Hall and Company.

Poloma, Margaret M., and Brian F. Pendleton. 1989. "Religious Experiences, Evangelism, and Institutional Growth within the Assemblies of God." *Journal for the Scientific Study of Religion* 28(4): 415–31.

Porter, Judith R., and Robert E. Washington. 1993. "Minority Identity and Self-Esteem." *Annual Review of Sociology* 19: 139–61.

Poulson, Stephen C., and Colin Campbell. 2010. "Isomorphism, Institutional Parochialism, and the Sociology of Religion." *American Sociologist* 41: 31–47.

Predelli, Line Nyhagen. 2004. "Interpreting Gender in Islam: A Case Study of Immigrant Muslim Women in Oslo, Norway." *Gender and Society* 18(4): 473–93.

Preston, David. 1988. *The Social Organization of Zen Practice: Constructing Transcultural Reality.* Cambridge: Cambridge University Press.

Rappaport, Roy A. 1999. *Ritual and Religion in the Making of Humanity.* Cambridge: Cambridge University Press.

Rawls, Anne Warfield. 1996. "Durkheim's Epistemology: The Neglected Argument." *American Journal of Sociology* 102(2): 430–82.

———. 1997a. "Durkheim and Pragmatism: An Old Twist on a Contemporary Debate." *Sociological Theory* 15(1): 5–29.

———. 1997b. "Durkheim's Epistemology: The Initial Critique, 1915–1924." *The Sociological Quarterly* 38(1): 111–45.

———. 2003. "Conflict as a Foundation for Consensus: Contradictions of Industrial Capitalism in Book III of Durkheim's Division of Labor." *Critical Sociology* 29(3): 295–335.

———. 2004. *Epistemology and Practice: Durkheim's The Elementary Forms of Religious Life.* Cambridge: Cambridge University Press.

Ray, Reginald. 2004. *In the Presence of Masters: Wisdom from 30 Contemporary Tibetan Buddhist Teachers.* Boston: Shambhala Publications, Inc.

Read, Jen'nan Ghazal. 2004. "Family, Religion, and Work among Arab American Women." *Journal of Marriage and Family* 66(4): 1042–50.

Read, Jen'nan Ghazal, and John Bartkowski. 2000. "To Veil or Not to Veil? A Case Study of Identity Negotiation among Muslim Women in Austin, Texas." *Gender and Society* 14(3): 395–417.

Reddy, William M. 1997. "Against Constructionism: The Historical Ethnography of Emotions." *Current Anthropology* 38(3): 327–51.

Ribiat, Rabbi Dovid. 1999. *The 39 Melochos.* Jerusalem: Feldheim Publishers.

Riis, Ole, and Linda Woodhead. 2010. *A Sociology of Religious Emotion.* New York: Oxford University Press.

Rizzuto, Ana-Maria. 1974. "Object Relations and the Formation of the Image of God." *British Journal of Medical Psychology* 47: 83–94.

Robinson, Haddon. 2001. *Expository Preaching: Principles and Practice.* Downers Grove: InterVarsity Press.

Rorty, Richard. 1979. *Philosophy and the Mirror of Nature.* Princeton: Princeton University Press.

Rubenstein, William B. 2004. "The Real Story of U.S. Hate Crimes Statistics: An Empirical Analysis." *Tulane Law Review* 78: 1213–46.

Sahlins, Peter. 1989. *Boundaries: The Making of France and Spain in the Pyrenees.* Berkeley: University of California Press.

Sánchez Jankowski, Martín. 1991. *Islands in the Street: Gangs and American Urban Society.* Berkeley: The Regents of the University of California.

Sandford, Christopher. 1999. *Springsteen: Point Blank.* London: Little, Brown, and Co.

Scheff, Thomas J. 1990. *Micro-Sociology: Discourse, Emotion and Social Structure.* Chicago: University of Chicago Press.

Schegloff, Emanuel. 1992. "Repair after Last Turn: The Last Structurally Provided Defense of Intersubjectivity in Conversation." *American Journal of Sociology* 97: 1295–1345.

Sharp, Shane. 2010. "How Does Prayer Help Manage Emotions?" *Social Psychology Quarterly* 73: 417–37.

Shibley, Mark. 1998. "Contemporary Evangelicals: Born Again and World Affirming." *The Annals of the American Academy of Political and Social Science* 558(1): 67–87.

Siddiqui, Abdul Hamid. 2005. "Translation of Sahih Muslim." http://www.documentacatholicaomnia.eu/03d/0834-0893,_Sahih_Muslim,_Hadith,_EN.pdf.

Simmel, Georg. (1922) 1955. *Conflict and the Web of Group Affiliations.* Translated by Kurt Wolff. Glencoe: Free Press.

Singh, Amardeep. 2002. "'We Are Not the Enemy': Hate Crimes against Arabs, Muslims, and Those Perceived to be Arab or Muslim after September 11." *Human Rights Watch Report* 14(6). http://www.hrw.org/sites/default/files/reports/usa1102.pdf

Smith, Buster. 2007. "Variety in the Sangha: A Survey of Buddhist Organizations in America." *Review of Religious Research* 48(3): 308–17.

Smith, Buster, and Paul Froese. 2008. "The Sociology of Buddhism: Theoretical Implications of Current Scholarship." *Interdisciplinary Journal of Research on Religion* 4(2).

Smith, Christian, Michael O. Emerson, Sally Gallagher, Paul Kennedy, and David Sikkink. 1998. *American Evangelicalism: Embattled and Thriving*. Chicago: University of Chicago Press.

Smith, Tom. 2002. "Religious Diversity in America: The Emergence of Muslims, Buddhists, Hindus, and Others." *Journal for the Scientific Study of Religion* 41(3): 577–85.

Snow, David, E. Burke Rochford, Jr., Steven Worden, and Robert Benford. 1986. "Frame Alignment Processes, Micromobilization, and Movement Participation." *American Sociological Review* 51(4): 464–81.

Spencer, Anne Cottrell. 2014. "Diversification in the Buddhist Churches of America: Demographic Trends and Their Implications for the Future Study of U.S. Buddhist Groups." *Journal of Global Buddhism* 15: 35–61.

Spilka, Bernard, Philip Armatas, and June Nussbaum. 1964. "The Concept of God: A Factor-Analytic Approach." *Review of Religious Research* 6(1): 28–36.

St. Clair, Michael. 2004. *Human Relationships and the Experience of God: Object Relations and Religion*. Eugene: Wipf and Stock Publishers.

Stark, Rodney. 1996. *The Rise of Christianity: How the Obscure, Marginal Jesus Movement Became the Dominant Religious Force in the Western World in a Few Centuries*. Princeton: Princeton University Press.

———. 2001a. "Gods, Rituals, and the Moral Order." *Journal for the Scientific Study of Religion* 40(4): 619–36.

———. 2001b. *One True God: Historical Consequences of Monotheism*. Princeton: Princeton University Press.

———. 2003. "Why Gods Should Matter in Social Science." *The Chronicle Review*, June 4. Retrieved June 20, 2017. http://freerepublic.com/focus/f-religion/922971/posts

Stark, Rodney, and William Sims Bainbridge. (1987) 1996. *A Theory of Religion*. New Brunswick: Rutgers University Press.

Stark, Rodney, and Roger Finke. 2000. *Acts of Faith: Explaining the Human Side of Religion*. Berkeley: University of California Press.

Stark, Rodney, and Charles Glock. 1968. *American Piety: The Nature of Religious Commitment*. Berkeley: University of California Press.

Stott, John. 1982. *Between Two Worlds: The Art of Preaching in the Twentieth Century*. Grand Rapids: William. B. Eerdmans Publishing Company.

Stroope, Samuel, Scott Draper, and Andrew Whitehead. 2013. "Images of a Loving God and Sense of Meaning in Life." *Social Indicators Research* 111(1): 25–44.

Summers Effler, Erika. 2010. *Laughing Saints and Righteous Heroes: Emotional Rhythms in Social Movement Groups*. Chicago: University of Chicago Press.

Sumner, William. 1906. *Folkways: A Study of the Sociological Importance of Usages, Manners, Customs, Mores, and Morals*. Boston: Ginn and Co.

Taves, Ann. 2009. *Religious Experiences Reconsidered: A Building-Block Approach to the Study of Religion and Other Special Things*. Princeton: Princeton University Press.

Taylor, Charles. 1989. *Sources of the Self: The Making of Modern Identity.* Cambridge: Harvard University Press.

Thompson, Robert, and Paul Froese. 2017. "God Versus Party: Competing Effects on Attitudes Concerning Criminal Punishment, National Security, and Military Service." *Journal for the Scientific Study of Religion* 55(4): 839–58.

Thumma, Scott, and Dave Travis. 2007. *Beyond Megachurch Myths: What We Can Learn from America's Largest Churches.* San Francisco: Jossey-Bass.

Troeltsch, Ernst. 1932. *The Social Teaching of the Christian Churches.* Translated by Olive Wyon. New York: Macmillan.

Trungpa, Chogyam. 1973. *Cutting through Spiritual Materialism.* Boulder: Shambhala Publications.

Turner, Edith. 2012. *Communitas: The Anthropology of Collective Joy.* New York: Palgrave Macmillan.

Turner, Victor. 1969. *The Ritual Process: Structure and Anti-Structure.* New Brunswick: Aldine Transaction.

———. 1974. *Dramas, Fields, and Metaphors: Symbolic Action in Human Society.* Ithaca: Cornell University Press.

United States Census Bureau. 2010. http://2010.census.gov/2010census/.

United States Department of Justice Federal Bureau of Investigation. 2010. *Uniform Crime Report.* http://www.fbi.gov/about-us/cjis/ucr/hate-crime/2010/narratives/hate-crime-2010-victims.

Vergote, Antoine. 1969. *The Religious Man: A Psychological Study of Religious Attitudes.* Dayton: Pflaum Press.

Vergote, Antoine, Alvaro Tamayo, Luiz Pasquali, Michel Bonami, Marie-Rose Pattyn, and Anne Custers. 1969. "Concept of God and Parental Images." *Journal for the Scientific Study of Religion* 8(1): 79–87.

Wacquant, Loïc. 2004. *Body and Soul: Notebooks of an Apprentice Boxer.* New York: Oxford University Press.

Wakin, Daniel. 2002. "For Muslims, an Uneasy Anniversary; Urge to Speak Out Conflicts with Low-Profile Instincts." *New York Times*, August 19, 2002. http://www.nytimes.com/2002/08/19/nyregion/for-muslims-uneasy-anniversary-urge-speak-conflicts-with-low-profile-instincts.html?pagewanted=all&src=pm.

Warren, Rick. 1995. *The Purpose Driven Church: Growth without Compromising Your Message and Mission.* Grand Rapids: Zondervan.

Webber, Robert. 1985. *Evangelicals on the Canterbury Trail: Why Evangelicals are Attracted to the Liturgical Church.* Waco: Word.

———. 2002. *The Younger Evangelicals: Facing the Challenges of the New World.* Grand Rapids: Baker.

Weber, Max. (1904) 2001. *The Protestant Ethic and the Spirit of Capitalism.* Translated by Stephen Kalberg. Chicago: Fitzroy Dearborn.

———. (1917–1919) 1952. *Ancient Judaism.* Translated by Hans H. Gerth and Don Martindale. New York: The Free Press.

———. (1922a) 1968. *Economy and Society.* Translated by Guenther Roth and Klaus Wittich. New York: Bedminster Press.

———. (1922b) 1968. *The Sociology of Religion. Economy and Society*. Translated by Guenther Roth and Klaus Wittich, 399–634. New York: Bedminster Press.

———. (1923) 1961. *General Economic History*. Translated by Frank H. Knight. New York: Collier-Macmillan.

Wellman Jr., James, Katie Corcoran, and Kate Stockly-Meyerdirk. 2014. "'God is Like a Drug. . . .': Explaining Interaction Ritual Chains in American Megachurches." *Sociological Forum* 29(3): 650–72.

Western, Bruce, and Jake Rosenfeld. 2012. "Workers of the World Divide: The Decline of Labor and the Future of the Middle Class." *Foreign Affairs* 91(3): 88–99.

Whitehead, Andrew. 2010. "Financial Commitment within Federations of Small Groups: The Effect of Cell-Based Congregational Structure on Individual Giving." *Journal for the Scientific Study of Religion* 49(4): 640–56.

———. 2012. "Gender Ideology and Religion: Does a Masculine Image of God Matter?" *Review of Religious Research* 54(2): 139–56.

Wiist, Bill, Bruce M. Sullivan, Diane M. St. George, and Heidi A. Wayment. 2012. "Buddhists' Religious and Health Practices." *Journal of Religion and Health* 51(1): 132–47.

Wiley, Norbert. 1994. *The Semiotic Self*. Chicago: University of Chicago Press.

Williams, Rhys. 2004. "Review: *Divided by Faith: Evangelical Religion and the Problem of Race in America*." *Sociology of Religion* 65(2): 178–79.

Winchester, Daniel. 2008. "Embodying the Faith: Religious Practice and the Making of a Muslim Moral Habitus." *Social Forces* 86(4): 1753–80.

Wollschleger, Jason. 2012. "Interaction Ritual Chains and Religious Participation." *Sociological Forum* 27(4): 896–912.

Wuthnow, Robert, ed. 1994. *"I Come Away Stronger": How Small Groups Are Shaping American Religion*. Grand Rapids: Eerdmans.

———. 2005. *America and the Challenges of Religious Diversity*. Princeton: Princeton University Press.

Wuthnow, Robert, and Wendy Cadge. 2004. "Buddhists and Buddhism in the United States: The Scope of Influence." *Journal for the Scientific Study of Religion* 43(3): 363–80.

Index

Page references for figures are italicized.

191

About the Author

Scott Draper serves as associate professor of sociology at The College of Idaho. His research examines a wide variety of contemporary religious phenomena, with an emphasis on emotions and religious experiences. Past publications include studies in *Sociological Forum, Journal for the Scientific Study of Religion, Social Indicators Research,* and several other journals. He also contributed a chapter to *What Americans Really Believe*, edited by Rodney Stark and published by Baylor University Press in 2008.